PRACTICE – ASSESS – DIAGNOSE

180 Days of MATH for Fourth Grade

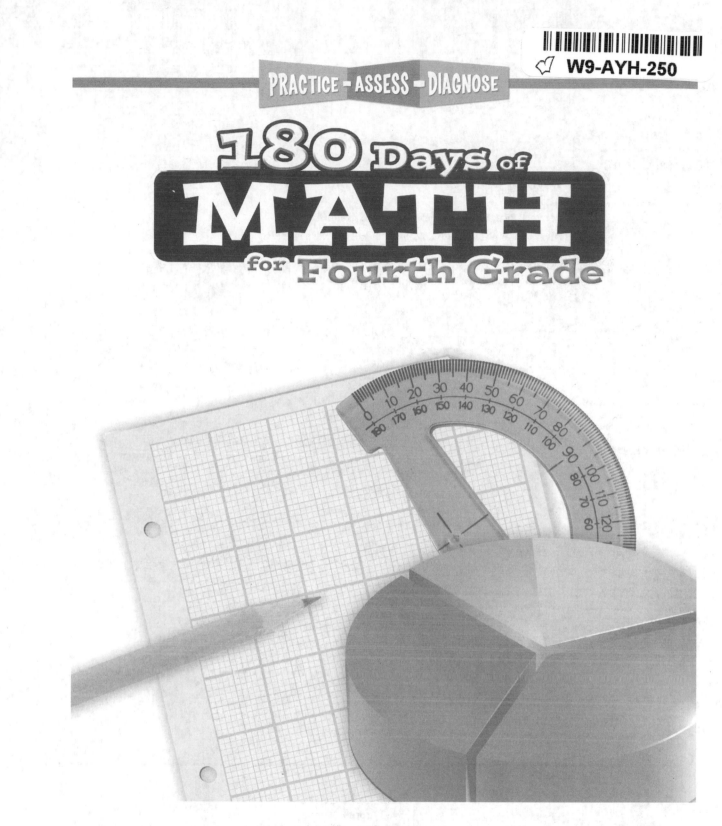

Developed by
Jodene Smith

Shell Education

Publishing Credits

Dona Herweck Rice, *Editor-in-Chief*; Lee Aucoin, *Creative Director*;
Don Tran, *Print Production Manager*; Timothy J. Bradley, *Illustration Manager*;
Chris McIntyre, M.A.Ed., *Editorial Director*; Sara Johnson, M.S.Ed., *Senior Editor*;
Aubrie Nielsen, M.S.Ed., *Associate Education Editor*; Juan Chavolla, *Cover/Interior Layout Designer*;
Robin Erickson, *Production Artist*; Corinne Burton, M.A.Ed., *Publisher*

Shell Education

5482 Argosy Avenue
Huntington Beach, CA 92649-1030
www.tcmpub.com/shell-education

ISBN 978-1-4258-0807-5

©2011 Shell Education Publishing, Inc.

TABLE OF CONTENTS

Introduction and Research 3

How to Use This Book 4

Daily Practice Pages 11

Answer Key....................................191

References Cited 207

Digital Resources...............................208

INTRODUCTION AND RESEARCH

The Need for Practice

In order to be successful in today's mathematics classroom, students must deeply understand both concepts and procedures so that they can discuss and demonstrate their understanding. Demonstrating understanding is a process that must be continually practiced in order for students to be successful. According to Marzano (2010, 83), "practice has always been, and will always be, a necessary ingredient to learning procedural knowledge at a level at which students execute it independently." Practice is especially important to help students apply their concrete, conceptual understanding to a particular procedural skill.

Understanding Assessment

In addition to providing opportunities for frequent practice, teachers must be able to assess students' understanding of mathematical procedures, terms, concepts, and reasoning (Kilpatrick, Swafford, and Findell 2001). This is important so that teachers can adequately address students' misconceptions, build on their current understanding, and challenge them appropriately.

Assessment is a long-term process that often involves careful analysis of student responses from a lesson discussion, project, practice sheet, or test. When analyzing the data, it is important for teachers to reflect on how their teaching practices may have influenced students' responses and to identify those areas where additional instruction may be required. In short, the data gathered from assessments should be used to inform instruction: slow down, speed up, or reteach. This type of assessment is called *formative assessment* and is used to provide a seamless connection between instruction and assessment (McIntosh 1997).

HOW TO USE THIS BOOK

180 Days of Math for Fourth Grade offers teachers and parents a full page of mathematics practice activities for each day of the school year.

Easy to Use and Standards-Based

These activities reinforce grade-level skills across a variety of mathematical concepts. The questions are provided as a full practice page, making them easy to prepare and implement as part of a classroom morning routine, at the beginning of each mathematics lesson, or as homework.

Every fourth-grade practice page provides 10 questions, each tied to a specific mathematical concept. Students are provided the opportunity for regular practice in each mathematical concept, allowing them to build confidence through these quick, standards-based activities.

Question	Mathematics Concept	NCTM Standard
1	**Addition or Subtraction**	Understands meanings of operations such as addition and subtraction and how they relate to one another
2	**Multiplication or Fractions, Decimals, Percents**	Understands various meanings of multiplication; Recognizes and generates equivalent forms of fractions, decimals, and percents
3	**Division**	Understands various meanings of division; Understands meanings of operations and how they relate to one another; Computes fluently and makes reasonable estimates
4		
5	**Place Value or Number Sense**	Understands representations of numbers, relationships among numbers, and number systems; Understands place-value structure of the base-ten number system
6	**Algebra and Algebraic Thinking**	Understands patterns, relations, and functions; Represents and analyzes patterns and functions, using words, tables, and graphs
7	**Measurement**	Applies appropriate techniques and formulas to determine measurements; Understands measurable attributes of objects and the units, systems, and processes of measurement
8		
9	**Geometry or Data Analysis**	Uses visualization and spacial reasoning to solve problems; Analyzes properties of two- and three-dimensional geometric shapes
10	**Word/Logic Problem or Mathematical Reasoning**	Solves problems that arise in mathematics and in other contexts

Standards are listed with the permission of the National Council of Teachers of Mathematics (NCTM). NCTM does not endorse the content or validity of these alignments.

HOW TO USE THIS BOOK *(cont.)*

Using the Practice Pages

As outlined on page 4, every question is aligned to a mathematics concept and standard.

Practice pages provide instruction and assessment opportunities for each day of the school year.

Each question ties student practice to a specific mathematics concept.

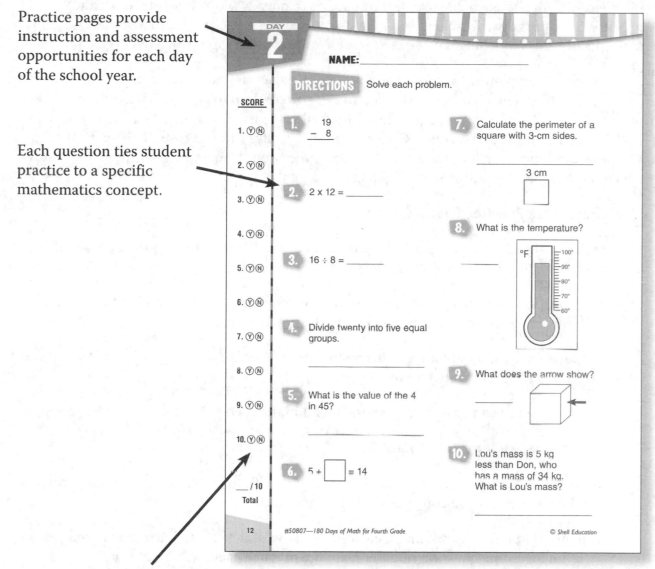

Using the Scoring Guide

Use the scoring guide along the side of each practice page to check answers and see at a glance which skills may need more reinforcement.

Fill in the appropriate circle for each problem to indicate correct (Y) or incorrect (N) responses. You might wish to indicate only incorrect responses to focus on those skills. (For example, if students consistently miss numbers 2 and 6, they may need additional help with those concepts as outlined in the table on page 4.) Use the answer key at the back of the book to score the problems, or you may call out answers to have students self-score or peer-score their work.

HOW TO USE THIS BOOK *(cont.)*

Diagnostic Assessment

Teachers can use the practice pages as diagnostic assessments. The data analysis tools included with the book enable teachers or parents to quickly score students' work and monitor their progress. Teachers and parents can see at a glance which mathematics concepts or skills students may need to target in order to develop proficiency.

After students complete a practice page, grade each page using the answer key (pages 191–206). Then, complete the *Practice Page Item Analysis* (page 7) for the whole class, or the *Student Item Analysis* (page 8) for individual students. These charts are also provided in the digital resources (filenames: G4_practicepage_analysis.pdf, G4_student_analysis.pdf). Teachers can input data into the electronic files directly on the computer or they can print the pages and analyze students' work using paper and pencil.

To complete the Practice Page Item Analysis:

- Write or type students' names in the far-left column. Depending on the number of students, more than one copy of the form may be needed or you may need to add rows.

- The question numbers are included across the top of the chart. Each item correlates with the matching question number from the practice page.

- For each student, record an *X* in the column if the student has the item incorrect. If the item is correct, leave the item blank.

- Count the *X*s in each row and column and fill in the correct boxes.

To complete the Student Item Analysis:

- Write or type the student's name on the top row. This form tracks the ongoing progress of each student, so one copy per student is necessary.

- The question numbers are included across the top of the chart. Each item correlates with the matching question number from the practice page.

- For each day, record an *X* in the column if the student has the item incorrect. If the item is correct, leave the item blank.

- Count the *X*s in each row and column and fill in the correct boxes.

Practice Page Item Analysis

Directions: Record an *X* in cells to indicate where students have missed questions. Add up the totals. You can view: (1) which questions/concepts were missed per student; (2) the total correct score for each student; and (3) the total number of students who missed each question.

Day: _____

Student Name	Question # 1	2	3	4	5	6	7	8	9	10	# correct
Sample Student		X			X	X				X	6/10
# of students missing each question											

HOW TO USE THIS BOOK (cont.)

Student Item Analysis

Directions: Record an *X* in cells to indicate where the student has missed questions. Add up the totals. You can view: (1) which questions/concepts the student missed; (2) the total correct score per day; and (3) the total number of times each question/concept was missed.

Student Name: Sample Student										
Question	1	2	3	4	5	6	7	8	9	10	# correct
Day											
1		X			X						8/10
Total											

HOW TO USE THIS BOOK *(cont.)*

Using the Results to Differentiate Instruction

Once results are gathered and analyzed, teachers can use the results to inform the way they differentiate instruction. The data can help determine which concepts are the most difficult for students and which need additional instructional support and continued practice. Depending on how often the practice pages are scored, results can be considered for instructional support on a daily or weekly basis.

Whole-Class Support

The results of the diagnostic analysis may show that the entire class is struggling with a particular concept or group of concepts. If these concepts have been taught in the past, this indicates that further instruction or reteaching is necessary. If these concepts have not been taught in the past, this data is a great pre-assessment and demonstrates that students do not have a working knowledge of the concepts. Thus, careful planning for the length of the unit(s) or lesson(s) must be considered, and extra frontloading may be required.

Small-Group or Individual Support

The results of the diagnostic analysis may show that an individual or small group of students is struggling with a particular concept or group of concepts. If these concepts have been taught in the past, this indicates that further instruction or reteaching is necessary. Consider pulling aside these students while others are working independently to instruct further on the concept(s). Teachers can also use the results to help identify individuals or groups of proficient students who are ready for enrichment or above-grade level instruction. These students may benefit from independent learning contracts or more challenging activities. Students may also benefit from extra practice using games or computer-based resources.

Digital Resources

Reference page 208 for information about accessing the digital resources and an overview of the contents.

HOW TO USE THIS BOOK (*cont.*)

NCTM Standards

The lessons in this book are aligned to the National Council of Teachers of Mathematics (NCTM) standards. The standards listed on page 4 support the concepts and skills that are consistently presented on each of the practice pages.

Standards Correlations

Shell Education is committed to producing educational materials that are research and standards based. In this effort, we have correlated all of our products to the academic standards of all 50 states, the District of Columbia, and the Department of Defense Dependent Schools, as well as to the college and career readiness standards.

How to Find Standards Correlations

To print a customized correlation report of this product for your state, visit our website at **www.tcmpub.com/shell-education** and follow the on-screen directions. If you require assistance in printing correlation reports, please contact Customer Service at 1-877-777-3450.

Purpose and Intent of Standards

The No Child Left Behind legislation mandates that all states adopt academic standards that identify the skills students will learn in kindergarten through grade twelve. While many states had already adopted academic standards prior to NCLB, the legislation set requirements to ensure the standards were detailed and comprehensive.

Standards are designed to focus instruction and guide adoption of curricula. Standards are statements that describe the criteria necessary for students to meet specific academic goals. They define the knowledge, skills, and content students should acquire at each level. Standards are also used to develop standardized tests to evaluate students' academic progress.

Teachers are required to demonstrate how their lessons meet state standards. State standards are used in development of all of our products, so educators can be assured they meet the academic requirements of each state.

NAME: _____

DIRECTIONS Solve each problem.

1. 18 + 5 = _23_

2. Color $\frac{4}{5}$ of the rectangle.

3. Share 8 equally between 2.

_64_

4. 8 ÷ 4 = _2_

5. Is 15 smaller than 51?

yes

6. Fill in the missing number.

45, 50, 55, _60_, 65, 70

7. Write the line length in centimeters.

_45_

cm 1 2 3 4 5

8. Do you use A.M. or P.M. to write 7:00 in the morning?

_A.M._

9. How many sides does a pentagon have?

_5_

10. Complete the addition grid.

+	8	14	17	19	22	36
19	27	33	36	38	41	55
29	36	43	46	48	51	65
39	47	53	56	58	61	85

1. Y N
2. Y N
3. Y N
4. Y N
5. Y N
6. Y N
7. Y N
8. Y N
9. Y N
10. Y N

_8_ / 10

Total

NAME:_____

DIRECTIONS Solve each problem.

SCORE

1. Ⓨ Ⓝ

2. Ⓨ Ⓝ

3. Ⓨ Ⓝ

4. Ⓨ Ⓝ

5. Ⓨ Ⓝ

6. Ⓨ Ⓝ

7. Ⓨ Ⓝ

8. Ⓨ Ⓝ

9. Ⓨ Ⓝ

10. Ⓨ Ⓝ

___ / 10
Total

1.
$$\begin{array}{r} 19 \\ -8 \\ \hline \end{array}$$

2. 2 x 12 = _____

3. 16 ÷ 8 = _____

4. Divide twenty into five equal groups.

_____

5. What is the value of the 4 in 45?

_____

6. 5 + ☐ = 14

7. Calculate the perimeter of a square with 3-cm sides.

_____

3 cm

8. What is the temperature?

_____

°F

100°
90°
80°
70°
60°

9. What does the arrow show?

_____

10. Lou's mass is 5 kg less than Don, who has a mass of 34 kg. What is Lou's mass?

_____

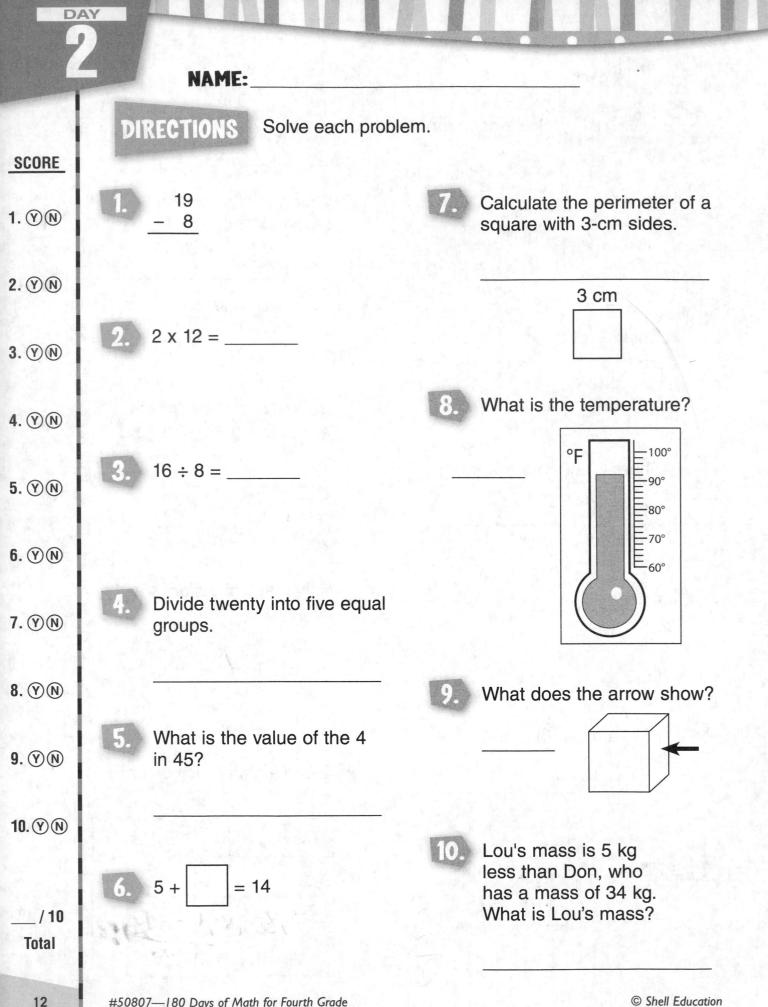

NAME: _____

DIRECTIONS Solve each problem.

1.
$$\begin{array}{r} 500 \\ +\ 400 \\ \hline 900 \end{array}$$

6. $8 = 10 - \boxed{2}$

1. (Y) (N)

2. (Y) (N)

2. $\frac{1}{2}$ of 16 is ___8___.

7. Write the time.

7:06

_____ past _____

3. (Y) (N)

4. (Y) (N)

5. (Y) (N)

3. Divide 18 into 9 equal groups.

_____2 groves_____

4. $16 \div 2 =$ ___8___

8. How many seconds are in 1 minute?

60

9. Do parallel lines intersect?

no

6. (Y) (N)

7. (Y) (N)

8. (Y) (N)

9. (Y) (N)

10. (Y) (N)

5. Circle the smallest number.

471   741   (417)

10. Rex bought 4 pens at $1.50 each. How much did he spend?

$$\begin{array}{r} 50 \\ \times 4 \\ \hline 400 \end{array}$$

$1.50 \times 4 = 10.00

8 / 10
Total

NAME: _____

SCORE

1. Ⓨ Ⓝ
2. Ⓨ Ⓝ
3. Ⓨ Ⓝ
4. Ⓨ Ⓝ
5. Ⓨ Ⓝ
6. Ⓨ Ⓝ
7. Ⓨ Ⓝ
8. Ⓨ Ⓝ
9. Ⓨ Ⓝ
10. Ⓨ Ⓝ

6 / 10

Total

1. $26 - 9 =$ 17

2.
$$\begin{array}{r} \$2.00 \\ + \$1.25 \\ \hline \end{array}$$
3.25

3. $8\overline{)40}$
5
40
0

4. $32 \div 4 =$ 8

5. 6 tens + 4 ones = 64

6. $7 \times \boxed{4} = 28$

7. What is the term for the amount of space inside a container?

oil

8. ___ quarts = 1 gallon

9. Name this shape.

hexagon

10. $\frac{1}{10}$ of 20 = 2, so $\frac{3}{10}$ of 20 =

4

NAME: _____

DIRECTIONS Solve each problem.

1. $20 + 80 =$ _100_

1. (Y) (N)

2.
$$\begin{array}{r} 5 \\ \times\ 8 \\ \hline 48 \end{array}$$

2. (Y) (N)

3. $8\overline{)12}$ 1 R5
8
5

3. (Ⓨ) (N)

4. How many groups of 10 are in 40?

4 groups

4. (Y) (N)

5. Write 306 in words.

Three hundred AND six

5. (Ⓨ) (N)

6. $9 + \boxed{1} = 10$

6. (Ⓨ) (N)

7. Circle the best estimate for the area of a door.

2 m²   40 m²

7. (Y) (Ⓝ)

8. What day comes after Sunday?

Monday

8. (Ⓨ) (N)

9. Record the data in the chart using numbers.

Number of Pets				
Tyrone	Melissa	Aubrey	Mitch	Cara
3	6	0	2	3

Tyrone has 3 pets.

Melissa has 6 pets.

Aubrey has no pets.

Mitch has 2 pets.

Cara has 3 pets.

9. (Ⓨ) (N)

10. Complete the multiplication wheel.

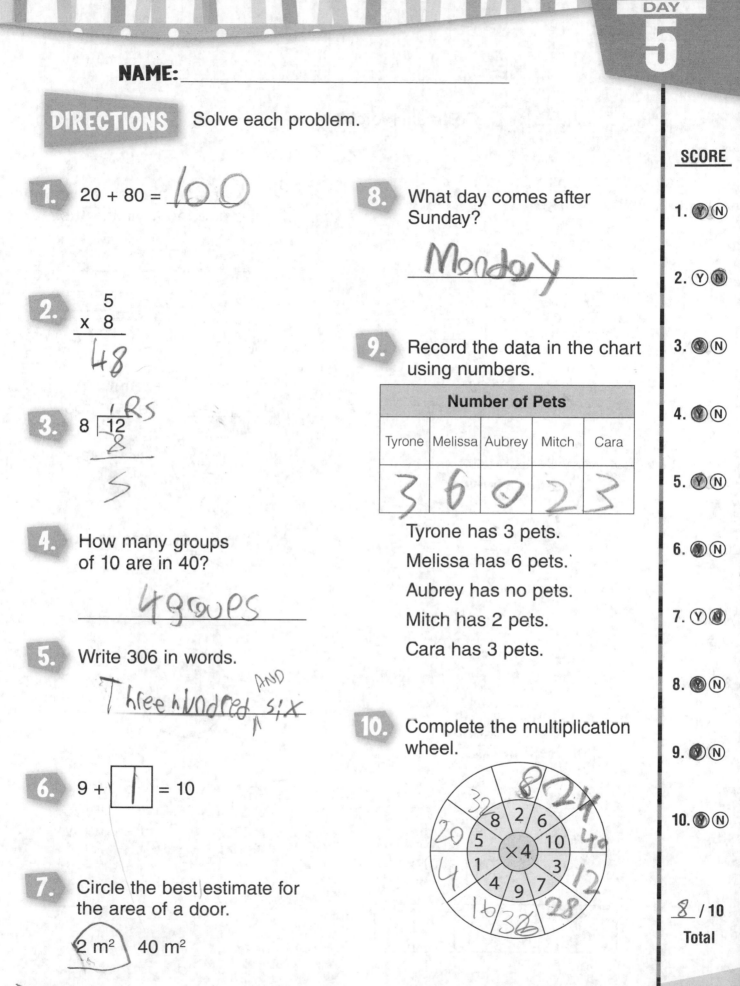

10. (Ⓨ) (N)

_8_ / 10
Total

NAME: _____

#50807—180 Days of Math for Fourth Grade

DIRECTIONS Solve each problem.

SCORE

1. (Y) (N)

2. (Y) (N)

3. (Y) (N)

4. (Y) (N)

5. (Y) (N)

6. (Y) (N)

7. (Y) (N)

8. (Y) (N)

9. (Y) (N)

10. (Y) (N)

2 / 10

Total

1.
$$\begin{array}{r} 24 \\ -13 \\ \hline 11 \end{array}$$

2. $\frac{1}{2}$ of 18 is ___9___.

3. Divide 28 into 4 equal groups.

$28 \div 4 = 7$

4. $8\overline{)63}$ 9 R1

5. What is the value of the 3 in 352?

hundreds

6. Complete the pattern.

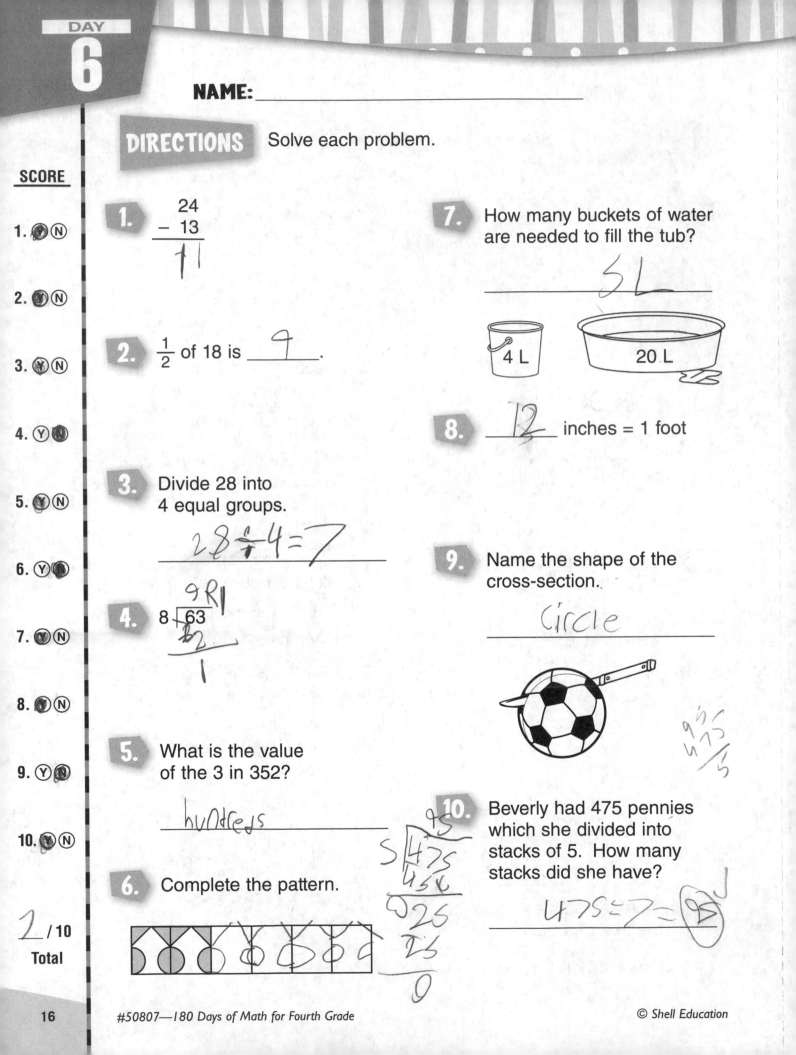

7. How many buckets of water are needed to fill the tub?

5 L

4 L   20 L

8. ___12___ inches = 1 foot

9. Name the shape of the cross-section.

Circle

10. Beverly had 475 pennies which she divided into stacks of 5. How many stacks did she have?

$475 \div 7 = 95$

NAME: _____

DIRECTIONS Solve each problem.

1.
$$\begin{array}{r} 6 \\ 4 \\ + \ 5 \\ \hline 15 \end{array}$$

2. Color $\frac{1}{4}$ of the pentagons.

3. $2\overline{)18}$ 9 / 18 / 18 / 0

4. 12 shared equally by 6 is

_____2_____.

5. Write 247 in expanded notation.

_____

6. 6 x [4] = 24

7. What is the date of the first Monday in February?

_____7_____

FEBRUARY						
Sun	Mon	Tue	Wed	Thu	Fri	Sat
		1	2	3	4	5
6	7	8	9	10	11	12
13	14	15	16	17	18	19
20	21	22	23	24	25	26
27	28	29				

8. What is the month before October?

_____September_____

9. Is the angle below a right angle?

_____Yes_____

10. If you add 9 to me, the sum is 43. What number am I?

_____33_____

43
9

34

SCORE

1. (Y) N
2. (Y) N
3. (Y) N
4. (Y) N
5. Y (N)
6. (Y) N
7. (Y) N
8. (Y) N
9. (Y) N
10. Y (N)

8 / 10
Total

NAME: _____

DIRECTIONS Solve each problem.

1. 50 − 15 = __35__

2. Is $\frac{1}{2}$ equal to 0.5?

__Yes__

3. 16 ÷ 4 = __4__

4. 56 ÷ 8 = __7__

5. Is 42 greater than 24?

__yes__

6. 1 × [8] = 8

7. Record the liquid amount in the pitcher in liters.

__1100__

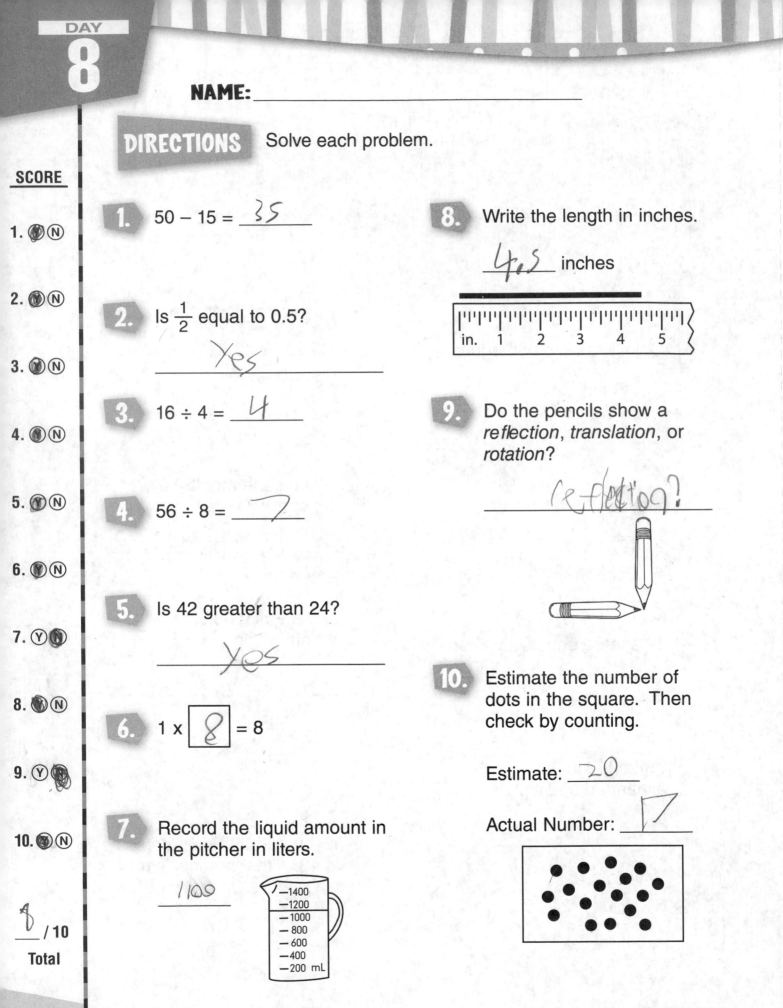

—1400
—1200
—1000
— 800
— 600
— 400
— 200 mL

8. Write the length in inches.

__4.5__ inches

in. 1 2 3 4 5

9. Do the pencils show a *reflection*, *translation*, or *rotation*?

__reflection?__

10. Estimate the number of dots in the square. Then check by counting.

Estimate: __20__

Actual Number: __17__

  #50807—180 Days of Math for Fourth Grade

NAME: _____

Solve each problem.

SCORE

1. Calculate the sum of 12, 4, and 8.

24

6. 2 x $\boxed{6}$ = 12

1. Y N

2. How many eighths are in one whole?

8eights

2. Y N

7. ___107___ mm = 1 cm

3. Y N

3. Divide 16 into 4 equal groups.

4

8. Which would be the best measuring tool for the length of a shoelace: a yardstick, a scale, or a clock?

yardstick

4. Y N

5. Y N

4. 36 ÷ 4 = ___9___

9. Color the polygons.

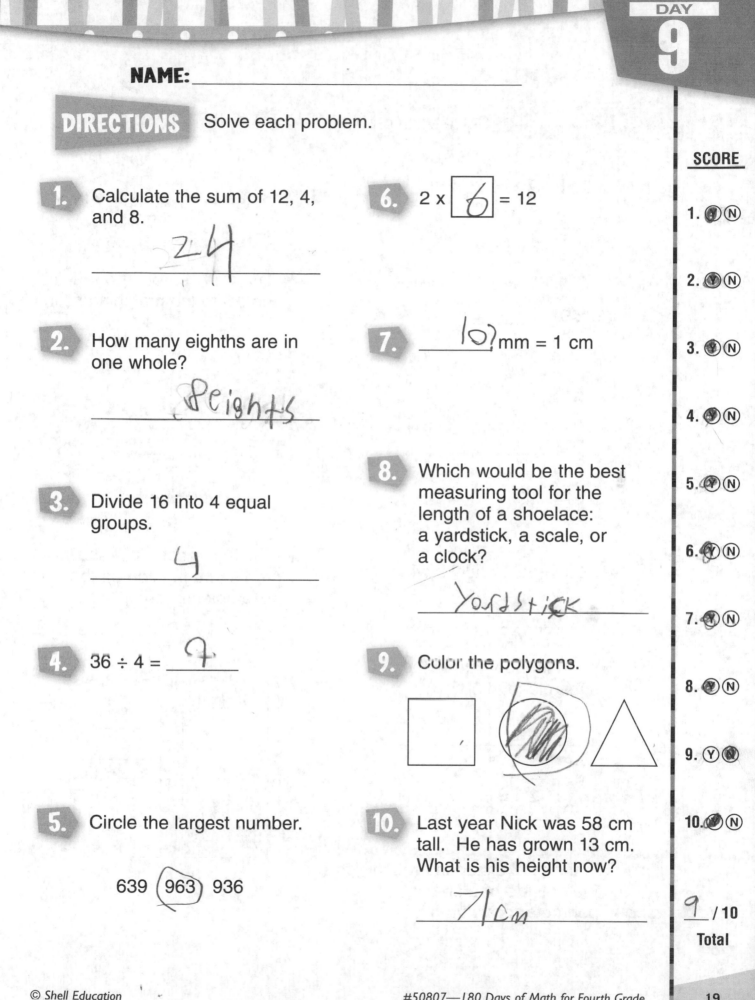

6. Y N

7. Y N

8. Y N

5. Circle the largest number.

639 (963) 936

10. Last year Nick was 58 cm tall. He has grown 13 cm. What is his height now?

71 cm

9. Y N

10. Y N

9 / 10

Total

NAME:_____

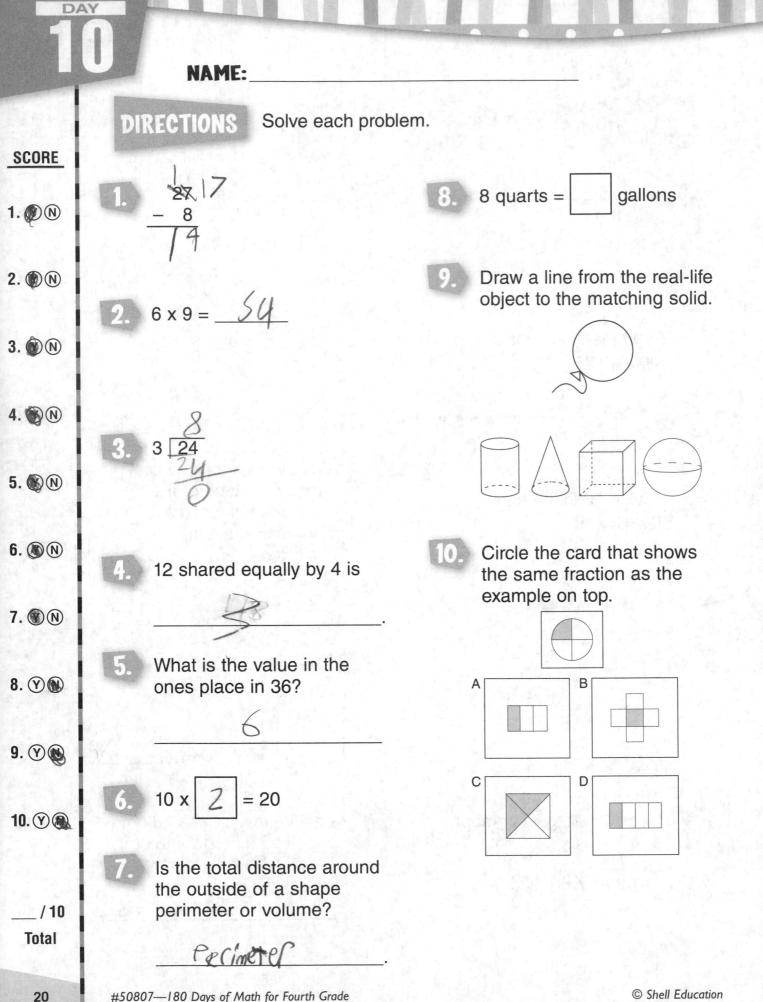

SCORE

1. (Y)(N)

2. (Y)(N)

3. (Y)(N)

4. (Y)(N)

5. (Y)(N)

6. (Y)(N)

7. (Y)(N)

8. (Y)(N)

9. (Y)(N)

10. (Y)(N)

___ / 10
Total

DIRECTIONS Solve each problem.

1. 27 17
  − 8
  14

2. 6 x 9 = 54

3. 3⟌24 8
  24
  0

4. 12 shared equally by 4 is _____.

5. What is the value in the ones place in 36?
  6

6. 10 x [2] = 20

7. Is the total distance around the outside of a shape perimeter or volume?
  Pecimeter.

8. 8 quarts = [ ] gallons

9. Draw a line from the real-life object to the matching solid.

10. Circle the card that shows the same fraction as the example on top.

A   B

C   D

NAME: _____

DIRECTIONS Solve each problem.

1.
```
   17
    5
 +  3
```
25

2. Is $\frac{1}{2}$ equal to $\frac{5}{10}$? _____ Yes

3. $16 \div 2 =$ _____ 8

4. $6 \overline{) 12}$ 2 ✓

5. What is the number right after 46?

47

6. Fill in the missing number.

3, 6, 9, _12_, 15, 18

7. Write the length in millimeters.

30mm?

8. Tom left home at 7:40 A.M. and reached school at 8:05 A.M. How many minutes did it take him to get to school?

25min

9. Mark the parallel lines with an X.

F

10. Write two odd numbers that total the even number 12.

13-1=12

1. (Y) N
2. (Y) N
3. (Y) N
4. (Y) N
5. (Y) N
6. (Y) N
7. (Y) N
8. (Y) N
9. (Y) N
10. (Y) (N)
9 /10
Total

NAME: _____

DIRECTIONS Solve each problem.

SCORE

1. $\textbf{Y}$ $\textbf{N}$

2. $\textbf{Y}$ $\textbf{N}$

3. $\textbf{Y}$ $\textbf{N}$

4. $\textbf{Y}$ $\textbf{N}$

5. $\textbf{Y}$ $\textbf{N}$

6. $\textbf{Y}$ $\textbf{N}$

7. $\textbf{Y}$ $\textbf{N}$

8. $\textbf{Y}$ $\textbf{N}$

9. $\textbf{Y}$ $\textbf{N}$

10. $\textbf{Y}$ $\textbf{N}$

9 / 10
Total

1. $36 - 7 =$ ___29___

2. $\frac{1}{4}$ of 28 is ___4___ .

3. Divide 24 into equal groups of 4.

___8___

4. $28 \div 4 =$ ___7___

5. What is the value of the 1 in 312?

___10___

6. $5 +$ ___29___ $= 25$

7. Calculate the area of the square.

___16cm___

4 cm

8. Would you use a scale or ruler to measure weight?

___scale___

9. What is the area of a rectangle that measures 4 cm by 12 cm?

___3cm___

10. There are 16 boys. A coach wants to form 4 equal teams. How many boys will be on each team?

___4___

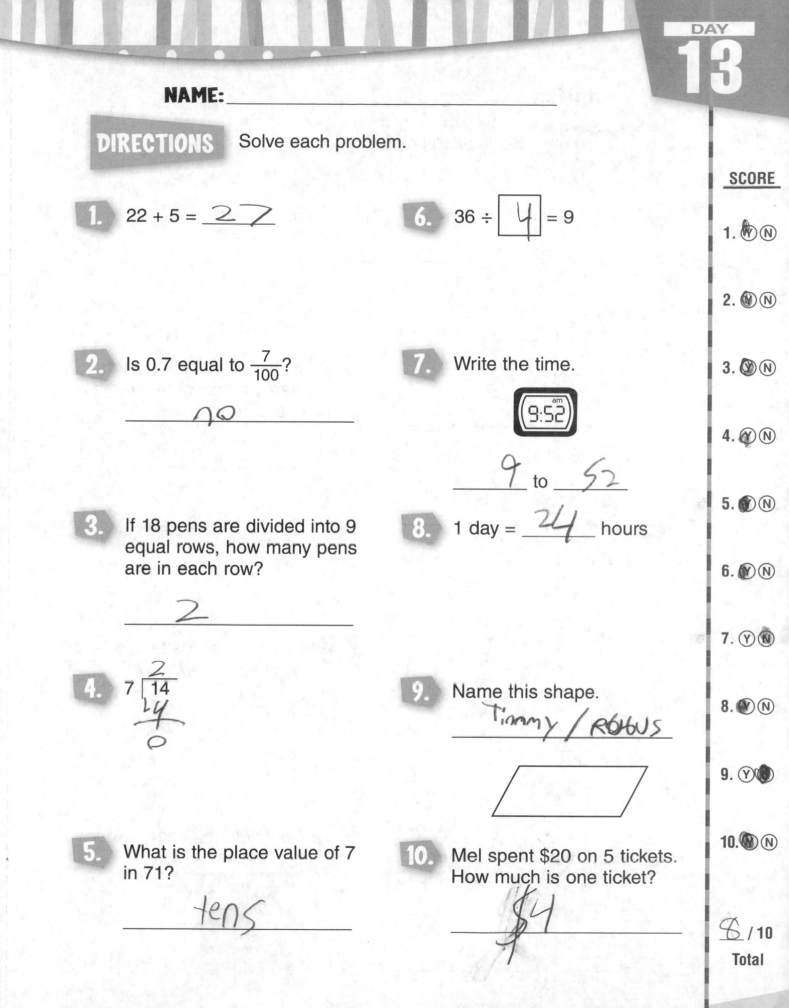

NAME: _____

DIRECTIONS Solve each problem.

SCORE

1. 22 + 5 = _27_

6. 36 ÷ |4| = 9

1. (Y) (N)

2. Is 0.7 equal to $\frac{7}{100}$?

___no___

7. Write the time.

9:52 am

___9___ to ___52___

2. (Y) (N)

3. (Y) (N)

4. (Y) (N)

3. If 18 pens are divided into 9 equal rows, how many pens are in each row?

___2___

8. 1 day = ___24___ hours

5. (Y) (N)

6. (Y) (N)

4. 7) 14

9. Name this shape.

Timmy / Rombus

7. (Y) (N)

8. (Y) (N)

9. (Y) (N)

5. What is the place value of 7 in 71?

___tens___

10. Mel spent $20 on 5 tickets. How much is one ticket?

$4

10. (Y) (N)

8 / 10

Total

NAME: _____

SCORE

DIRECTIONS Solve each problem.

1. (Y)(N)

2. (Y)(N)

3. (Y)(N)

4. (Y)(N)

5. (Y)(N)

6. (Y)(N)

7. (Y)(N)

8. (Y)(N)

9. (Y)(N)

10. (Y)(N)

___ / 10
Total

1.
$$\begin{array}{r} 43 \\ -\ 8 \\ \hline \end{array}$$

2. Is $\frac{1}{2}$ less than $\frac{1}{4}$?

_____

3. $5\overline{)40}$

4. How many 4s are in 20?

_____

5. Order the numbers from smallest to largest.

43, 73, 33

_____ _____ _____

6. $45 - \boxed{} = 39$

7. Would you use kilograms or grams to measure the mass of a banana?

_____

8. _____ pints = 1 quart

9. Circle the solids that have a rectangular top view.

A   B   C   D

10. Complete the chart. Round the number 423.

Tens	
Hundreds	

NAME:_____

DIRECTIONS Solve each problem.

1.
$$\begin{array}{r} 24 \\ +\ 7 \\ \hline \end{array}$$

6. ☐ x 4 = 24

1. Ⓨ Ⓝ

2. Ⓨ Ⓝ

7. Is the distance around a polygon called perimeter?

_____

2. Calculate the product of 9 and 6.

_____

3. Ⓨ Ⓝ

4. Ⓨ Ⓝ

8. _____ feet = 1 yard

3. 40 ÷ 10 = _____

5. Ⓨ Ⓝ

9. Circle the triangle that has 3 equal sides.

A   B   C

6. Ⓨ Ⓝ

7. Ⓨ Ⓝ

4. Divide 36 into 1 equal groups.

_____

8. Ⓨ Ⓝ

10. Use different colors to color pairs of numbers that equal the product shown in the center.

9. Ⓨ Ⓝ

① 1

⑮ 15 — ● 15 — ③ 3

⑤ 5

5. What is the value of the 9 in 892,135?

_____

10. Ⓨ Ⓝ

___ / 10
Total

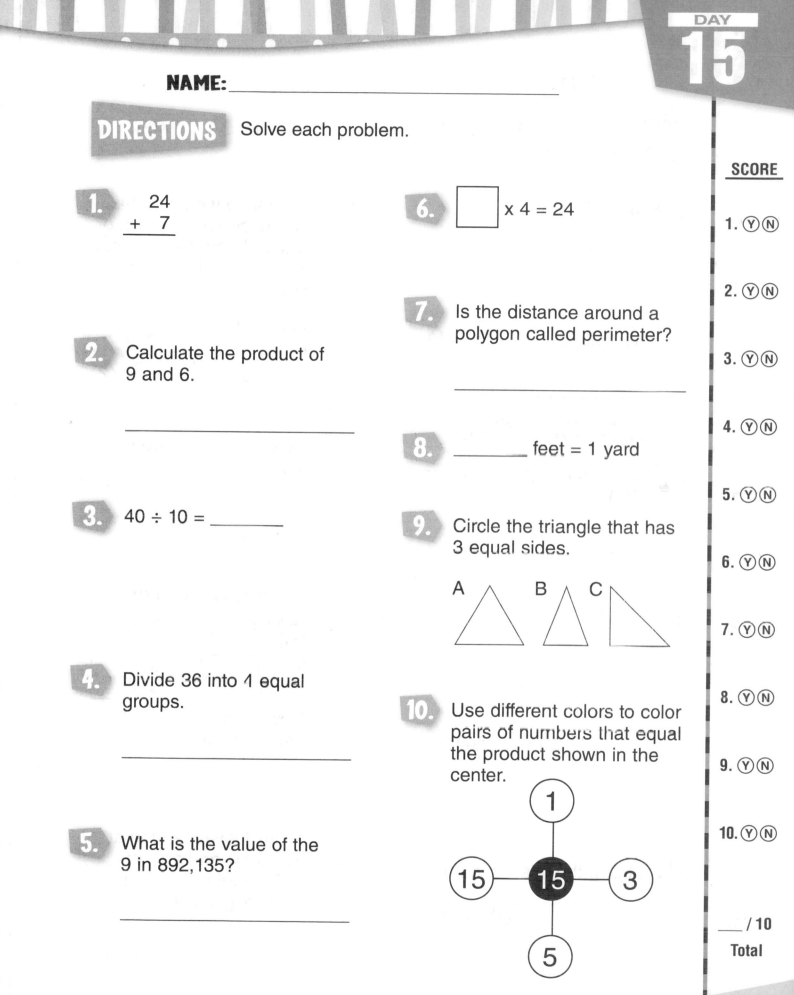

NAME: _____

DIRECTIONS Solve each problem.

1. Y N

2. Y N

3. Y N

4. Y N

5. Y N

6. Y N

7. Y N

8. Y N

9. Y N

10. Y N

____ / 10
Total

1.
$$20$$
$$-\ \ 5$$

2. Write $\frac{25}{100}$ as a decimal.

_____

3. Divide 40 into 10 equal groups.

_____

4. $80 \div 8 =$ _____

5. What is the next even number after 68?

_____

6. $24 \div \boxed{} = 6$

7. Can containers with a capacity of 1 liter have different shapes?

_____

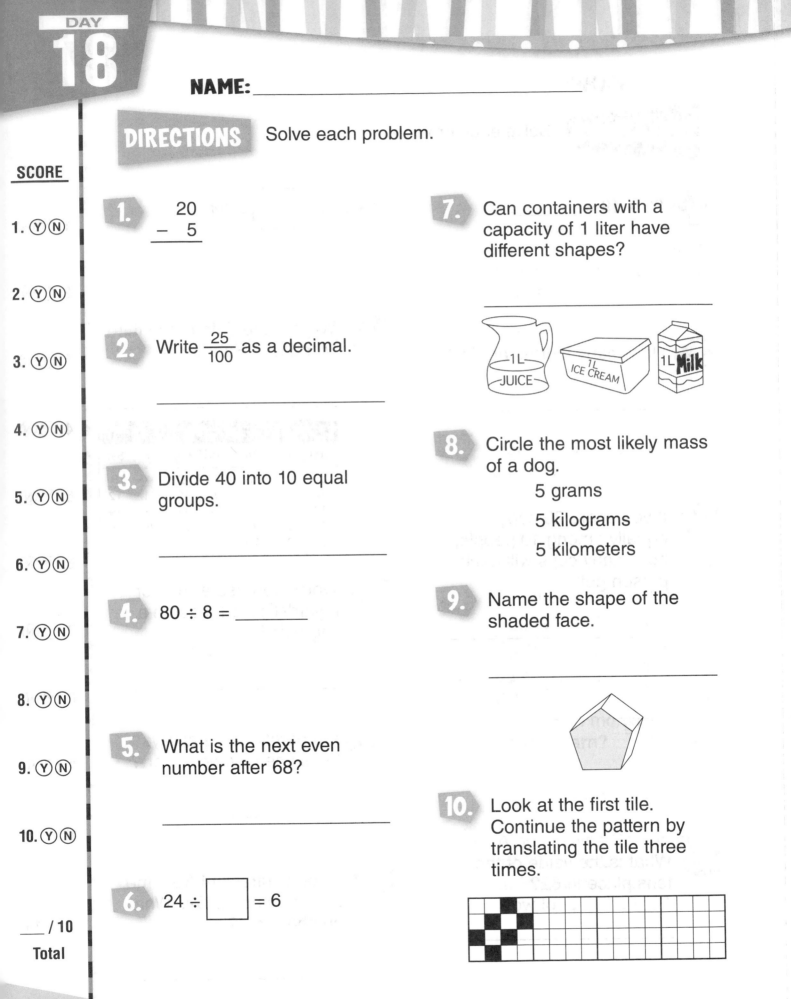

8. Circle the most likely mass of a dog.

    5 grams

    5 kilograms

    5 kilometers

9. Name the shape of the shaded face.

_____

10. Look at the first tile. Continue the pattern by translating the tile three times.

NAME: _____

DIRECTIONS Solve each problem.

1.
```
   21
+  14
```

2. $\frac{1}{4}$ of 24 is _____

3. $3\overline{)12}$

4. What is 48 books shared equally among 4 classes?

_____

5. Which is larger: 6 or 0.6?

_____

6. $15 + \boxed{} = 37$

7. Each cube has 1-cm sides. What is the volume of the model?

_____

8. Do you leave for school in the A.M. or P.M.?

_____

9. **Books Read in March**

Cathy	📖 📖 📖
Martin	📖 📖 📖 📖
Jose	📖 📖 📖

📖 = 5 books read

How many books did Cathy read?

_____

10. It takes Dad 20 minutes to drive to work. How long does he spend driving to and from work every day?

_____

SCORE

1. Ⓨ Ⓝ
2. Ⓨ Ⓝ
3. Ⓨ Ⓝ
4. Ⓨ Ⓝ
5. Ⓨ Ⓝ
6. Ⓨ Ⓝ
7. Ⓨ Ⓝ
0. Ⓨ Ⓝ
9. Ⓨ Ⓝ
10. Ⓨ Ⓝ

____ / 10
Total

NAME:_____

DIRECTIONS Solve each problem.

1. (Y)(N)

2. (Y)(N)

3. (Y)(N)

4. (Y)(N)

5. (Y)(N)

6. (Y)(N)

7. (Y)(N)

8. (Y)(N)

9. (Y)(N)

10. (Y)(N)

___ / 10
Total

1. 30 − 15 = _____

2.
$$\begin{array}{r} 8 \\ \times\ 8 \\ \hline \end{array}$$

3. 40 ÷ 4 = _____

4. 18 divided into 9 equal groups is

_____.

5. Fill in the missing number.

63, 64, 65, _____

6. 9 x ☐ = 18

7. Would the area of a stamp most likely be measured in cm² or m²?

_____

8. 60 minutes equals how many hours?

_____

9. Which numbers are inside the circle but not in the rectangle or triangle?

_____

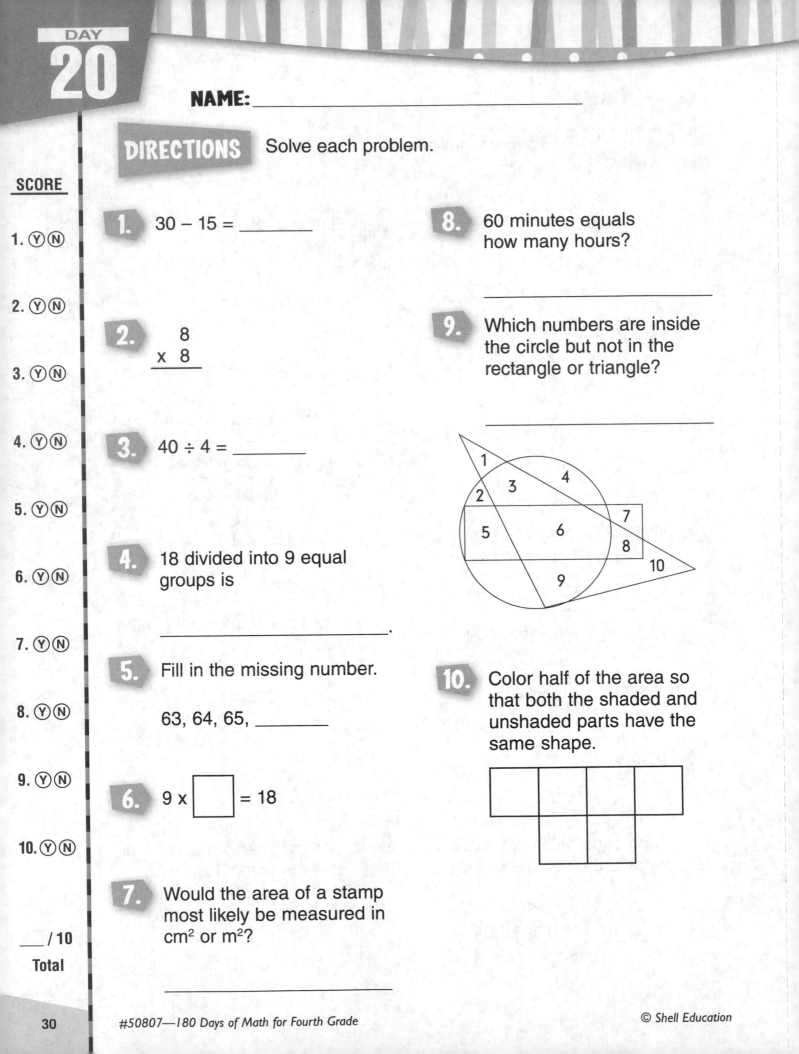

10. Color half of the area so that both the shaded and unshaded parts have the same shape.

NAME: _____

DIRECTIONS Solve each problem.

1. 26 + 13 = _____

6. Fill in the missing number.

8, 12, 16, _____, 24

2. $\frac{1}{8}$ of 24 is _____

7. Write the line length in centimeters.

3. 5)‾2‾0‾

8. If you wanted a glass of water, would you pour a cup or a gallon of water?

_____

4. 56 ÷ 8 = _____

9. Draw the axes of symmetry.

5. What is the place value of 9 in 918?

_____

10. Write two odd numbers that total the even number 8.

_____

1. Ⓨ Ⓝ

2. Ⓨ Ⓝ

3. Ⓨ Ⓝ

4. Ⓨ Ⓝ

5. Ⓨ Ⓝ

6. Ⓨ Ⓝ

7. Ⓨ Ⓝ

8. Ⓨ Ⓝ

9. Ⓨ Ⓝ

10. Ⓨ Ⓝ

___ / 10
Total

NAME: _____

DIRECTIONS Solve each problem.

1. Y N
2. Y N
3. Y N
4. Y N
5. Y N
6. Y N
7. Y N
8. Y N
9. Y N
10. Y N

___ / 10
Total

1. 20 − 17 = _____

2. Write the fraction for 0.27.

_____

3. 54 ÷ 6 = _____

4. 7 ⟌ 14

5. 300 + 80 + 6 = _____

6. ☐ − 4 = 12

7. Circle the best estimate for the weight of the object.

100 g   2 kg   5 kg   10 kg

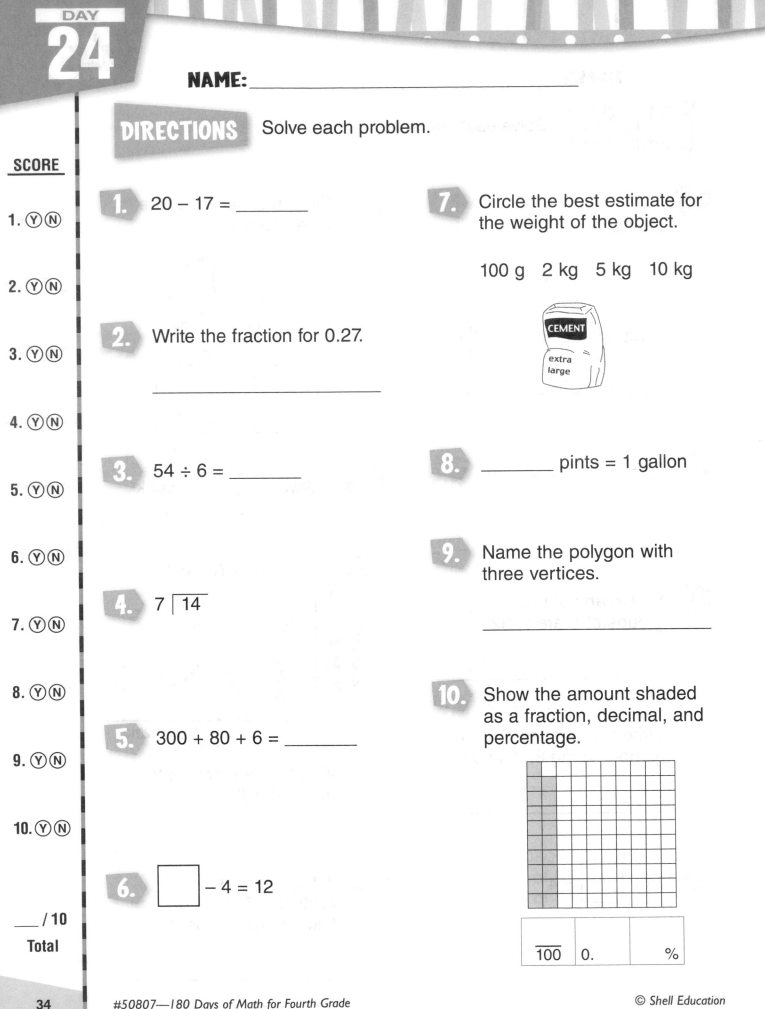

CEMENT
extra large

8. _____ pints = 1 gallon

9. Name the polygon with three vertices.

_____

10. Show the amount shaded as a fraction, decimal, and percentage.

$\overline{100}$	0.	%

#50807—180 Days of Math for Fourth Grade

NAME:_____

DIRECTIONS Solve each problem.

1. 32 + 26 = _____

6. 4 x ☐ = 40

1. Ⓨ Ⓝ

2. Ⓨ Ⓝ

2. 4
   x 3

7. How many millimeters are in 5 centimeters?

_____

3. Ⓨ Ⓝ

4. Ⓨ Ⓝ

8. _____ inches = 1 yard

3. How many groups of three are in 30?

_____

5. Ⓨ Ⓝ

6. Ⓨ Ⓝ

7. Ⓨ Ⓝ

9. A parallelogram has:
_____ angles
_____ axes of symmetry

4. 7 ⟌ 70

8. Ⓨ Ⓝ

9. Ⓨ Ⓝ

10. Color the multiples of 4.

10. Ⓨ Ⓝ

5. Write 1,061 in expanded notation.

_____

1	2	3	4	5	6	7	8	9	10
11	12	13	14	15	16	17	18	19	20
21	22	23	24	25	26	27	28	29	30
31	32	33	34	35	36	37	38	39	40

___/ 10
Total

NAME: _____

SCORE

1. Ⓨ Ⓝ

2. Ⓨ Ⓝ

3. Ⓨ Ⓝ

4. Ⓨ Ⓝ

5. Ⓨ Ⓝ

6. Ⓨ Ⓝ

7. Ⓨ Ⓝ

8. Ⓨ Ⓝ

9. Ⓨ Ⓝ

10. Ⓨ Ⓝ

___ / 10
Total

1.
$$\begin{array}{r} 20 \\ -\ 15 \\ \hline \end{array}$$

2. Which is smaller: 0.6 or 0.16?

_____

3. How many groups of 6 are in 42?

_____

4. $25 \div 5 =$ _____

5. Is 75 less than 57?

_____

6. Fill in the missing number.

112, 102, _____, 82, 72

7. If 2 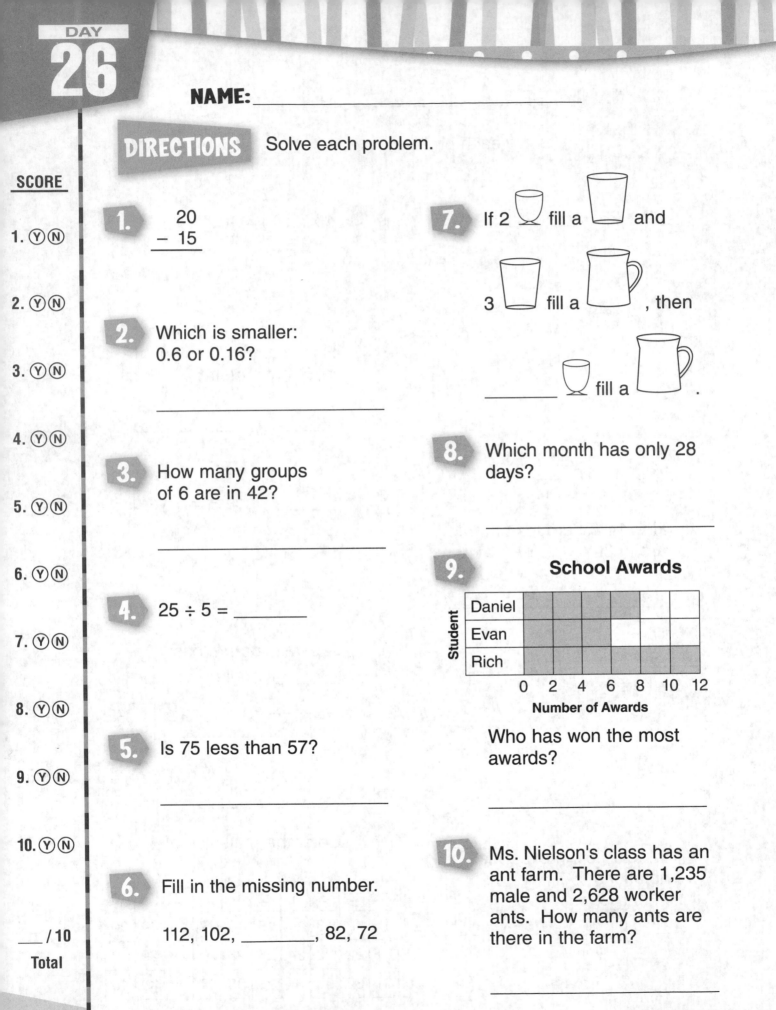 fill a ⎕ and

3 ⎕ fill a ⎕ , then

_____ ⎕ fill a ⎕ .

8. Which month has only 28 days?

_____

9. **School Awards**

Student						
Daniel						
Evan						
Rich						

0   2   4   6   8   10   12
Number of Awards

Who has won the most awards?

_____

10. Ms. Nielson's class has an ant farm. There are 1,235 male and 2,628 worker ants. How many ants are there in the farm?

_____

NAME: _____

DIRECTIONS Solve each problem.

1. 26 + 35 = _____

2. $\frac{1}{2}$ of 18 = _____

3. 8 ⟌ 24

4. 9 ÷ 3 = _____

5. What number is 100 more than 1,468?

_____

6. 18 + ☐ = 20

7. On what day of the week does January end?

_____

JANUARY						
Sun	Mon	Tue	Wed	Thu	Fri	Sat
		1	2	3	4	5
6	7	8	9	10	11	12
13	14	15	16	17	18	19
20	21	22	23	24	25	26
27	28	29	30	31		

8. Write the length in inches.

_____ inches

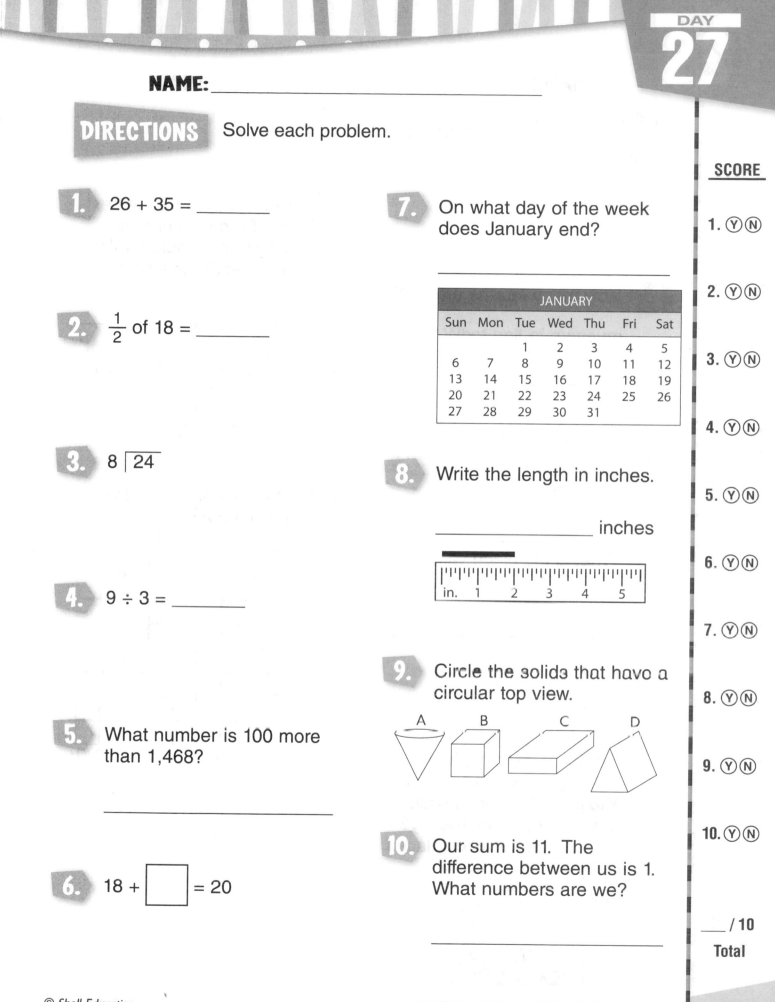

9. Circle the solids that have a circular top view.

A   B   C   D

10. Our sum is 11. The difference between us is 1. What numbers are we?

_____

SCORE

1. Ⓨ Ⓝ

2. Ⓨ Ⓝ

3. Ⓨ Ⓝ

4. Ⓨ Ⓝ

5. Ⓨ Ⓝ

6. Ⓨ Ⓝ

7. Ⓨ Ⓝ

8. Ⓨ Ⓝ

9. Ⓨ Ⓝ

10. Ⓨ Ⓝ

___ / 10
Total

NAME:_____

DIRECTIONS Solve each problem.

1.
$$\begin{array}{r} 30 \\ -9 \\ \hline \end{array}$$

2. $5 \times 7 =$ _____

3. Divide 16 into 4 equal groups.

_____

4. $28 \div 7 =$ _____

5. Is 63 closer to 60 or 70?

_____

6. $\boxed{} \times 6 = 36$

7. The area of the flower bed is 12 m² and the area of the grass is 24 m². What is their combined area?

_____

8. Is 12:00 P.M. a reasonable bedtime?

_____

9. **Sports Played Each Year**

	1st Trimester	2nd Trimester	3rd Trimester
Troy	soccer	basketball	baseball
Jessica	golf	basketball	track
Allison	soccer	diving	swimming

Which sport does Troy play in the 3rd trimester?

_____

10. $\frac{1}{10}$ of 60 = 6, so $\frac{7}{10}$ of 60 =

_____

NAME:_____

DIRECTIONS Solve each problem.

1.
```
  12
+ 14
```

2. $\frac{1}{4}$ of 36 is _____

3. Divide 20 by 5. _____

4. 8 ⟌ 40

5. Write the smallest 4-digit numeral using 0, 2, 8, and 7.

_____

6. Fill in the missing number.

20, 40, 60, _____, 100

7. Write the length in millimeters.

_____

```
cm  1   2   3   4   5
```

8. If the temperature were 89 degrees Fahrenheit, would you wear a bathing suit or a jacket?

_____

9. What type of prism is shown?

_____

10. Complete the subtraction grid.

−	44	48	53	61	72	75
19						
29						
39						

1. Ⓨ Ⓝ

2. Ⓨ Ⓝ

3. Ⓨ Ⓝ

4. Ⓨ Ⓝ

5. Ⓨ Ⓝ

6. Ⓨ Ⓝ

7. Ⓨ Ⓝ

8. Ⓨ Ⓝ

9. Ⓨ Ⓝ

10. Ⓨ Ⓝ

___ / 10
Total

NAME:_____

DIRECTIONS Solve each problem.

1. $43 - 17 =$ _____

2. Which is smaller: 0.4 or $\frac{3}{10}$?

_____

3. $15 \div 5 =$ _____

4. $3\overline{)18}$

5. Write 3,426 in expanded notation.

_____

_____

6. $25 + \boxed{} = 36$

7. Calculate the area of a square with 3 cm sides.

_____ $\boxed{}$ 3 cm

8. How many weeks are in one year?

_____

9. Circle the set of lines that are parallel.

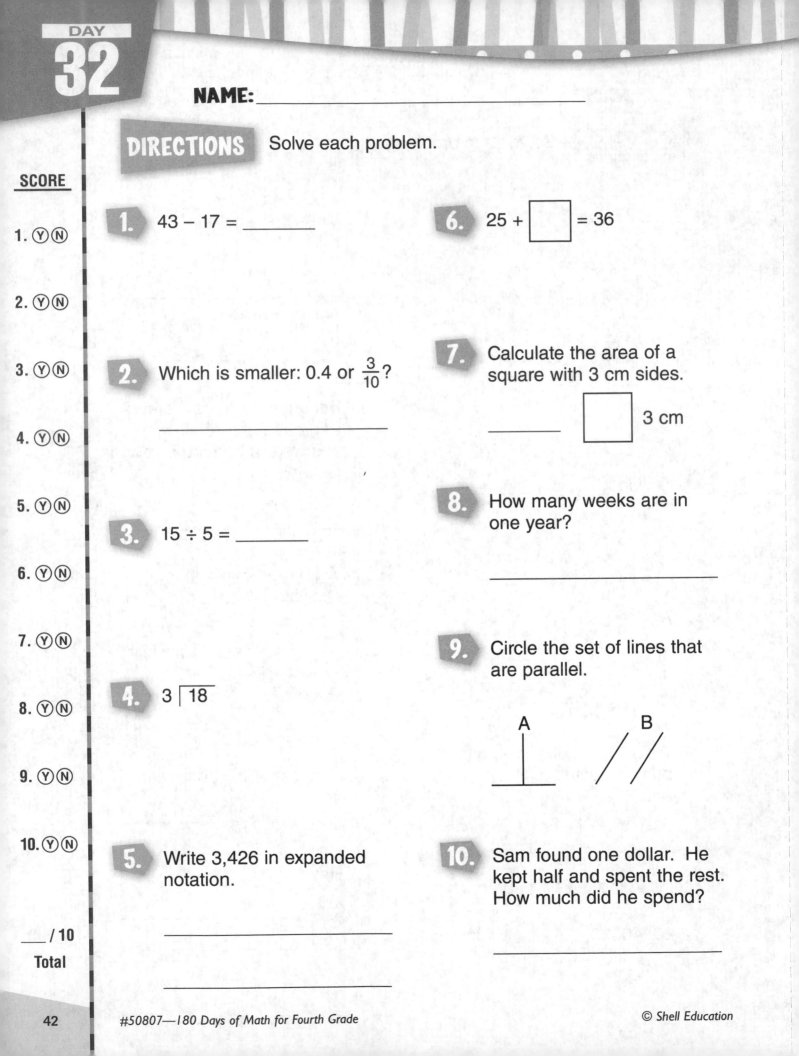

A   B

10. Sam found one dollar. He kept half and spent the rest. How much did he spend?

_____

NAME: _____

DIRECTIONS Solve each problem.

1. 23 + 7 = _____

6. 42 − □ = 15

1. Ⓨ Ⓝ

7. Show 20 to 3 on both clocks.

2. Ⓨ Ⓝ

2. Color $\frac{1}{2}$.

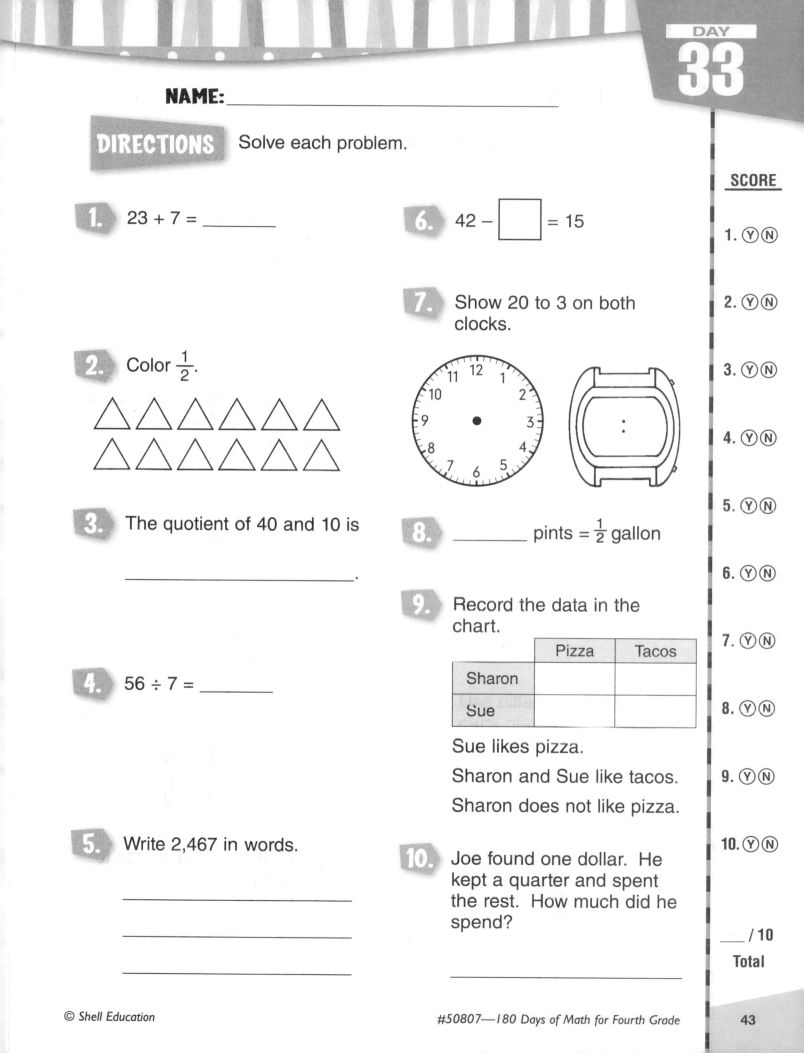

3. Ⓨ Ⓝ

4. Ⓨ Ⓝ

5. Ⓨ Ⓝ

3. The quotient of 40 and 10 is

_____.

8. _____ pints = $\frac{1}{2}$ gallon

6. Ⓨ Ⓝ

9. Record the data in the chart.

7. Ⓨ Ⓝ

	Pizza	Tacos
Sharon		
Sue		

4. 56 ÷ 7 = _____

8. Ⓨ Ⓝ

Sue likes pizza.

Sharon and Sue like tacos.

9. Ⓨ Ⓝ

Sharon does not like pizza.

5. Write 2,467 in words.

10. Ⓨ Ⓝ

10. Joe found one dollar. He kept a quarter and spent the rest. How much did he spend?

_____

_____

_____

____ / 10

Total

_____

NAME: _____

DIRECTIONS Solve each problem.

1. 27 – 15 = _____

2. $\frac{1}{4}$ of 28 is _____

3. 40 ÷ 4 = _____

4. List all the factors of 6.

_____

5. What is 200 more than 694?

_____

6. Fill in the missing number.

650, 700, _____, 800, 850

7. How many liters are in 7,000 milliliters?

_____

8. Would you use a ruler or a yardstick to measure the length of your shoe?

_____

9. Draw the top view of this solid.

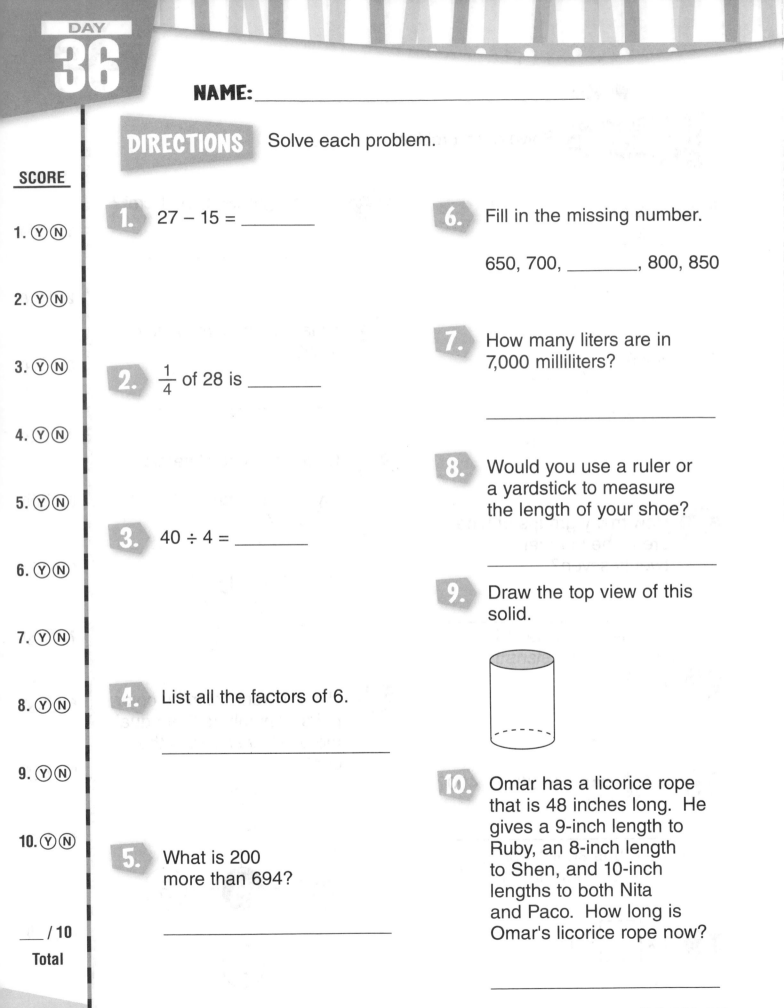

10. Omar has a licorice rope that is 48 inches long. He gives a 9-inch length to Ruby, an 8-inch length to Shen, and 10-inch lengths to both Nita and Paco. How long is Omar's licorice rope now?

_____

NAME:_____

DIRECTIONS Solve each problem.

1. 35 + 37 = _____

6. 15 ÷ ☐ = 5

2. Write the decimal for $\frac{3}{4}$.

_____

7. Look at the calendar below. What day of the week is January 31?

_____

FEBRUARY						
Sun	Mon	Tue	Wed	Thu	Fri	Sat
		1	2	3	4	5
6	7	8	9	10	11	12
13	14	15	16	17	18	19
20	21	22	23	24	25	26
27	28	29				

3. 7 ⟌ 14

8. Circle the most likely height of a door.

    6 inches

    6 feet

    6 centimeters

4. How many groups of 9 are in 81?

_____

9. Draw an obtuse angle.

5. Is 847 closer to 800 or 900?

_____

10. If you add me to 246, the sum is 473. What number am I?

_____

SCORE

1. Ⓨ Ⓝ
2. Ⓨ Ⓝ
3. Ⓨ Ⓝ
4. Ⓨ Ⓝ
5. Ⓨ Ⓝ
6. Ⓨ Ⓝ
7. Ⓨ Ⓝ
8. Ⓨ Ⓝ
9. Ⓨ Ⓝ
10. Ⓨ Ⓝ

___ / 10
Total

NAME:_____

DIRECTIONS
Solve each problem.

SCORE

1. Ⓨ Ⓝ

2. Ⓨ Ⓝ

3. Ⓨ Ⓝ

4. Ⓨ Ⓝ

5. Ⓨ Ⓝ

6. Ⓨ Ⓝ

7. Ⓨ Ⓝ

8. Ⓨ Ⓝ

9. Ⓨ Ⓝ

10. Ⓨ Ⓝ

___ / 10
Total

1.
$$\begin{array}{r} 24 \\ -\ 12 \\ \hline \end{array}$$

2. Write the fraction for 0.1.

_____

3. $16 \div 4 =$ _____

4. How many groups of 7 are in 42?

_____

5. $1,000 + 300 + 70 + 4 =$

_____

6. $56 -\boxed{}= 36$

7. How many milliliters are in 7 liters?

_____

8. Do you go home from school in the A.M. or P.M.?

_____

9. Name the quadrilateral with only one set of parallel sides.

_____

10. Follow the directions and color the path of the counter.

Directions

Move: 3 right, 3 up, 6 right, 4 down, 2 right, 2 down, 10 left, 1 down.

O

#50807—180 Days of Math for Fourth Grade

NAME: _____

DIRECTIONS Solve each problem.

1.
$$\begin{array}{r} 22 \\ + 19 \\ \hline \end{array}$$

6. $\boxed{} \times 5 = 30$

2. $\frac{1}{4}$ of 20 is _____

7. 100 _____ = 1 m

3. 6 ⟌ 36

8. If the outdoor temperature is 85°F, is it a warm or cold day?

_____

4. List all the factors of 4.

_____

9. How many right angles does a rectangle have?

_____

5. Is 265 less than 256?

_____

10. There are 8 squares. If 25% of the squares are red and the rest of them are blue, how many squares are red?

_____

1. Ⓨ Ⓝ

2. Ⓨ Ⓝ

3. Ⓨ Ⓝ

4. Ⓨ Ⓝ

5. Ⓨ Ⓝ

6. Ⓨ Ⓝ

7. Ⓨ Ⓝ

8. Ⓨ Ⓝ

9. Ⓨ Ⓝ

10. Ⓨ Ⓝ

___ / 10
Total

NAME: _____

SCORE

1. Ⓨ Ⓝ

2. Ⓨ Ⓝ

3. Ⓨ Ⓝ

4. Ⓨ Ⓝ

5. Ⓨ Ⓝ

6. Ⓨ Ⓝ

7. Ⓨ Ⓝ

8. Ⓨ Ⓝ

9. Ⓨ Ⓝ

10. Ⓨ Ⓝ

___ / 10
Total

1. What is the difference between 24 and 7?

_____ .

2. Calculate the product of 7 and 6.

_____

3. $35 \div 7 =$ _____

4. $6 \overline{)12}$

5. $1,000 + 300 + 20 =$

_____

6. ☐ $\times 4 = 32$

7. _____ is the longest dimension of an object.

8. 12 months = _____ year(s)

9. A cylinder has:

_____ surfaces

_____ edges

10. If the shaded area is equal to one, what is the area of the dotted region?

_____

NAME: _____

DIRECTIONS Solve each problem.

1. 35 + 18 = _____

7. Write the length in centimeters.

_____

cm 1   2   3   4   5

2. Which is larger: 0.6 or 0.16?

_____

8. _____ quarts = 2 gallons

3. List all the factors of 9.

_____

9.

Dollars Earned in May

Audrey	$15
Dameon	$23
Jason	$12
Lauren	$18

Who earned the most money?

_____

4. 70 ÷ 7 = _____

5. How many digits are in 600?

_____

10. Write two odd numbers that total the even number 20.

_____

6. Fill in the missing number.

32, 40, 48, _____, 64

1. Ⓨ Ⓝ

2. Ⓨ Ⓝ

3. Ⓨ Ⓝ

4. Ⓨ Ⓝ

5. Ⓨ Ⓝ

6. Ⓨ Ⓝ

7. Ⓨ Ⓝ

8. Ⓨ Ⓝ

9. Ⓨ Ⓝ

10. Ⓨ Ⓝ

___ / 10

Total

NAME:_____

DIRECTIONS Solve each problem.

1. Y N

2. Y N

3. Y N

4. Y N

5. Y N

6. Y N

7. Y N

8. Y N

9. Y N

10. Y N

___ / 10
Total

1.
$$\begin{array}{r} 46 \\ -\ 25 \\ \hline \end{array}$$

2. Color $\frac{3}{10}$.

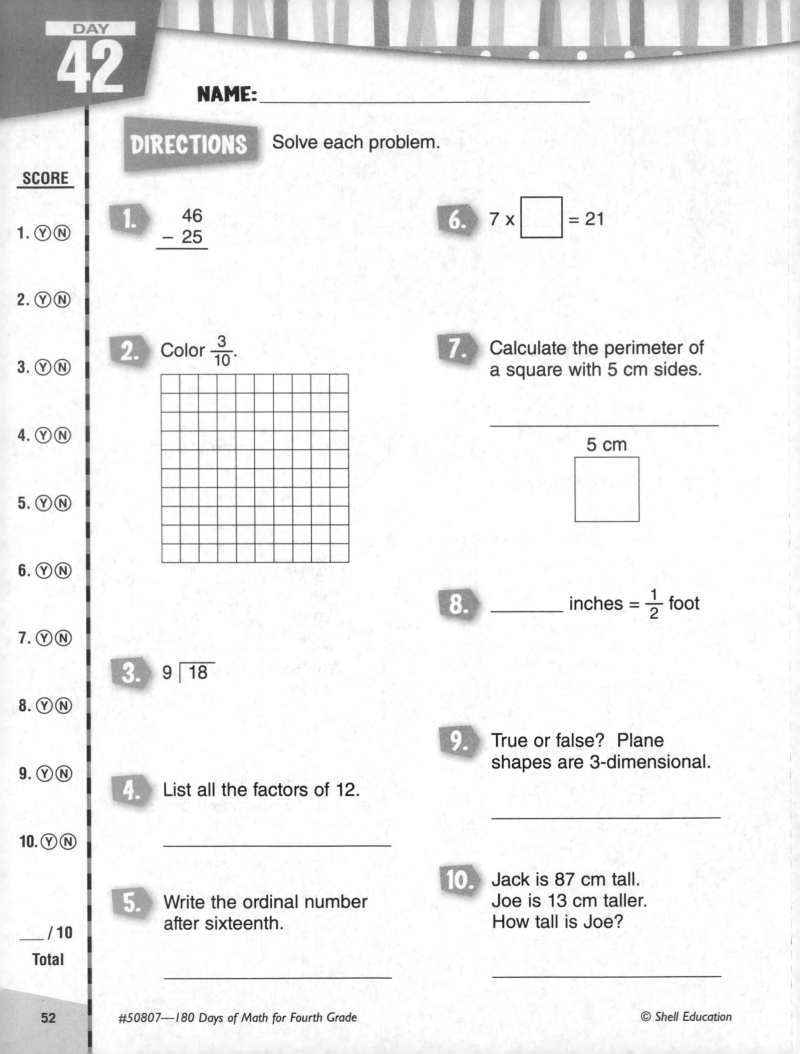

3. $9\overline{)18}$

4. List all the factors of 12.

_____

5. Write the ordinal number after sixteenth.

_____

6. $7 \times \boxed{} = 21$

7. Calculate the perimeter of a square with 5 cm sides.

_____

5 cm

8. _____ inches = $\frac{1}{2}$ foot

9. True or false? Plane shapes are 3-dimensional.

_____

10. Jack is 87 cm tall. Joe is 13 cm taller. How tall is Joe?

_____

NAME:_____

Solve each problem.

SCORE

1.
$$\begin{array}{r} 22 \\ + 17 \\ \hline \end{array}$$

1. Ⓨ Ⓝ

2. $\frac{1}{8}$ of 48 is _____

2. Ⓨ Ⓝ

3. List all the factors of 16.

_____

3. Ⓨ Ⓝ

4. 8 ⟌ 64

4. Ⓨ Ⓝ

5. Which is greater:
0.03 or 0.3?

_____

5. Ⓨ Ⓝ

6. 48 ÷ ⬚ = 12

6. Ⓨ Ⓝ

7. Fill in the blanks for the time shown.

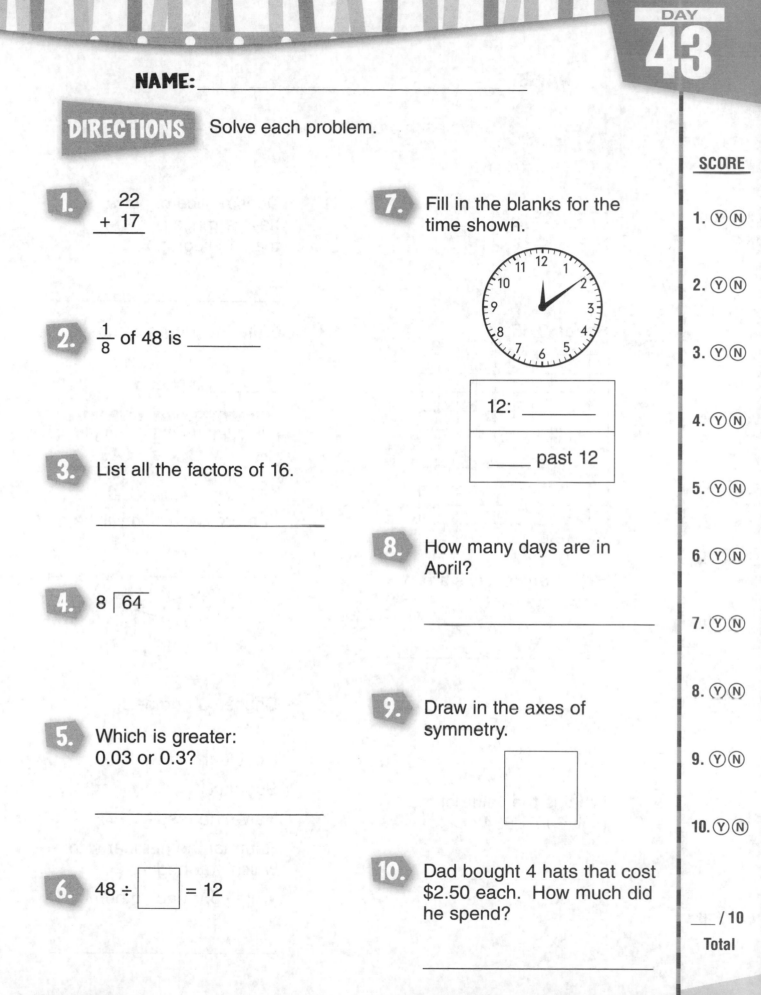

12: _____
_____ past 12

7. Ⓨ Ⓝ

8. How many days are in April?

_____

8. Ⓨ Ⓝ

9. Draw in the axes of symmetry.

9. Ⓨ Ⓝ

10. Ⓨ Ⓝ

10. Dad bought 4 hats that cost $2.50 each. How much did he spend?

_____

___ / 10
Total

NAME:_____

DIRECTIONS Solve each problem.

1. (Y) (N)

1. 37 − 23 = _____

2. (Y) (N)

2. Shade 0.53.

3. (Y) (N)

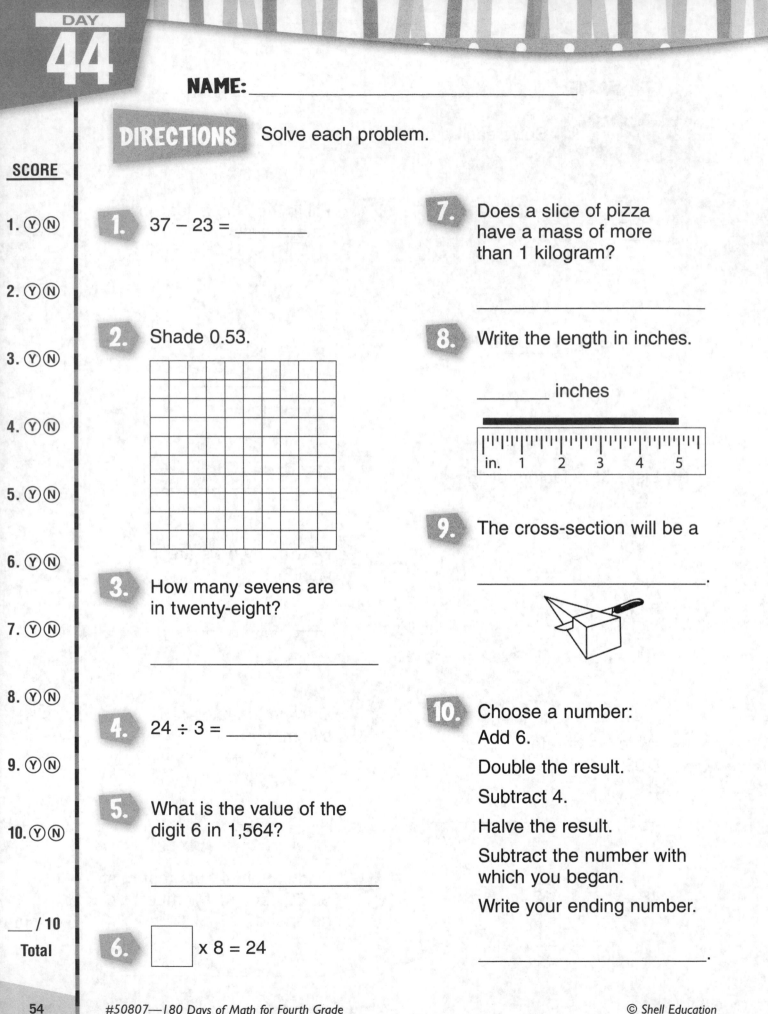

4. (Y) (N)

5. (Y) (N)

6. (Y) (N)

3. How many sevens are in twenty-eight?

7. (Y) (N)

_____

8. (Y) (N)

4. 24 ÷ 3 = _____

9. (Y) (N)

5. What is the value of the digit 6 in 1,564?

10. (Y) (N)

_____

___ / 10
Total

6. ☐ x 8 = 24

7. Does a slice of pizza have a mass of more than 1 kilogram?

_____

8. Write the length in inches.

_____ inches

9. The cross-section will be a

_____.

10. Choose a number:
Add 6.

Double the result.

Subtract 4.

Halve the result.

Subtract the number with which you began.

Write your ending number.

_____.

NAME: _____

DIRECTIONS Solve each problem.

1. Calculate the sum of 23 and 15.

_____

2. 6
     x 5

_____

3. 3 ⟌ 27

4. List all the factors of 18.

_____

5. 2,000 + 900 + 70 + 5 =

_____

6. 4 x ☐ = 36

7. What is the abbreviation for cubic centimeter?

_____

8. Which would be the best tool for measuring the temperature of water: a scale, a thermometer, or a meter stick?

_____

9.

Books Read in March

Cathy	📖 📖 📖
Martin	📖 📖 📖 📖
Jose	📖 📖 📖

📖 = 5 books read

Which children read the same number of books?

_____

10. Complete the multiplication wheel.

Wheel center: x 8
Outer numbers: 0, 5, 7, 4, 9, 6, 3, 10, 8, 2

SCORE
1. Y N
2. Y N
3. Y N
4. Y N
5. Y N
6. Y N
7. Y N
8. Y N
9. Y N
10. Y N
___ / 10
Total

NAME: _____

Solve each problem.

SCORE

1. Y N

2. Y N

3. Y N

4. Y N

5. Y N

6. Y N

7. Y N

8. Y N

9. Y N

10. Y N

___ / 10
Total

1.
  13
– 6

2. 0.5 of 18 is _____.

3. How many groups of 6 are in the number 36?

_____

4. 48 ÷ 6 = _____

5. What is the even number right before 36?

_____

6. Fill in the missing number.

129, 139, 149, _____, 169

7. How many full oil bottles can be poured into the bucket?

_____

OIL 4L   9 L

8. _____ inches = 2 feet

9. A regular octagon has:

_____ angles

_____ sides

_____ axes of symmetry

10. What fraction must be added to $\frac{3}{4}$ of a pizza to make 1 whole pizza?

_____

NAME: _____

Solve each problem.

SCORE

1. $4 + 7 + 6 =$ _____

1. Ⓨ Ⓝ

6. ☐ x 2 = 18

2. Ⓨ Ⓝ

2. What decimal is shaded?

_____

3. Ⓨ Ⓝ

7. What is the date of the first Monday in March?

4. Ⓨ Ⓝ

FEBRUARY						
Sun	Mon	Tue	Wed	Thu	Fri	Sat
		1	2	3	4	5
6	7	8	9	10	11	12
13	14	15	16	17	18	19
20	21	22	23	24	25	26
27	28	29				

5. Ⓨ Ⓝ

3. How many threes are in 21?

_____

8. A movie starts at 3:15 P.M. and ends at 5:30 P.M. How long is the movie?

_____

6. Ⓨ Ⓝ

7. Ⓨ Ⓝ

4. 6 ⟌ 60

9. How many pairs of opposite parallel sides does a parallelogram have?

_____

8. Ⓨ Ⓝ

9. Ⓨ Ⓝ

5. Is 42 smaller than 24?

_____

10. Our product is 72. The difference between us is 1. What numbers are we?

_____ _____

10. Ⓨ Ⓝ

_____ / 10
Total

NAME:_____

SCORE

DIRECTIONS Solve each problem.

1. $(Y)(N)$

2. $(Y)(N)$

3. $(Y)(N)$

4. $(Y)(N)$

5. $(Y)(N)$

6. $(Y)(N)$

7. $(Y)(N)$

8. $(Y)(N)$

9. $(Y)(N)$

10. $(Y)(N)$

___ / 10
Total

1. $33 - 7 = $ _____

2. $\frac{1}{5}$ of 15 is _____.

3. How many rows of 7 are in 49?

_____

4. $42 \div 6 = $ _____

5. Is 0.6 less than 0.06?

_____

6. $\boxed{} \div 7 = 6$

7. It took 4 buckets of water to fill a 20-liter tub. How many liters are in each bucket?

_____

8. What is the temperature?

_____

°F 60°
50°
40°
30°
20°

9. **Total Rainfall**

Inches of Rain
60
50
40
30
20
10
2007 2008 2009 2010
Year

Which year received the least rainfall?

_____

10. Use the same three colors for each flag. Color each flag in a different way.

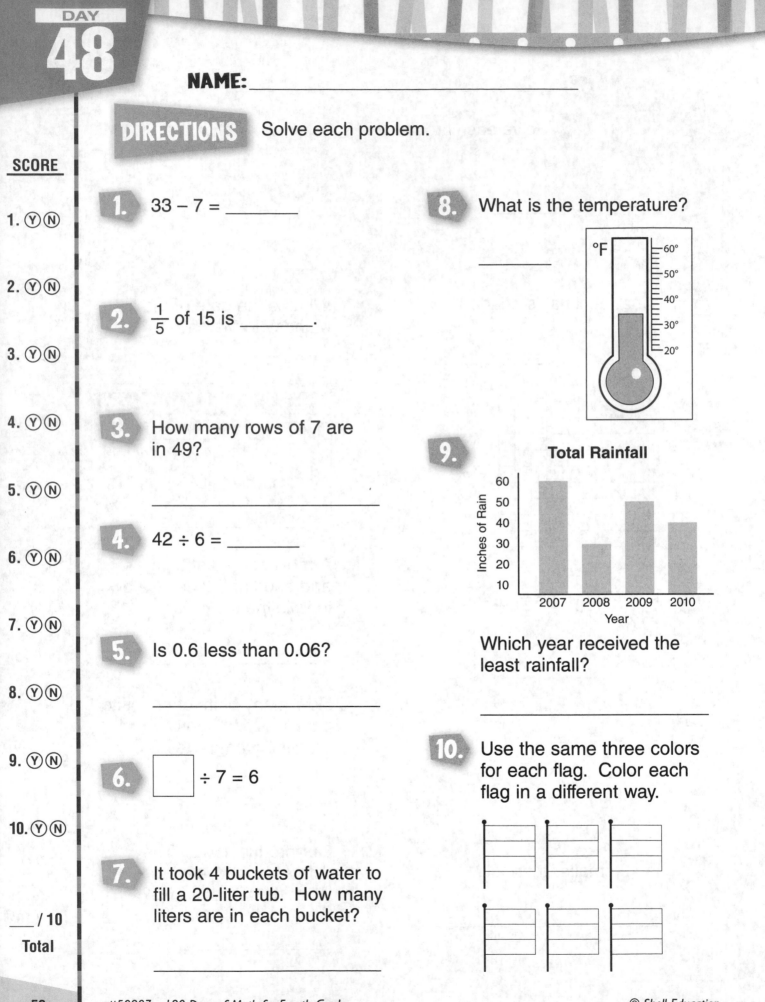

NAME: _____

DIRECTIONS Solve each problem.

1.
```
   16
 +  8
```

2. $\frac{1}{4}$ of 36 is _____.

3. List all the factors of 8.

_____

4. 9)‾45‾

5. What is the value of the digit 4 in 10,472?

_____

6. 36 + ☐ = 40

7. Each cube has 1-cm sides. What is the volume of the model?

_____

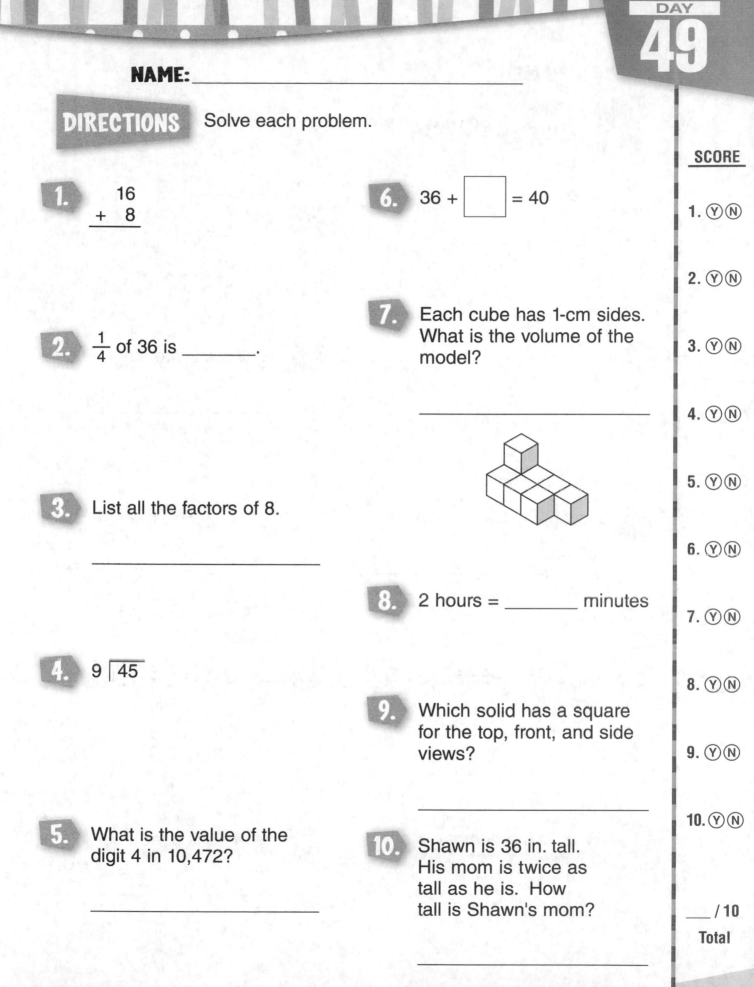

8. 2 hours = _____ minutes

9. Which solid has a square for the top, front, and side views?

_____

10. Shawn is 36 in. tall. His mom is twice as tall as he is. How tall is Shawn's mom?

_____

1. Y N

2. Y N

3. Y N

4. Y N

5. Y N

6. Y N

7. Y N

8. Y N

9. Y N

10. Y N

___ / 10

Total

NAME:_____

DIRECTIONS Solve each problem.

SCORE

1. Ⓨ Ⓝ

1.
28
− 9

6. $24 \div \boxed{} = 4$

2. Ⓨ Ⓝ

3. Ⓨ Ⓝ

2. 9 x 6 = _____

7. How many mm are in 2 cm?

_____

4. Ⓨ Ⓝ

5. Ⓨ Ⓝ

3. How many twos are in 18?

8. _____ quarts = $\frac{1}{2}$ gallon

6. Ⓨ Ⓝ

_____

7. Ⓨ Ⓝ

8. Ⓨ Ⓝ

4. List all the factors of 24.

9. Circle the right angles.

A.   B.   C.

_____

9. Ⓨ Ⓝ

10. Ⓨ Ⓝ

5. What is the number after 3,899?

10. $\frac{1}{5}$ of 45 is 9, so $\frac{4}{5}$ of 45 is

_____

___ / 10

Total

_____

#50807—180 Days of Math for Fourth Grade
© Shell Education

NAME: _____

DIRECTIONS Solve each problem.

1. 16 + 8 + 14 = _____

2. Is $\frac{3}{10}$ larger than $\frac{29}{100}$?

_____

3. 9 $\overline{)81}$

4. 54 divided by 9 is _____

5. What is the next odd number after 421?

_____

6. Write the number that comes next in the pattern.
41, 31, 21, 11,

_____

7. Write the line length in millimeters.

_____

cm 1   2   3   4   5

8. _____ yard = 18 inches

9. Draw in tho diagonals for the shape.

10. Write two odd numbers that total the even number 16.

_____

1. Ⓨ Ⓝ

2. Ⓨ Ⓝ

3. Ⓨ Ⓝ

4. Ⓨ Ⓝ

5. Ⓨ Ⓝ

6. Ⓨ Ⓝ

7. Ⓨ Ⓝ

8. Ⓨ Ⓝ

9. Ⓨ Ⓝ

10. Ⓨ Ⓝ

___ / 10

Total

NAME: _____

DIRECTIONS Solve each problem.

1. $41 - 8 =$ _____

1. Ⓨ Ⓝ

2. Ⓨ Ⓝ

2. $\$1.50 + \$1.25 =$ _____

3. Ⓨ Ⓝ

4. Ⓨ Ⓝ

3. How many sixes are in 30?

5. Ⓨ Ⓝ

_____

6. Ⓨ Ⓝ

4. $72 \div 9 =$ _____

7. Ⓨ Ⓝ

8. Ⓨ Ⓝ

5. Circle the larger number.

9. Ⓨ Ⓝ

    2,463   2,634

10. Ⓨ Ⓝ

6. ☐ $\times 4 = 24$

_____ / 10
Total

7. Calculate the area of a square with 9-cm sides.

_____

            ☐ 9 cm

8. How many months are in a year?

_____

9. **School Awards**

Student	Number of Awards
Daniel	
Evan	
Rich	

0 2 4 6 8 10 12
Number of Awards

How many awards did Daniel win?

_____

10. Follow the pattern in the first circle to complete the second circle.

NAME: _____

DIRECTIONS Solve each problem.

1.
$$\begin{array}{r} 24 \\ +9 \\ \hline \end{array}$$

2. $\frac{4}{5}$ of 30 is _____

3. Divide 36 in 4 equal rows.

_____

4. $7\overline{)28}$

5. What is the value of the tens place in 1,906?

_____

6. $\boxed{} \div 5 = 6$

7. Draw and write the time that is 15 minutes later.

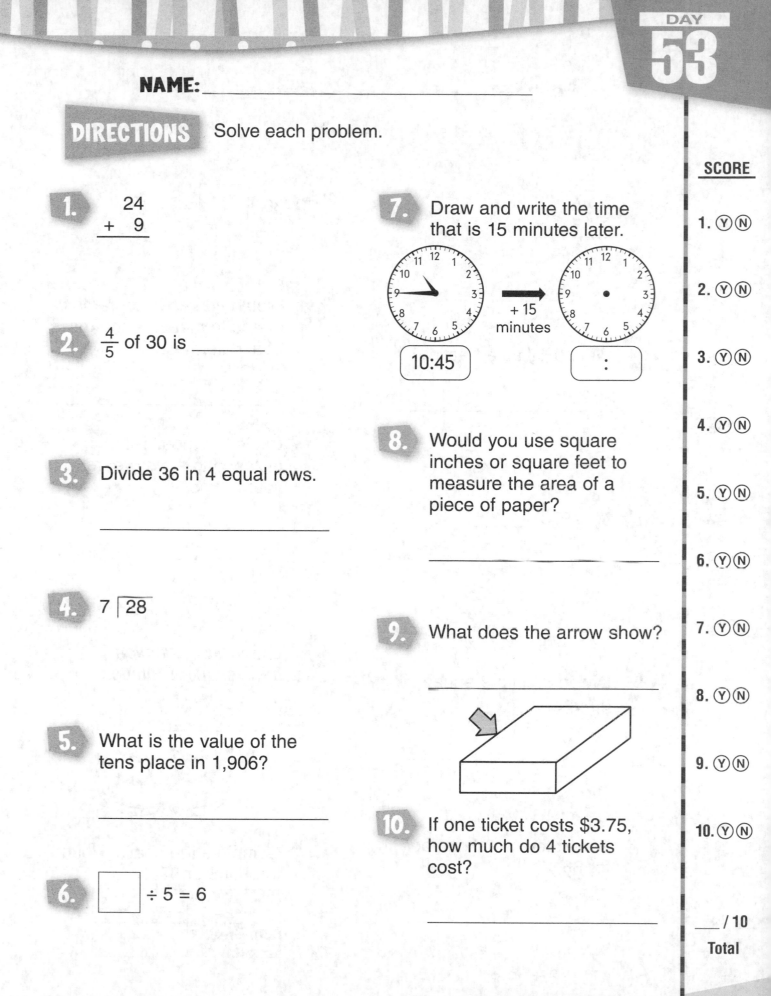

10:45 → + 15 minutes → :

8. Would you use square inches or square feet to measure the area of a piece of paper?

_____

9. What does the arrow show?

_____

10. If one ticket costs $3.75, how much do 4 tickets cost?

_____

1. Ⓨ Ⓝ

2. Ⓨ Ⓝ

3. Ⓨ Ⓝ

4. Ⓨ Ⓝ

5. Ⓨ Ⓝ

6. Ⓨ Ⓝ

7. Ⓨ Ⓝ

8. Ⓨ Ⓝ

9. Ⓨ Ⓝ

10. Ⓨ Ⓝ

___ / 10
Total

NAME: _____

SCORE

DIRECTIONS Solve each problem.

1. Ⓨ Ⓝ

2. Ⓨ Ⓝ

3. Ⓨ Ⓝ

4. Ⓨ Ⓝ

5. Ⓨ Ⓝ

6. Ⓨ Ⓝ

7. Ⓨ Ⓝ

8. Ⓨ Ⓝ

9. Ⓨ Ⓝ

10. Ⓨ Ⓝ

___ / 10
Total

1.
```
   45
 −  7
```

2. Write 0.67 as a fraction.

_____

3. $56 \div 7 = $ _____

4. Divide 63 into 9 equal groups.

_____

5. Write the ordinal number for 36.

_____

6. $36 \div \boxed{} = 6$

7. Would you use kilograms or grams to measure the mass of a watermelon?

_____

8. Circle the most likely distance to the store from your house.

  1 kilometer

  1 meter

  1 gram

9. Label with *reflection*, *translation*, or *rotation*.

_____

10. Complete the chart. Round the number 872.

Tens	
Hundreds	

NAME: _____

DIRECTIONS Solve each problem.

1. Find the sum of 496 and 784

_____

2.
```
    3
  x 8
```

3. 7 ⟌ 14

4. Divide 54 into 6 equal groups.

_____

5. Is 36 an even number?

_____

6. To find 12 ÷ 4, we say

☐ x 4 = 12

7. Ezra takes 2 steps to cover a meter. She walks 500 meters to the bus stop. How many steps does she take?

_____

8. 24 inches = _____ feet

9. **Sports Played Each Year**

	1st Trimester	2nd Trimester	3rd Trimester
Troy	soccer	basketball	baseball
Jessica	golf	basketball	track
Allison	soccer	diving	swimming

Which 3 sports does Allison play?

_____

_____

10. Use different colors to color pairs of numbers that equal the product shown in the center.

30
6   1
30
15   2
5

1. Y N
2. Y N
3. Y N
4. Y N
5. Y N
6. Y N
7. Y N
8. Y N
9. Y N
10. Y N
____ / 10
Total

NAME:_____

DIRECTIONS Solve each problem.

1. 62 − 8 = _____

2. Color $\frac{3}{100}$.

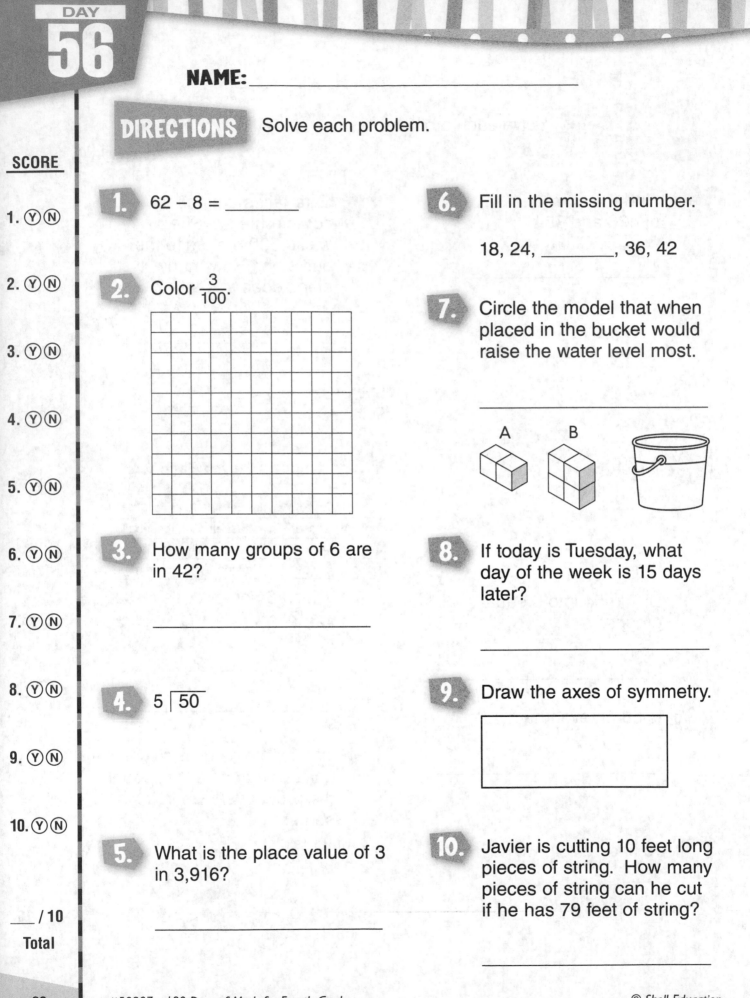

3. How many groups of 6 are in 42?

_____

4. 5 $\overline{)50}$

5. What is the place value of 3 in 3,916?

_____

6. Fill in the missing number.

18, 24, _____, 36, 42

7. Circle the model that when placed in the bucket would raise the water level most.

_____

A   B

8. If today is Tuesday, what day of the week is 15 days later?

_____

9. Draw the axes of symmetry.

10. Javier is cutting 10 feet long pieces of string. How many pieces of string can he cut if he has 79 feet of string?

_____

NAME: _____

DIRECTIONS Solve each problem.

1.   59
      + 9

2. $5.00 - $2.25 = _____

3. Share 63 equally among 7.

_____

4. 49 ÷ 7 = _____

5. Round 132 to the nearest ten.

_____

6. 18 + ☐ = 25

7. On what day of the week is March 15th?

_____

FEBRUARY						
Sun	Mon	Tue	Wed	Thu	Fri	Sat
		1	2	3	4	5
6	7	8	9	10	11	12
13	14	15	16	17	18	19
20	21	22	23	24	25	26
27	28	29				

8. Do you go to bed in the A.M. or P.M.?

_____

9. Draw a line from the real-life object to the solid.

10. If you add me to 493, the sum is 1,221. What number am I?

_____

1. Ⓨ Ⓝ
2. Ⓨ Ⓝ
3. Ⓨ Ⓝ
4. Ⓨ Ⓝ
5. Ⓨ Ⓝ
6. Ⓨ Ⓝ
7. Ⓨ Ⓝ
8. Ⓨ Ⓝ
9. Ⓨ Ⓝ
10. Ⓨ Ⓝ

___ / 10
Total

NAME: _____

DIRECTIONS Solve each problem.

1. (Y)(N)

1.
$$\begin{array}{r} 53 \\ -7 \\ \hline \end{array}$$

2. (Y)(N)

2. Write 0.99 as a fraction.

3. (Y)(N)

_____

4. (Y)(N)

3. $8\overline{)24}$

5. (Y)(N)

4. How many sevens are in 70?

6. (Y)(N)

_____

7. (Y)(N)

5. Write the smallest 3-digit number using 2, 8, and 1.

8. (Y)(N)

_____

6. $72 \div \boxed{} = 9$

9. (Y)(N)

10. (Y)(N)

7. Record in milliliters.

_____ mL

_____ / 10
Total

8. What is the temperature?

_____

°C
60°
50°
40°
30°
20°

9. Record the data in the chart.

Child's Name	Number of CDs

Jahir has 23 music CDs.
Olivia has 15 music CDs.
Gerald has 35 music CDs.
Mimi has 3 music CDs.

10. Plot each set of coordinates to make a rectangle.
(A, 2); (A, 5); (E, 2); (E, 5)

8
7
6
5
4
3
2
1
A B C D E F G H

NAME: _____

Solve each problem.

SCORE

1. 35 + 8 = _____

6. ☐ − 16 = 23

1. Ⓨ Ⓝ

2. Ⓨ Ⓝ

2. $\frac{8}{10}$ of 90 = _____

7. Each cube has 1-cm sides. What is the volume of the model?

3. Ⓨ Ⓝ

_____

4. Ⓨ Ⓝ

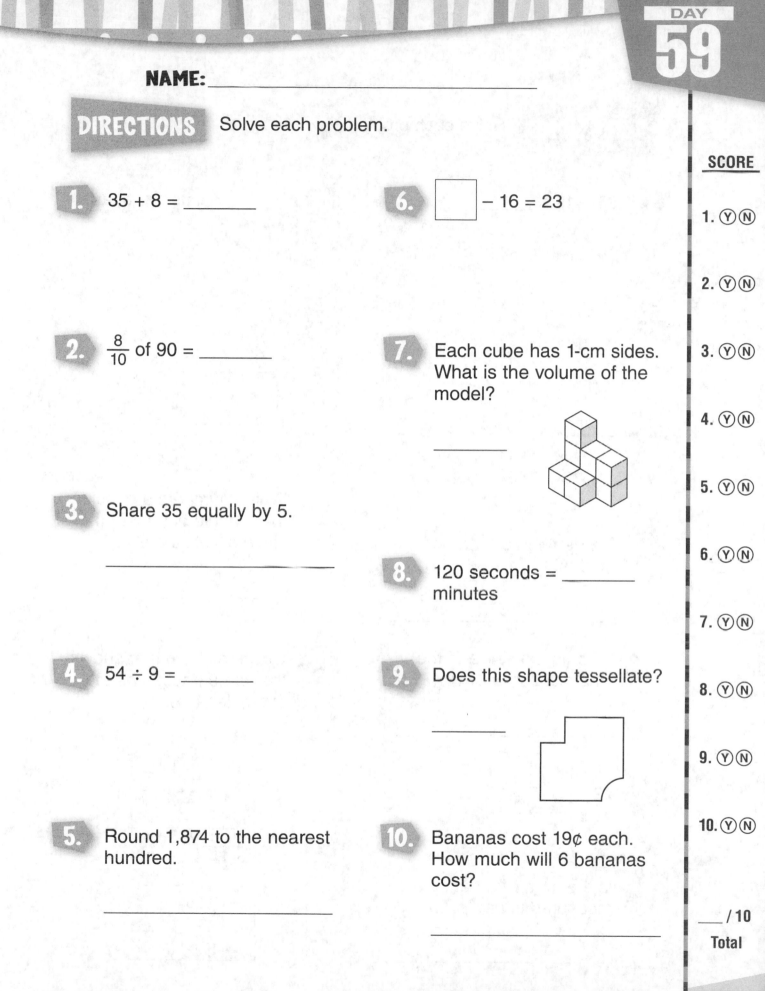

5. Ⓨ Ⓝ

3. Share 35 equally by 5.

_____

8. 120 seconds = _____ minutes

6. Ⓨ Ⓝ

7. Ⓨ Ⓝ

4. 54 ÷ 9 = _____

9. Does this shape tessellate?

8. Ⓨ Ⓝ

_____

9. Ⓨ Ⓝ

5. Round 1,874 to the nearest hundred.

10. Bananas cost 19¢ each. How much will 6 bananas cost?

10. Ⓨ Ⓝ

_____

_____

___/ 10
Total

NAME:_____

DIRECTIONS Solve each problem.

1. (Y)(N)

2. (Y)(N)

3. (Y)(N)

4. (Y)(N)

5. (Y)(N)

6. (Y)(N)

7. (Y)(N)

8. (Y)(N)

9. (Y)(N)

10.(Y)(N)

___/ 10
Total

1. 28 − 19 = _____

2.
$$\begin{array}{r} 7 \\ \times\ 3 \\ \hline \end{array}$$

3. 8$\overline{)32}$

4. Divide 45 into 5 equal groups.

_____

5. What is the value of the tens place in 3,571?

_____

6. 72 − ☐ = 12

7. Is the area of a handprint measured in cm^2 or m^2?

_____

8. _____ pints = 2 quarts

9.

Which numbers are inside the triangle but not in the circle or rectangle?

_____

10. Circle the card that shows the same fraction as the example on top.

NAME: _____

DIRECTIONS Solve each problem.

1.
```
   56
+   8
```

2. Color $\frac{30}{100}$.

3. 50 ÷ 5 = _____

4. 63 ÷ 9 = _____

5. What is the first odd number before 81?

_____

6. Fill in the missing number.

200, 400, _____, 800, 1,000

7. Write the length in centimeters.

_____

cm 1   2   3   4   5

8. _____ yards = 72 inches

9. What shape is the base of a cylinder?

_____

10. Complete the addition grid.

+	7	15	18	23	25	28
19						
29						
39						

1. Ⓨ Ⓝ
2. Ⓨ Ⓝ
3. Ⓨ Ⓝ
4. Ⓨ Ⓝ
5. Ⓨ Ⓝ
6. Ⓨ Ⓝ
7. Ⓨ Ⓝ
8. Ⓨ Ⓝ
9. Ⓨ Ⓝ
10. Ⓨ Ⓝ

___ / 10
Total

NAME: _____

DIRECTIONS Solve each problem.

SCORE

1. Ⓨ Ⓝ

2. Ⓨ Ⓝ

3. Ⓨ Ⓝ

4. Ⓨ Ⓝ

5. Ⓨ Ⓝ

6. Ⓨ Ⓝ

7. Ⓨ Ⓝ

8. Ⓨ Ⓝ

9. Ⓨ Ⓝ

10. Ⓨ Ⓝ

___ / 10

Total

1.
$$\begin{array}{r} 17 \\ -9 \\ \hline \end{array}$$

2. Circle the greater number.

0.02   0.2

3. 12 ⟌ 84

4. $36 \div 6 =$ _____

5. Write 2,365 in expanded notation.

_____

_____

6. $23 +$ ☐ $= 50$

7. Calculate the perimeter of a square with 2-cm sides.

_____

☐ 2 cm

8. How many faces does a rectangular prism have?

_____

9. Draw intersecting lines.

10. It takes 5 bottles of juice to fill a 20-liter tank. How many liters are in each bottle?

_____

NAME: _____

DIRECTIONS Solve each problem.

1. 13 + 4 + 17 = _____

7. Complete the labels for the time shown.

7: _____

_____ past 7

2. $\frac{8}{10}$ of 70 is _____

3. 60 ÷ 6 = _____

8. Write the length in inches.

_____ inches

4. 63 ÷ 7 = _____

9. Are these lines perpendicular? _____

5. What is the value of the digit 5 in 42,562?

_____

6. ☐ x 5 = 10

10. Michael buys 1 notebook and 5 pencils. If the notebook costs $3.50 and the pencils are 25¢ each, what is the total he spent?

_____

1. Ⓨ Ⓝ

2. Ⓨ Ⓝ

3. Ⓨ Ⓝ

4. Ⓨ Ⓝ

5. Ⓨ Ⓝ

6. Ⓨ Ⓝ

7. Ⓨ Ⓝ

8. Ⓨ Ⓝ

9. Ⓨ Ⓝ

10. Ⓨ Ⓝ

___ / 10
Total

NAME: _____

DIRECTIONS Solve each problem.

SCORE

1. Y N

2. Y N

3. Y N

4. Y N

5. Y N

6. Y N

7. Y N

8. Y N

9. Y N

10. Y N

___ / 10
Total

1. Subtract 19 from 36.

_____

2. Is 0.4 less than 0.04?

_____

3. 81 ÷ 9 = _____

4. Divide 27 into 3 equal groups.

_____

5. Order the numbers from smallest to largest.
1,624; 1,264; 1,426

_____ _____ _____

6. 8 × ☐ = 64

7. Circle the best estimate for the weight of the object.

100 g   2 kg   5 kg   10 kg

8. Which would be the best measure for the width of your pointer finger: a foot, a degree, or a centimeter?

_____

9. Does an angle get bigger if you make its lines longer?

_____

10. Complete the chart below to represent the shaded part of the hundred grid.

100	0.	%

NAME: _____

DIRECTIONS Solve each problem.

1. 18
      + 13

2. 10 rows of 6 is _____.

3. 5 ⟌ 45

4. 56 ÷ 7 = _____

5. Is 2,509 less than 2,590?

_____

6. 12 x ☐ = 36

7. Circle the best estimate for the area of a handprint.

75 cm²   750 cm²

8. 108 inches equals how many yards?

_____

9. What type of prism is shown?

_____

10. Complete the multiplication wheel.

1. Ⓨ Ⓝ

2. Ⓨ Ⓝ

3. Ⓨ Ⓝ

4. Ⓨ Ⓝ

5. Ⓨ Ⓝ

6. Ⓨ Ⓝ

7. Ⓨ Ⓝ

8. Ⓨ Ⓝ

9. Ⓨ Ⓝ

10. Ⓨ Ⓝ

___ / 10
Total

NAME: _____

SCORE

DIRECTIONS Solve each problem.

1. (Y)(N)

1.   43
      − 29

2. (Y)(N)

3. (Y)(N)

2. $\frac{3}{5}$ of 35 is _____

4. (Y)(N)

5. (Y)(N)

3. The quotient of 35 and 7 is

6. (Y)(N)

_____.

7. (Y)(N)

8. (Y)(N)

4. 9$\overline{)72}$

9. (Y)(N)

10. (Y)(N)

5. Write the numeral for
two thousand three.

_____ / 10
Total

6. Fill in the missing number.

4, 8, _____, 16, 20

7. How many 250-milliliter
bottles are needed to
fill a 5-liter bucket?

_____

8. Calculate the number
of seconds there
are in 2 minutes.

_____

9. **Dollars Earned in May**

Audrey	$15
Dameon	$23
Jason	$12
Lauren	$18

How much more did Audrey
earn than Jason?

_____

10. Find the perimeter of a
figure with these 4 sides:
3 cm, 5 cm, 7 cm, 4 cm.

_____

NAME: _____

DIRECTIONS Solve each problem.

1. 23 + 17 = _____

2. $\frac{1}{2}$ of 14 is _____

3. 14 ÷ 2 = _____

4. Divide 50 by 10. _____

5. How many digits are in the number 2,967?

_____

6. 45 − ☐ = 40

7. How many Mondays are in February?

_____

FEBRUARY						
Sun	Mon	Tue	Wed	Thu	Fri	Sat
		1	2	3	4	5
6	7	8	9	10	11	12
13	14	15	16	17	18	19
20	21	22	23	24	25	26
27	28	29				

8. Trish starts to watch TV at 7:30 P.M. and ends at 8:10 P.M. How long did she watch?

_____

9. Name this shape.

_____

10. Our sum is 13. The difference between us is 1. What numbers are we?

_____

1. Ⓨ Ⓝ

2. Ⓨ Ⓝ

3. Ⓨ Ⓝ

4. Ⓨ Ⓝ

5. Ⓨ Ⓝ

6. Ⓨ Ⓝ

7. Ⓨ Ⓝ

8. Ⓨ Ⓝ

9. Ⓨ Ⓝ

10. Ⓨ Ⓝ

___ / 10
Total

NAME: _____

DIRECTIONS Solve each problem.

1. 18 – 9 = _____

2. What decimal is shaded?

_____

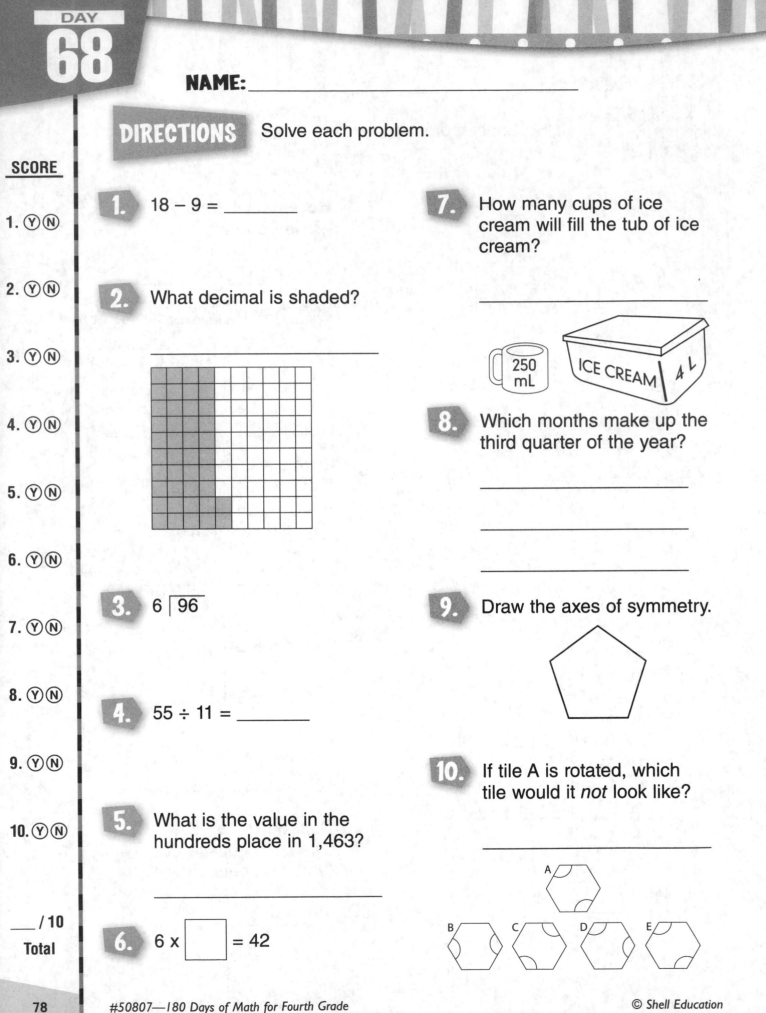

3. 6 ⟌ 96

4. 55 ÷ 11 = _____

5. What is the value in the hundreds place in 1,463?

_____

6. 6 x ☐ = 42

7. How many cups of ice cream will fill the tub of ice cream?

_____

8. Which months make up the third quarter of the year?

_____

_____

_____

9. Draw the axes of symmetry.

10. If tile A is rotated, which tile would it *not* look like?

_____

NAME: _____

DIRECTIONS Solve each problem.

1.
$$\begin{array}{r} 42 \\ +\ 19 \\ \hline \end{array}$$

6. $70 - \boxed{} = 55$

7. Is this a leap year?

_____

FEBRUARY						
Sun	Mon	Tue	Wed	Thu	Fri	Sat
		1	2	3	4	5
6	7	8	9	10	11	12
13	14	15	16	17	18	19
20	21	22	23	24	25	26
27	28	29				

2. $\frac{1}{4}$ of 28 = _____

3. How many threes are in the number twelve?

_____

8. If the outdoor temperature were 32°F, would you more likely build a snowman or go swimming in the ocean?

_____

4. $58 \div 6 =$ _____

9. Color the solids that have a triangle for a front view.

A.   B.   C.

5. Write the largest 4-digit number using 3, 7, 2, and 5.

_____

10. It takes David 15 minutes to ride his bike around the block. How many times can he ride around the block in 45 minutes?

_____

1. Ⓨ Ⓝ

2. Ⓨ Ⓝ

3. Ⓨ Ⓝ

4. Ⓨ Ⓝ

5. Ⓨ Ⓝ

6. Ⓨ Ⓝ

7. Ⓨ Ⓝ

8. Ⓨ Ⓝ

9. Ⓨ Ⓝ

10. Ⓨ Ⓝ

___ / 10
Total

NAME: _____

DIRECTIONS Solve each problem.

SCORE

1. Ⓨ Ⓝ

2. Ⓨ Ⓝ

3. Ⓨ Ⓝ

4. Ⓨ Ⓝ

5. Ⓨ Ⓝ

6. Ⓨ Ⓝ

7. Ⓨ Ⓝ

8. Ⓨ Ⓝ

9. Ⓨ Ⓝ

10. Ⓨ Ⓝ

___/ 10
Total

1. $34 - 19 =$ _____

2. Write 0.3 as a fraction.

_____

3. Divide 64 into eight groups.

_____

4. $3 \overline{)24}$

5. Order the numbers from largest to smallest.

2,097; 2,079; 2,907

_____ _____ _____

6. $4 \times \boxed{} = 28$

7. Calculate the area of a square with 6-cm sides.

_____

6 cm

8. 3 yards = _____ feet

9. Name the angle found at the corner of this page.

_____

10. Follow the pattern in the first circle to complete the second circle.

NAME:_____

DIRECTIONS Solve each problem.

1. 28 + 12 = _____

6. 4 x ☐ = 28

1. Ⓨ Ⓝ

2. Shade 0.65.

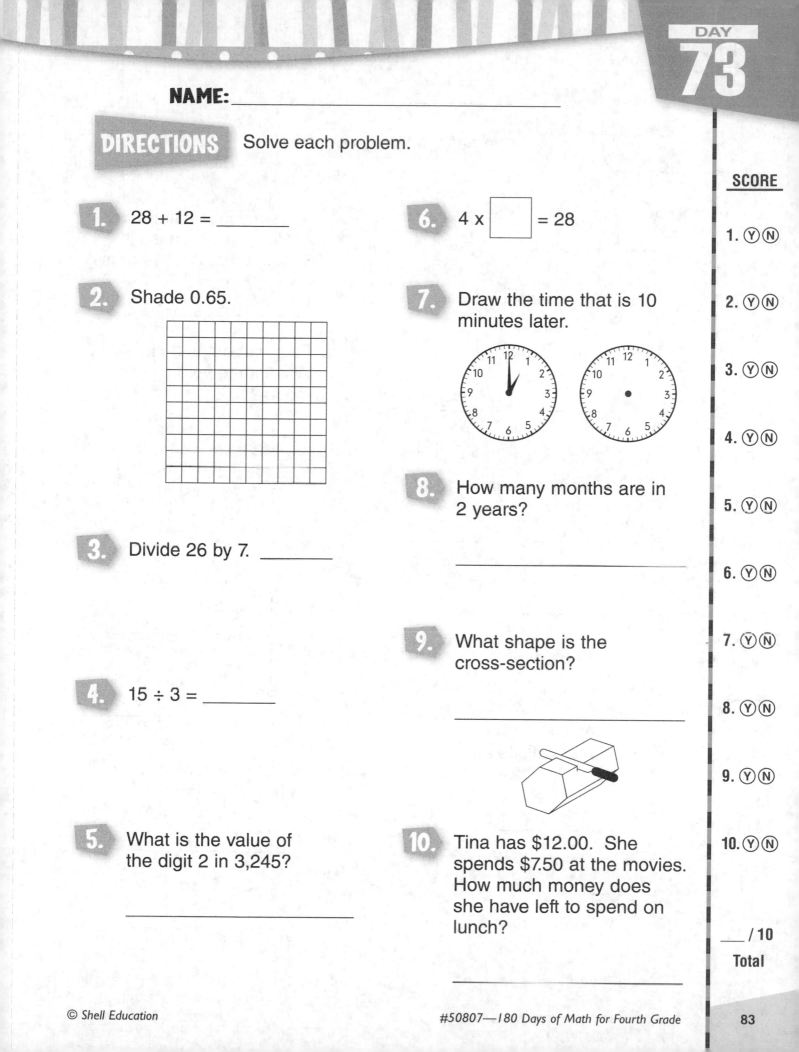

7. Draw the time that is 10 minutes later.

2. Ⓨ Ⓝ

3. Ⓨ Ⓝ

4. Ⓨ Ⓝ

8. How many months are in 2 years?

5. Ⓨ Ⓝ

3. Divide 26 by 7. _____

_____

6. Ⓨ Ⓝ

9. What shape is the cross-section?

7. Ⓨ Ⓝ

4. 15 ÷ 3 = _____

_____

8. Ⓨ Ⓝ

9. Ⓨ Ⓝ

5. What is the value of the digit 2 in 3,245?

10. Tina has $12.00. She spends $7.50 at the movies. How much money does she have left to spend on lunch?

10. Ⓨ Ⓝ

_____

____ / 10

Total

_____

NAME: _____

DIRECTIONS Solve each problem.

SCORE

1. Ⓨ Ⓝ

2. Ⓨ Ⓝ

3. Ⓨ Ⓝ

4. Ⓨ Ⓝ

5. Ⓨ Ⓝ

6. Ⓨ Ⓝ

7. Ⓨ Ⓝ

8. Ⓨ Ⓝ

9. Ⓨ Ⓝ

10. Ⓨ Ⓝ

___ / 10
Total

1.
$$\begin{array}{r} 46 \\ -\ 29 \\ \hline \end{array}$$

2. Is 0.3 equal to $\frac{3}{100}$?

_____

3. How many sixes are in 24?

_____

4. $3\overline{\smash{)}16}$

5. How many digits are in the number 3,090?

_____

6. $36 \div \boxed{} = 6$

7. Jon's mass is half the mass of Nick, whose mass is 86 kg. What is Jon's mass?

_____

8. Each cube has 3-cm sides. What is the volume of the model?

_____

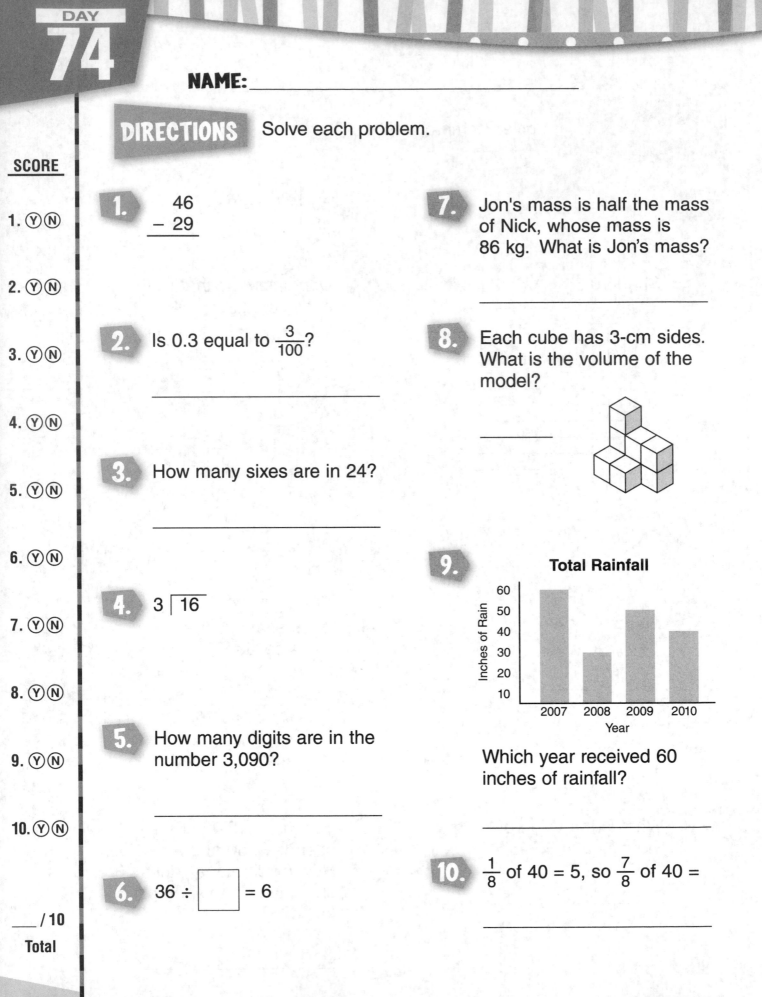

9. **Total Rainfall**

Which year received 60 inches of rainfall?

_____

10. $\frac{1}{8}$ of 40 = 5, so $\frac{7}{8}$ of 40 =

_____

NAME: _____

Solve each problem.

SCORE

1.
34
+ 16

1. Ⓨ Ⓝ

2. Ⓨ Ⓝ

2. 8 x 9 = _____

3. Ⓨ Ⓝ

3. 42 ÷ 6 = _____

4. Ⓨ Ⓝ

4. How many groups of 8 are in 72?

_____

5. Write 3,058 in words.

_____

_____

_____

6. ☐ x 2 = 18

7. Is 100 cm equal to 1 m?

_____

8. Would you use a ruler or a yardstick to measure the height of a person?

_____

9. Are parallel lines always straight?

_____

10. Use different colors to color pairs of numbers that equal the product shown in the center.

5. Ⓨ Ⓝ

6. Ⓨ Ⓝ

7. Ⓨ Ⓝ

8. Ⓨ Ⓝ

32

8   2

32

16   1

4

9. Ⓨ Ⓝ

10. Ⓨ Ⓝ

___ / 10
Total

SCORE

DIRECTIONS Solve each problem.

1. (Y) (N)

2. (Y) (N)

3. (Y) (N)

4. (Y) (N)

5. (Y) (N)

6. (Y) (N)

7. (Y) (N)

8. (Y) (N)

9. (Y) (N)

10. (Y) (N)

___ / 10
Total

1. $\begin{array}{r} 19 \\ -\ 17 \\ \hline \end{array}$

2. Is $\frac{1}{2}$ greater than $\frac{1}{3}$?

    _____

3. $34 \div 5 =$ _____

4. Divide 70 by 10. _____

5. Is 2,194 less than 2,914?

    _____

6. $81 \div \boxed{} = 9$

7. Does 1 liter equal 1,000 milliliters?

    _____

8. 3 yards = _____ inches

9. **School Awards**

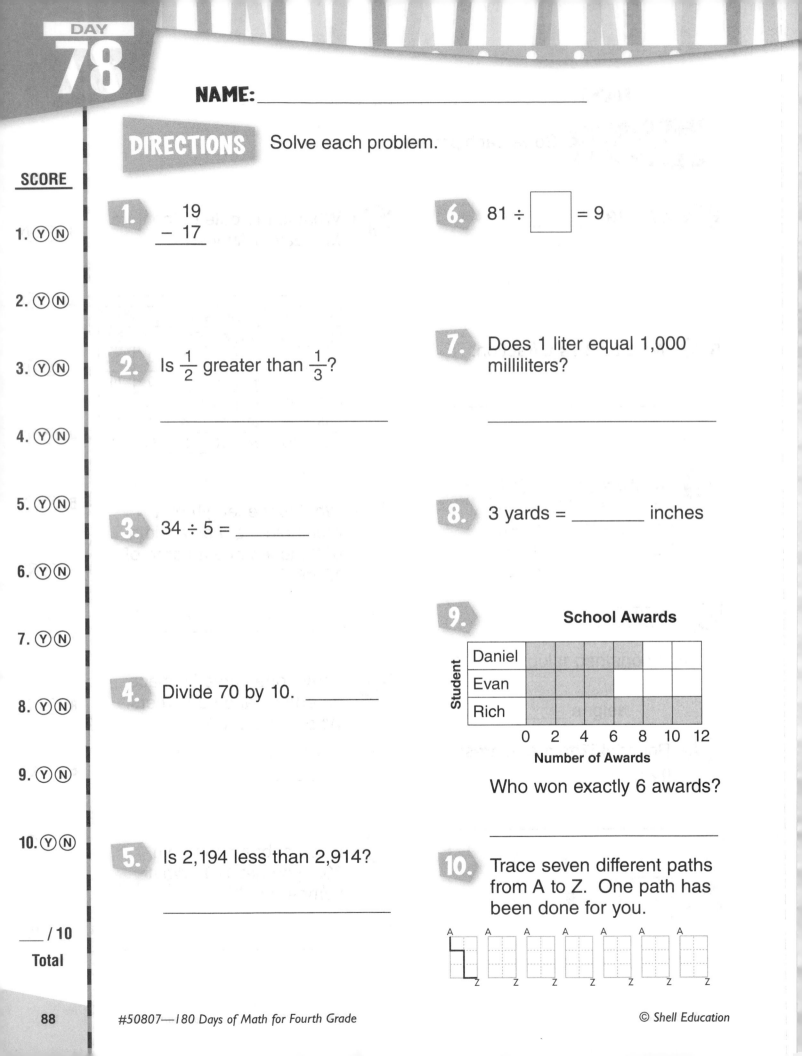

    Who won exactly 6 awards?

    _____

10. Trace seven different paths from A to Z. One path has been done for you.

NAME: _____

DIRECTIONS Solve each problem.

1.
$$35$$
$$+\ 25$$

6. $7 \times \boxed{} = 21$

7. Each cube has 2-cm sides. What is the volume of the model?

_____

2. Write $\frac{6}{10}$ as a decimal.

_____

3. $10\overline{)75}$

8. You wake up at 6:28 A.M. and go to bed at 9:30 P.M. How long are you awake?

_____

9. If you turn around a given point, are you *reflecting*, *translating*, or *rotating*?

_____

4. What is the quotient of 80 and 10?

_____

5. What is the value of the tens place in 1,378?

_____

10. Three sisters are each making themselves one beaded necklace. They use 125 beads on each necklace. How many beads do they need?

_____

1. Ⓨ Ⓝ

2. Ⓨ Ⓝ

3. Ⓨ Ⓝ

4. Ⓨ Ⓝ

5. Ⓨ Ⓝ

6. Ⓨ Ⓝ

7. Ⓨ Ⓝ

8. Ⓨ Ⓝ

9. Ⓨ Ⓝ

10. Ⓨ Ⓝ

___ / 10
Total

NAME: _____

DIRECTIONS Solve each problem.

SCORE

1. Ⓨ Ⓝ

2. Ⓨ Ⓝ

3. Ⓨ Ⓝ

4. Ⓨ Ⓝ

5. Ⓨ Ⓝ

6. Ⓨ Ⓝ

7. Ⓨ Ⓝ

8. Ⓨ Ⓝ

9. Ⓨ Ⓝ

10. Ⓨ Ⓝ

___ / 10
Total

1. 24 − 6 = _____

2.
$$\begin{array}{r} 9 \\ \times\ 7 \\ \hline \end{array}$$

3. 2 ⟌ 10

4. 87 ÷ 10 = _____

5. Write the largest 4-digit numeral using 1, 0, 7, and 9.

_____

6. ☐ x 8 = 32

7. Is the area of the cover of a book measured in cm² or m²?

_____

8. Would you use a thermometer or a ruler to measure temperature?

_____

9. Complete around the axis of symmetry.

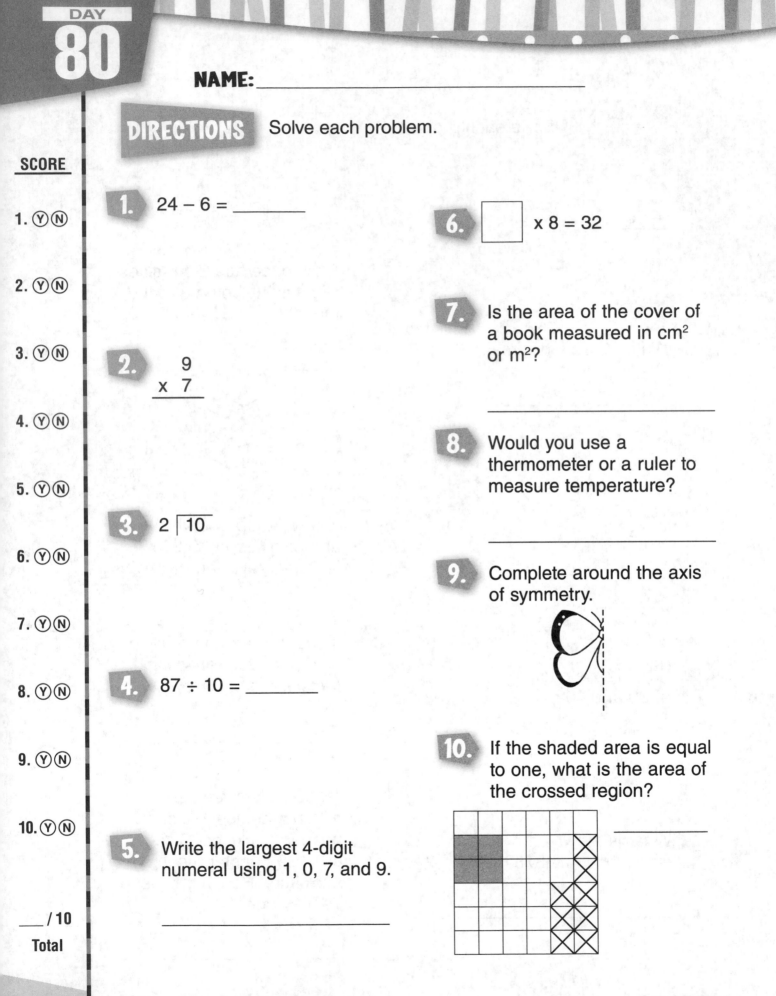

10. If the shaded area is equal to one, what is the area of the crossed region?

_____

NAME:_____

DIRECTIONS Solve each problem.

1. 31 + 29 = _____

6. Fill in the missing number.

60, 54, _____, 42, 36

2. Is $\frac{7}{10}$ equal to $\frac{7}{100}$?

_____

7. Write the length in millimeters.

cm 1 2 3 4 5

_____

3. Divide 50 into 10 equal groups.

_____

8. 2 hours = _____ minutes

4. 100 ÷ 10 = _____

9. A cylinder has:

_____ faces

_____ vertices

_____ edges

5. What is the first odd number before 291?

_____

10. Write two odd numbers that total the even number 50.

_____

1. Ⓨ Ⓝ

2. Ⓨ Ⓝ

3. Ⓨ Ⓝ

4. Ⓨ Ⓝ

5. Ⓨ Ⓝ

6. Ⓨ Ⓝ

7. Ⓨ Ⓝ

8. Ⓨ Ⓝ

9. Ⓨ Ⓝ

10. Ⓨ Ⓝ

___ / 10
Total

NAME:_____

DIRECTIONS Solve each problem.

1. (Y)(N)

2. (Y)(N)

3. (Y)(N)

4. (Y)(N)

5. (Y)(N)

6. (Y)(N)

7. (Y)(N)

8. (Y)(N)

9. (Y)(N)

10. (Y)(N)

___ / 10
Total

1.   36
       − 19

2. Which is greater:
$\frac{3}{10}$ or $\frac{3}{100}$?

_____

3. 24 ÷ 7 = _____

4. 10 ⟌ 57

5. What is 100 more than 1,706?

_____

6. 25 ÷ ☐ = 5

7. Would you use kilograms or grams to measure the mass of a slice of cheese?

_____

8. How many days are in December?

_____

9. How many angles are in a triangle?

_____

10. Complete the chart by rounding 2,176 to the specified places.

Ten	
Hundred	
Thousand	

NAME:_____

DIRECTIONS Solve each problem.

1. 42 + 28 = _____

7. Is the area of a room measured in cm^2 or m^2?

_____

2.
$$\begin{array}{r} 8 \\ \times\ 7 \\ \hline \end{array}$$

8. Write the length in inches.

_____ inches

3. What is the quotient of 15 and 7?

_____.

9. What shape forms the base of this pyramid?

_____

4. 37 ÷ 7 = _____

5. What is the place value of 6 in 3,698?

_____

10. Color the multiples of 3.

1	2	3	4	5	6	7	8	9	10
11	12	13	14	15	16	17	18	19	20
21	22	23	24	25	26	27	28	29	30
31	32	33	34	35	36	37	38	39	40

6. 82 − 15 = 73 − ☐

1. Ⓨ Ⓝ
2. Ⓨ Ⓝ
3. Ⓨ Ⓝ
4. Ⓨ Ⓝ
5. Ⓨ Ⓝ
6. Ⓨ Ⓝ
7. Ⓨ Ⓝ
8. Ⓨ Ⓝ
9. Ⓨ Ⓝ
10. Ⓨ Ⓝ
___ / 10
Total

NAME: _____

DIRECTIONS Solve each problem.

1. Y N

2. Y N

3. Y N

4. Y N

5. Y N

6. Y N

7. Y N

8. Y N

9. Y N

10. Y N

___ / 10
Total

1. 45 − 29 = _____

2. What is $\frac{1}{10}$ of 50? _____

3. 7 ⟌ 65

4. 88 ÷ 9 = _____

5. What is the value of the 7 in 2,738?

_____

6. Fill in the missing number.

54, _____, 42, 36, 30

7. How many 20-liter containers can be filled from a 90-liter tank?

_____

8. What is the most likely mass of a boy?

45 kilograms

45 grams

45 liters

9. Record the data in the pictograph.
Cheryl has been in 4 plays.
Brooke has been in 8 plays

Number of Plays

Cheryl	
Brooke	

☺ = 2 plays

10. What number means five ten thousands, three thousands, two hundreds, one ten, and no ones?

_____

NAME:_____

DIRECTIONS Solve each problem.

1. What is the sum of 26 and 7?

_____

2. $\frac{6}{10}$ of $1 is _____.

3. 49 ÷ 9 = _____

4. 24 ÷ 9 = _____

5. Is 316 an even number?

_____

6. 8 x ▢ = 32

7. On which day of the week is September 1st?

_____

August						
Sun	Mon	Tues	Wed	Thurs	Fri	Sat
				1	2	3
4	5	6	7	8	9	10
11	12	13	14	15	16	17
18	19	20	21	22	23	24
25	26	27	28	29	30	31

8. How many days are in 2 weeks?

_____

9. Is a square a regular shape?

_____

10. Our product is 132. The difference between us is 1. What numbers are we?

_____

1. Ⓨ Ⓝ
2. Ⓨ Ⓝ
3. Ⓨ Ⓝ
4. Ⓨ Ⓝ
5. Ⓨ Ⓝ
6. Ⓨ Ⓝ
7. Ⓨ Ⓝ
8. Ⓨ Ⓝ
9. Ⓨ Ⓝ
10. Ⓨ Ⓝ

___ / 10
Total

NAME:_____

SCORE

DIRECTIONS Solve each problem.

1. Y N

1. 56
    − 19

2. Y N

2. $\frac{1}{3}$ of 30 is _____.

3. Y N

4. Y N

3. 9 ⟌ 30

5. Y N

6. Y N

4. 68 ÷ 9 = _____

7. Y N

8. Y N

5. Write 2,064 in words.

9. Y N

_____

10. Y N

6. To find 60 ÷ 6, we say

[ ] × 6 = 60

___ / 10
Total

7. I put 500 mL of water in the jug. Next, I put a toy in the jug. How much water was displaced by the toy?

_____ mL

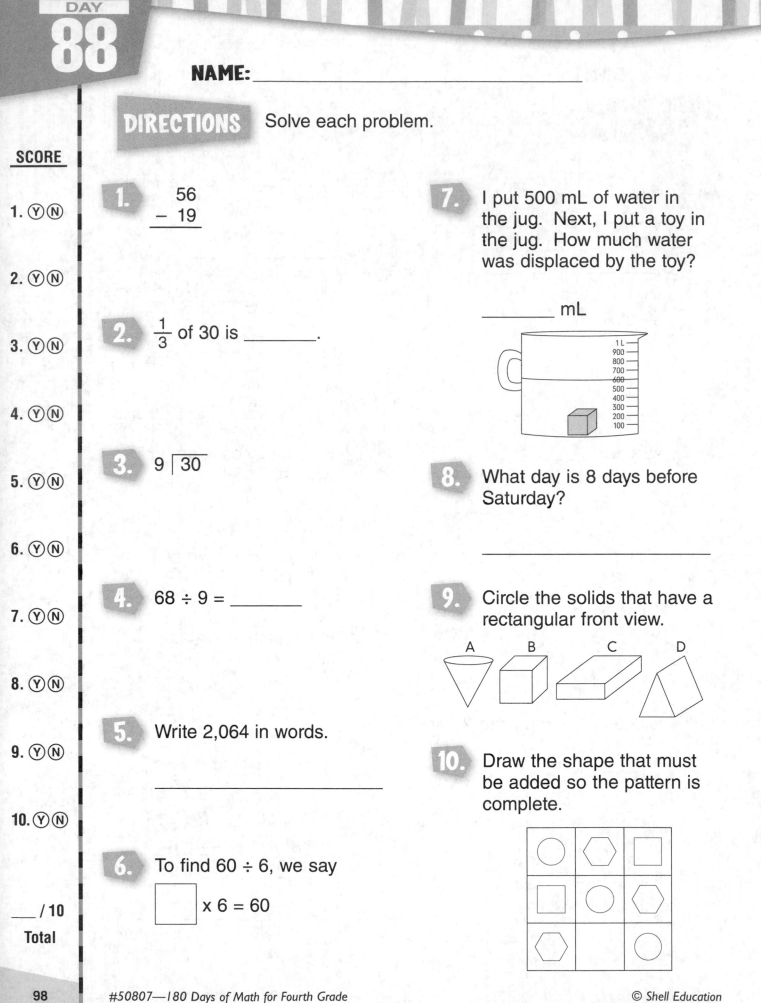

1 L
900
800
700
600
500
400
300
200
100

8. What day is 8 days before Saturday?

_____

9. Circle the solids that have a rectangular front view.

A   B   C   D

10. Draw the shape that must be added so the pattern is complete.

NAME: _____

Solve each problem.

SCORE

1.
23
+ 8

2. Is 0.6 equal to $\frac{6}{100}$?

_____

3. Divide 49 into 7 equal groups.

_____

4. $9\overline{\smash{)}76}$

5. How many digits are in 3,333?

_____

6. $\boxed{} \div 8 = 3$

7. How many seasons are in a year?

_____

8. 2 pints = _____ quart(s)

9. Draw a 180° angle.

10. A pound of ground beef costs $2.00. You have a coupon for 25% off. How much will you pay for a pound of beef?

_____

1. Ⓨ Ⓝ
2. Ⓨ Ⓝ
3. Ⓨ Ⓝ
4. Ⓨ Ⓝ
5. Ⓨ Ⓝ
6. Ⓨ Ⓝ
7. Ⓨ Ⓝ
8. Ⓨ Ⓝ
9. Ⓨ Ⓝ
10. Ⓨ Ⓝ

___ / 10
Total

NAME: _____

DIRECTIONS Solve each problem.

SCORE

1. Ⓨ Ⓝ

2. Ⓨ Ⓝ

3. Ⓨ Ⓝ

4. Ⓨ Ⓝ

5. Ⓨ Ⓝ

6. Ⓨ Ⓝ

7. Ⓨ Ⓝ

8. Ⓨ Ⓝ

9. Ⓨ Ⓝ

10. Ⓨ Ⓝ

___ / 10
Total

1. $33 - 17 =$ _____

2. How many objects are in 4 columns of 7?

_____

3. $9 \overline{)60}$

4. $40 \div 9 =$ _____

5. Round 372 to the nearest hundred.

_____

6. $6 \times \boxed{} = 42$

7. To find the height of a door, is the unit of measure m or m²?

_____

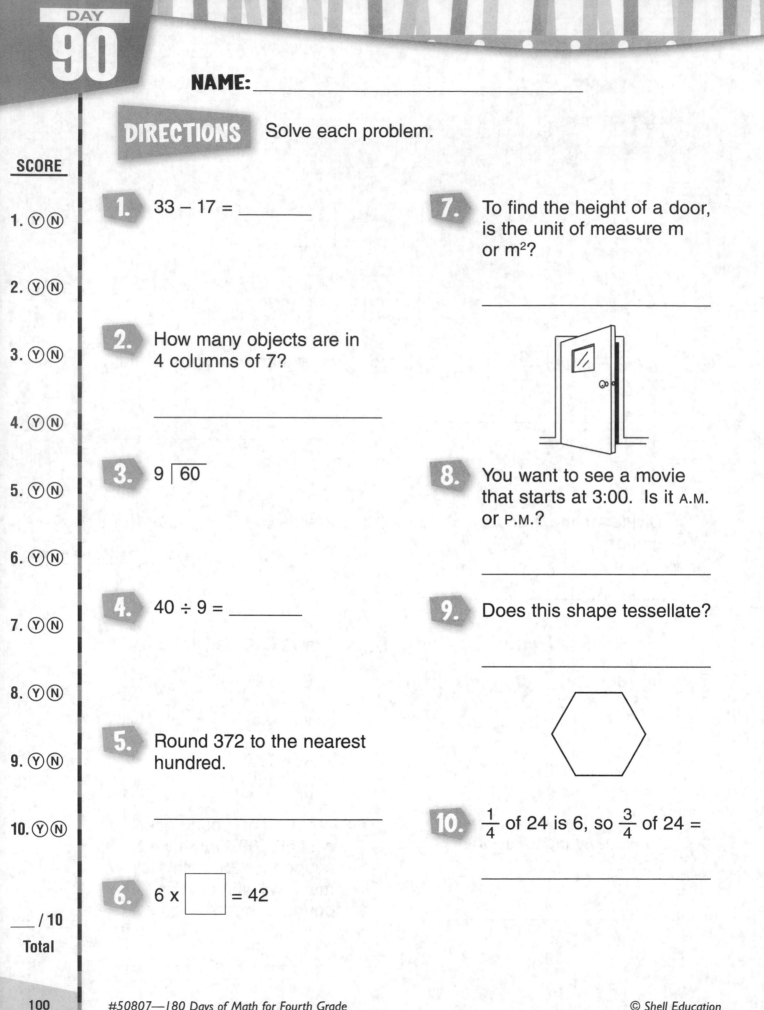

8. You want to see a movie that starts at 3:00. Is it A.M. or P.M.?

_____

9. Does this shape tessellate?

_____

10. $\frac{1}{4}$ of 24 is 6, so $\frac{3}{4}$ of 24 =

_____

 #50807—180 Days of Math for Fourth Grade

NAME: _____

DIRECTIONS Solve each problem.

1. 24 + 33 = _____

2.
$2.50
− $1.25

3. Divide 30 by 8. _____

4. 4 ⟌ 36

5. 700 + 40 + 6 = _____

6. Fill in the missing number.

56, 49, _____, 35, 28

7. Write the length in centimeters.

_____

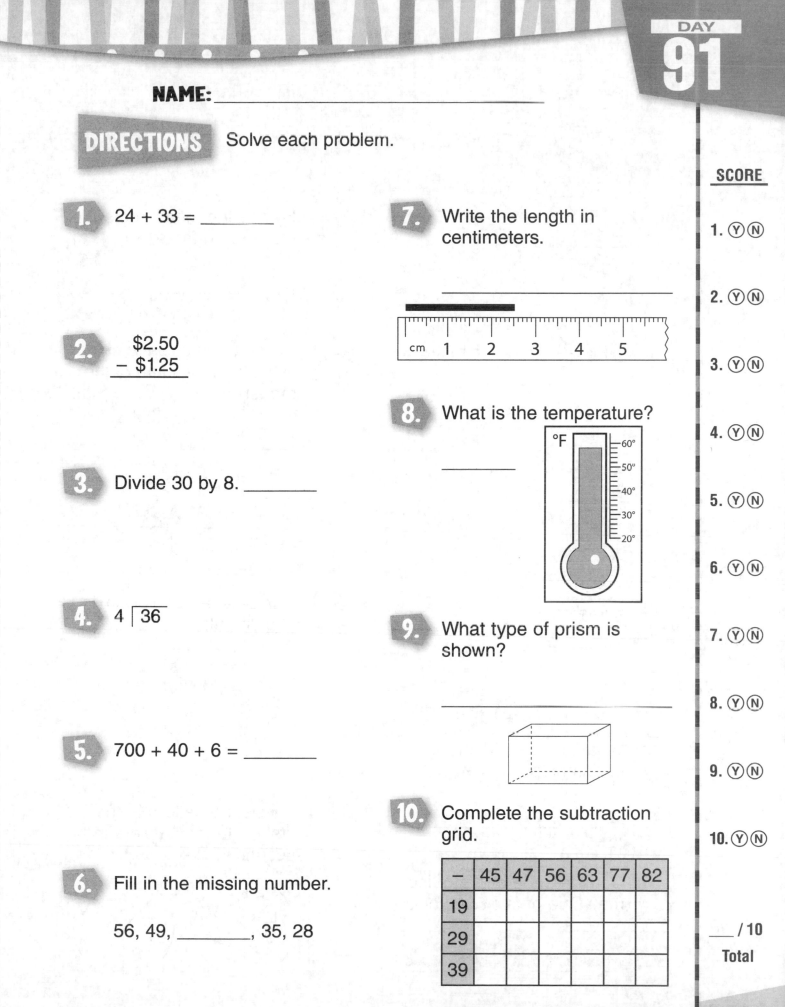

cm 1   2   3   4   5

8. What is the temperature?

_____

°F
60°
50°
40°
30°
20°

9. What type of prism is shown?

_____

10. Complete the subtraction grid.

−	45	47	56	63	77	82
19						
29						
39						

1. Ⓨ Ⓝ

2. Ⓨ Ⓝ

3. Ⓨ Ⓝ

4. Ⓨ Ⓝ

5. Ⓨ Ⓝ

6. Ⓨ Ⓝ

7. Ⓨ Ⓝ

8. Ⓨ Ⓝ

9. Ⓨ Ⓝ

10. Ⓨ Ⓝ

___ / 10
Total

NAME: _____

DIRECTIONS Solve each problem.

1. Ⓨ Ⓝ

2. Ⓨ Ⓝ

3. Ⓨ Ⓝ

4. Ⓨ Ⓝ

5. Ⓨ Ⓝ

6. Ⓨ Ⓝ

7. Ⓨ Ⓝ

8. Ⓨ Ⓝ

9. Ⓨ Ⓝ

10. Ⓨ Ⓝ

___ / 10
Total

1.
$$\begin{array}{r} 45 \\ -\ 26 \\ \hline \end{array}$$

2. Write $\frac{5}{100}$ as a decimal.

_____

3. 42 ÷ 8 = _____

4. 5⟌23

5. What is the value of the hundreds place in 1,573?

_____

6. Complete the chart to find the value of five 50¢ coins.

1 Coin	2 Coins	3 Coins	4 Coins	5 Coins
50¢				

7. Is area the measurement of mass or surface?

_____

8. Each cube has 1-cm sides. What is the volume of the model?

_____

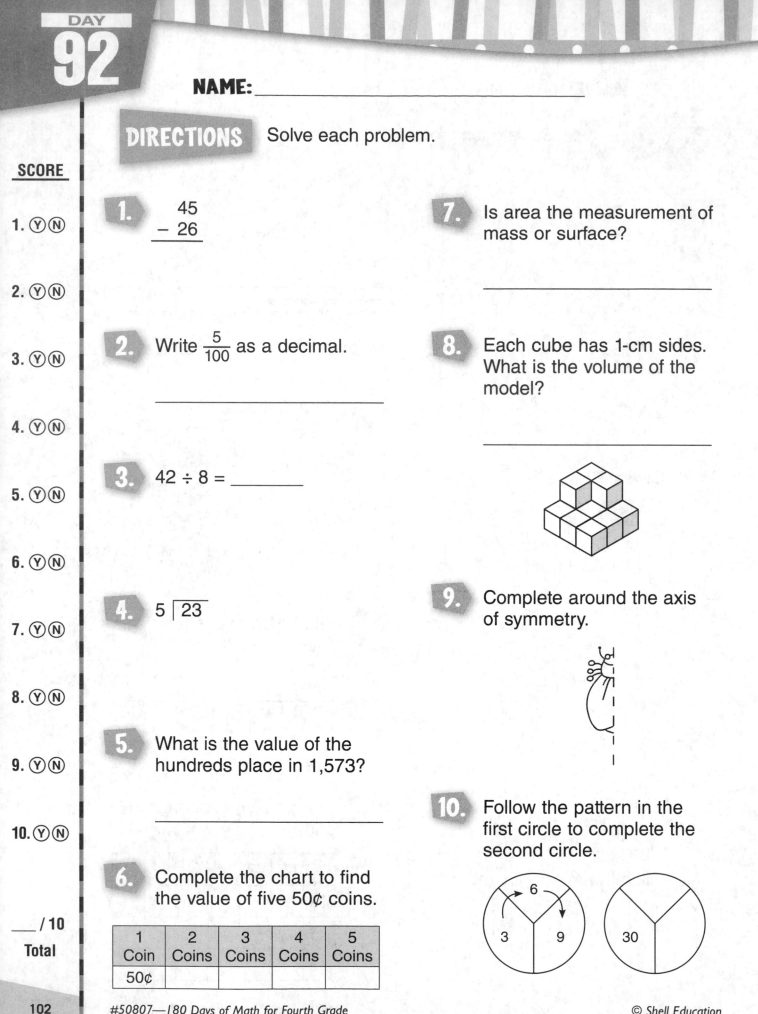

9. Complete around the axis of symmetry.

10. Follow the pattern in the first circle to complete the second circle.

NAME: _____

Solve each problem.

1.
```
   16
    7
+ 14
```

2. Which is larger: $\frac{4}{100}$ or $\frac{4}{10}$?

_____

3. 36 ÷ 8 = _____

4. 36 ÷ 9 = _____

5. Write the smallest 3-digit number using 2, 8, 1, and 4.

_____

6. 15 + 5 = 18 + ☐

7. Draw the time that is 20 minutes later.

8. 1 _____ = 60 seconds

9. **Dollars Earned in May**

Audrey	$15
Dameon	$23
Jason	$12
Lauren	$18

What was the total amount of money earned in May by the children?

_____

10. If one ticket costs $2.50, how many tickets can be bought with $15.00?

_____

1. Ⓨ Ⓝ

2. Ⓨ Ⓝ

3. Ⓨ Ⓝ

4. Ⓨ Ⓝ

5. Ⓨ Ⓝ

6. Ⓨ Ⓝ

7. Ⓨ Ⓝ

8. Ⓨ Ⓝ

9. Ⓨ Ⓝ

10. Ⓨ Ⓝ

___ / 10
Total

NAME: _____

SCORE

DIRECTIONS Solve each problem.

1. (Y)(N)

1. $63 - 9 =$ _____

6. $10 - x = 2$

$x =$ _____

2. (Y)(N)

3. (Y)(N)

2. What is one-fourth of 12?

_____

7. Sam's mass is 8 kg greater than Joe's, whose mass is 34 kg. What is Sam's mass?

4. (Y)(N)

_____

5. (Y)(N)

3. $8\overline{)65}$

8. How many gallons make up four quarts?

6. (Y)(N)

_____

7. (Y)(N)

8. (Y)(N)

4. Divide 5 into 43.

9. Name this shape. _____

_____

9. (Y)(N)

10. (Y)(N)

5. What is the next even number after 398?

10. Complete the chart. Round the number 4,832.

Tens	
Hundreds	
Thousands	

_____

_____ / 10
Total

NAME: _____

DIRECTIONS Solve each problem.

1. 25 + 8 = _____

7. How many centimeters are in 6 meters?

_____

2. 4 x 9 = _____

8. What month is 4 months after September?

_____

3. Share 24 equally among 4 groups.

_____

9. Draw the top view of the solid.

4. 77 ÷ 8 = _____

5. What is 300 more than 2,476?

_____

10. Use different colors to color pairs of numbers that equal the product shown in the center.

6. 9 + 4 = 13 – ☐

1. Ⓨ Ⓝ

2. Ⓨ Ⓝ

3. Ⓨ Ⓝ

4. Ⓨ Ⓝ

5. Ⓨ Ⓝ

6. Ⓨ Ⓝ

7. Ⓨ Ⓝ

8. Ⓨ Ⓝ

9. Ⓨ Ⓝ

10. Ⓨ Ⓝ

___ / 10
Total

NAME: _____

SCORE

1. Ⓨ Ⓝ

2. Ⓨ Ⓝ

3. Ⓨ Ⓝ

4. Ⓨ Ⓝ

5. Ⓨ Ⓝ

6. Ⓨ Ⓝ

7. Ⓨ Ⓝ

8. Ⓨ Ⓝ

9. Ⓨ Ⓝ

10. Ⓨ Ⓝ

___ / 10
Total

1.
$$\begin{array}{r} 25 \\ -6 \\ \hline \end{array}$$

2. $1.20 + $1.15 = _____

3. $8\overline{)60}$

4. Calculate the quotient of 56 and 4.

_____

5. Write 3,642 in expanded notation.

_____

_____

6. Fill in the missing number.

28, 35, 42, _____, 56

7. How many liters are in 8,000 milliliters?

_____

8. 48 inches = _____ feet

9. Is this a *reflection*, *translation*, or *rotation*?

_____

10. A telephone costs $9.89. A calendar costs $5.99. A watch costs $19.50. What is the total cost of the items?

_____

_____

#50807—180 Days of Math for Fourth Grade

NAME: _____

DIRECTIONS Solve each problem.

1. 17 + 9 = _____

2. Write $\frac{7}{10}$ as a decimal.

_____

3. How many 4s are in 16?

_____

4. 52 ÷ 8 = _____

5. What is 10 more than 437?

_____

6. Does 6 + 4 = 3 + 7?

_____

7. On which day of the week is the last day of August?

_____

August						
Sun	Mon	Tues	Wed	Thurs	Fri	Sat
				1	2	3
4	5	6	7	8	9	10
11	12	13	14	15	16	17
18	19	20	21	22	23	24
25	26	27	28	29	30	31

8. Would you use a ruler or a yardstick to measure the height of a drinking glass?

_____

9.

Books Read in March

Cathy	📖 📖 📖
Martin	📖 📖 📖 📖
Jose	📖 📖 📖

📖 = 5 books read

Who read the most books?

_____

10. If you subtract me from 1,437, you get 422. What number am I?

_____

1. Y N
2. Y N
3. Y N
4. Y N
5. Y N
6. Y N
7. Y N
8. Y N
9. Y N
10. Y N

___ / 10
Total

NAME: _____

1. Ⓨ Ⓝ

2. Ⓨ Ⓝ

3. Ⓨ Ⓝ

4. Ⓨ Ⓝ

5. Ⓨ Ⓝ

6. Ⓨ Ⓝ

7. Ⓨ Ⓝ

8. Ⓨ Ⓝ

9. Ⓨ Ⓝ

10. Ⓨ Ⓝ

___ / 10
Total

DIRECTIONS Solve each problem.

1. $47 - 29 =$ _____

2. Is $\frac{1}{8}$ more than $\frac{1}{4}$?

_____

3. $8\overline{)20}$

4. $42 \div 4 =$ _____

5. Write the number for five thousand two hundred fifty-three.

_____

6. $6 + 5 = 17 -$ ☐

7. How many milliliters are in half a liter?

_____

8. Circle the most likely time for a 1-mile run.

12 minutes

12 seconds

12 inches

9. Draw the diagonals in the shape.

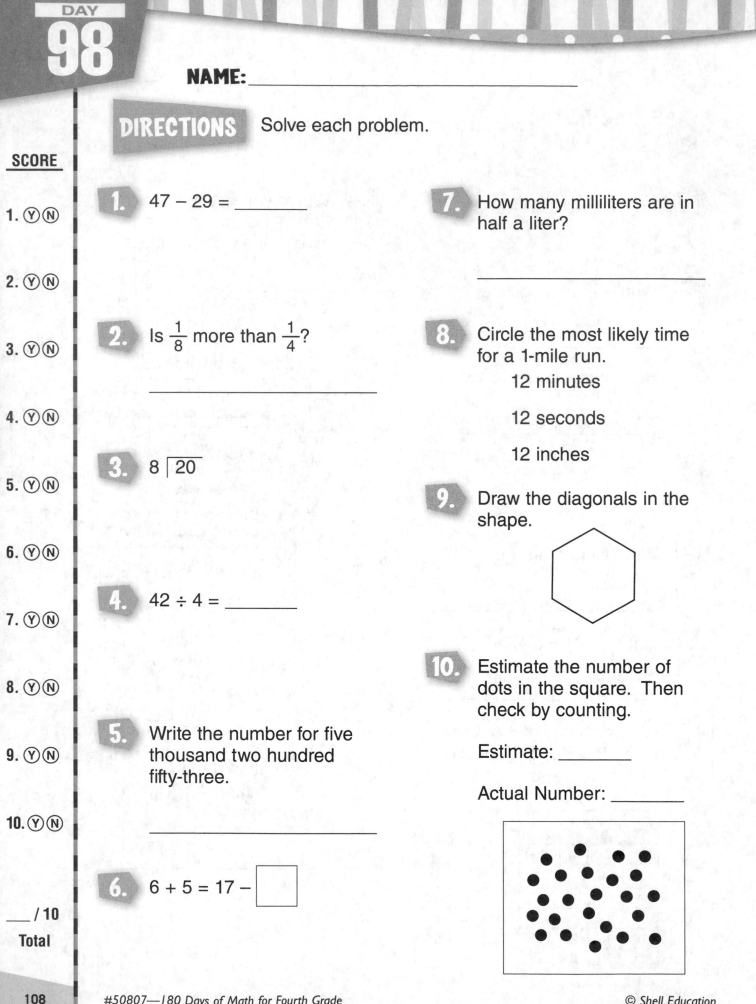

10. Estimate the number of dots in the square. Then check by counting.

Estimate: _____

Actual Number: _____

#50807—180 Days of Math for Fourth Grade   © Shell Education

NAME: _____

DIRECTIONS Solve each problem.

1.   52
      + 9

6. 22 − x = 13

x = _____

2. Write 0.62 as a fraction.

_____

7. Which months are in the second quarter of the year?

_____

_____

3. List all the factors of 20.

_____

8. Each cube has 1-cm sides. What is the volume of the model?

_____

4. 12 ÷ 4 = _____

9. A cone has:

_____ surfaces

_____ edges

5. Write the ordinal number for forty-two.

_____

10. There are 5 toys in a bag. Shelly buys 8 bags of toys. She then divides the toys evenly among 4 friends. How many toys did each friend get?

_____

1. Ⓨ Ⓝ

2. Ⓨ Ⓝ

3. Ⓨ Ⓝ

4. Ⓨ Ⓝ

5. Ⓨ Ⓝ

6. Ⓨ Ⓝ

7. Ⓨ Ⓝ

8. Ⓨ Ⓝ

9. Ⓨ Ⓝ

10. Ⓨ Ⓝ

___ / 10
Total

NAME: _____

DIRECTIONS Solve each problem.

SCORE

1. Ⓨ Ⓝ

2. Ⓨ Ⓝ

3. Ⓨ Ⓝ

4. Ⓨ Ⓝ

5. Ⓨ Ⓝ

6. Ⓨ Ⓝ

7. Ⓨ Ⓝ

8. Ⓨ Ⓝ

9. Ⓨ Ⓝ

10. Ⓨ Ⓝ

___ / 10
Total

1.
$$\begin{array}{r} 27 \\ -\ 19 \\ \hline \end{array}$$

2. $7 \times 6 = $ _____

3. $4\overline{)28}$

4. List all the factors of 36.

_____

5. What is the value of the 7 in 374?

_____

6. $15 - 6 = \boxed{} - 9$

7. My garden bed has an area of 18 m². I planted 10 m² with peas. What area is left?

_____

8. How many weekdays are there?

_____

9.

Total Rainfall

How much did it rain in all the years combined?

_____

10. Circle the card that shows the same fraction as the example.

NAME: _____

DIRECTIONS Solve each problem.

1. 45 + 7 = _____

7. Write the length in millimeters.

_____

cm 1   2   3   4   5

2. $\frac{1}{8}$ of 48 is _____.

8. Maggie works on her homework from 2:35 P.M. until 3:15 P.M. How long does she spend on homework?

3. 32 ÷ 4 = _____

_____

9. Circle the sets of parallel lines.

4. 7)‾56‾

A   B   C   D

5. Round 756 to the nearest hundred.

_____

10. Use each of the 5 numbers once and any operations to solve the problem below. You may also add parentheses.

6. Fill in the missing number.

42, _____, 28, 21, 14

⬡10⬡13⬡1⬡4⬡12⬡

⬡ ⬡ ⬡ ⬡ ⬡ = 3

1. Ⓨ Ⓝ
2. Ⓨ Ⓝ
3. Ⓨ Ⓝ
4. Ⓨ Ⓝ
5. Ⓨ Ⓝ
6. Ⓨ Ⓝ
7. Ⓨ Ⓝ
8. Ⓨ Ⓝ
9. Ⓨ Ⓝ
10. Ⓨ Ⓝ

___ / 10
Total

NAME: _____

DIRECTIONS Solve each problem.

1. (Y)(N)

2. (Y)(N)

3. (Y)(N)

4. (Y)(N)

5. (Y)(N)

6. (Y)(N)

7. (Y)(N)

8. (Y)(N)

9. (Y)(N)

10. (Y)(N)

___ / 10
Total

1. $63 - 9 =$ _____

2. Is 0.4 greater than 0.29?

_____

3. $43 \div 8 =$ _____

4. How many groups of eight are in sixteen?

_____

5. Write 8,091 in words.

_____

6. $32 + 8 = \boxed{} - 8$

7. Calculate the area of a square with 5-cm sides.

_____

5 cm

8. If the temperature were 53 degrees Fahrenheit, would you be more likely to wear a bathing suit or a jacket?

_____

9. Draw the shape made if you fold along the axis of symmetry.

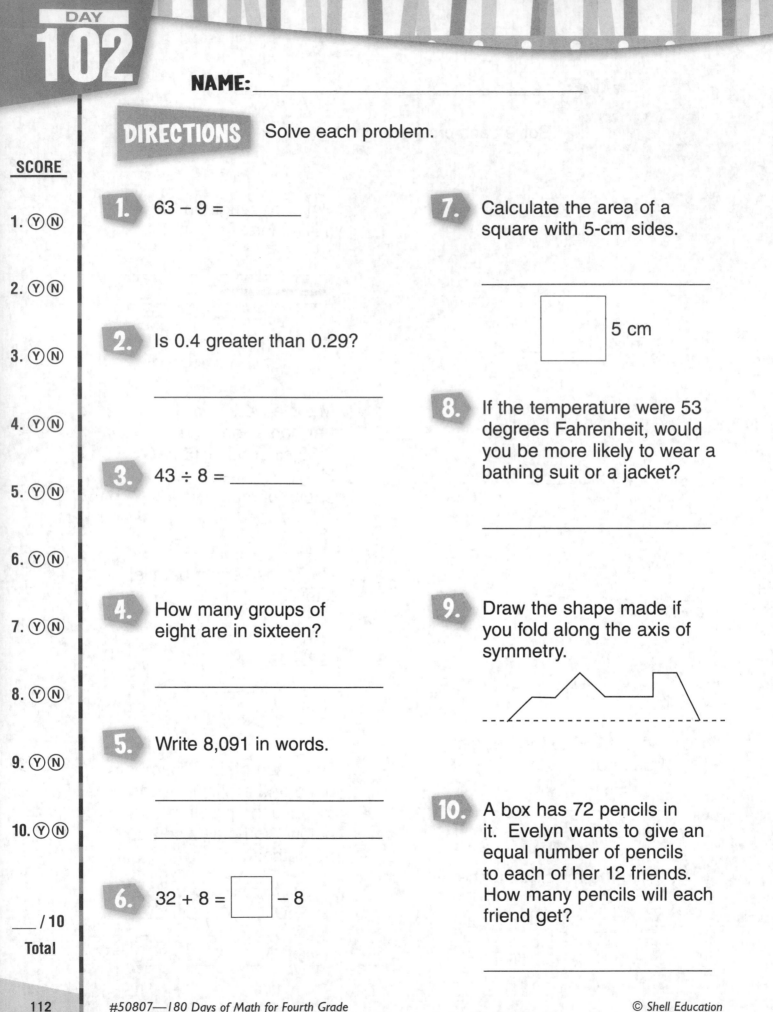

10. A box has 72 pencils in it. Evelyn wants to give an equal number of pencils to each of her 12 friends. How many pencils will each friend get?

_____

NAME: _____

DIRECTIONS
Solve each problem.

SCORE

1.
```
   43
+  18
```

2. Which is smaller:

$\frac{9}{10}$ or $\frac{9}{100}$?

_____

3. Divide 48 into
8 equal groups.

_____

4. $8\overline{)72}$

5. Write 386 in expanded
notation.

_____

6. Is 7 x 9 equal to 9 x 7?

_____

7. Fill in the blanks for the
time shown.

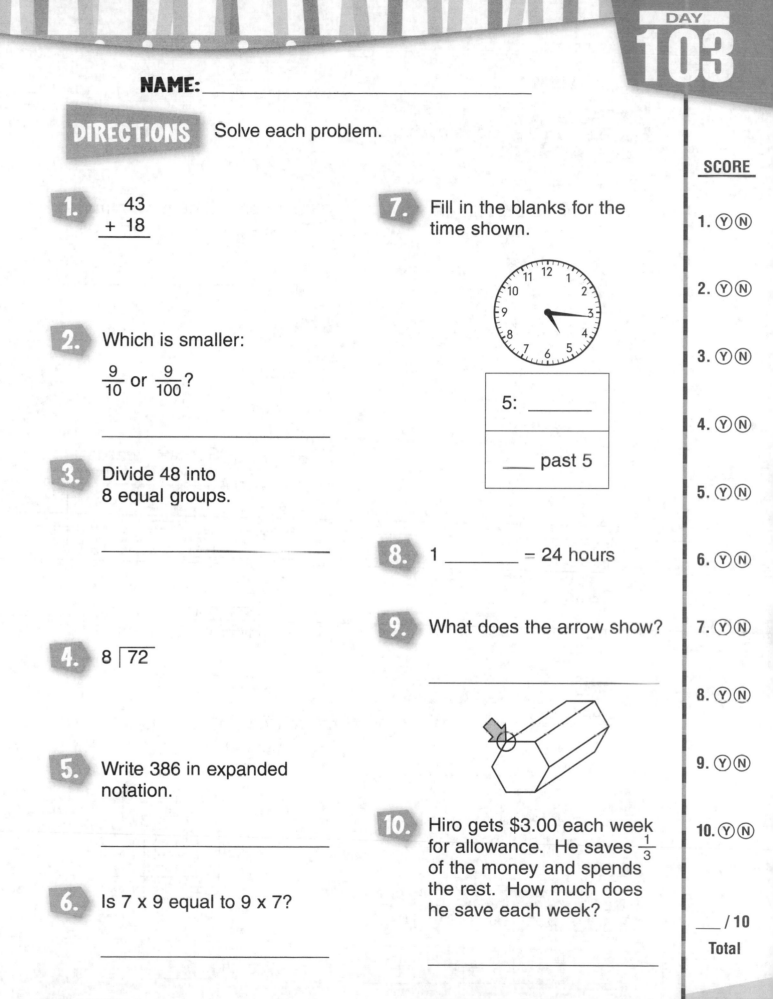

5: _____

_____ past 5

8. 1 _____ = 24 hours

9. What does the arrow show?

_____

10. Hiro gets $3.00 each week
for allowance. He saves $\frac{1}{3}$
of the money and spends
the rest. How much does
he save each week?

_____

1. Ⓨ Ⓝ

2. Ⓨ Ⓝ

3. Ⓨ Ⓝ

4. Ⓨ Ⓝ

5. Ⓨ Ⓝ

6. Ⓨ Ⓝ

7. Ⓨ Ⓝ

8. Ⓨ Ⓝ

9. Ⓨ Ⓝ

10. Ⓨ Ⓝ

___ / 10
Total

NAME: _____

SCORE

1. Ⓨ Ⓝ

2. Ⓨ Ⓝ

3. Ⓨ Ⓝ

4. Ⓨ Ⓝ

5. Ⓨ Ⓝ

6. Ⓨ Ⓝ

7. Ⓨ Ⓝ

8. Ⓨ Ⓝ

9. Ⓨ Ⓝ

10. Ⓨ Ⓝ

___ / 10
Total

1. $24 - 8 =$ _____

2. $\$1.50 + \$1.75 =$ _____

3. $72 \div 9 =$ _____

4. Calculate the quotient of 32 and 8.

_____

5. What is the next number after 809?

_____

6. Complete the chart to find the cost of 6 bags at $20 each.

1 Bag	2 Bags	3 Bags	4 Bags	5 Bags	6 Bags
$20					

7. Does a shoe have a mass less than 1 kilogram?

_____

8. 6 pints = _____ quart(s)

9.

School Awards

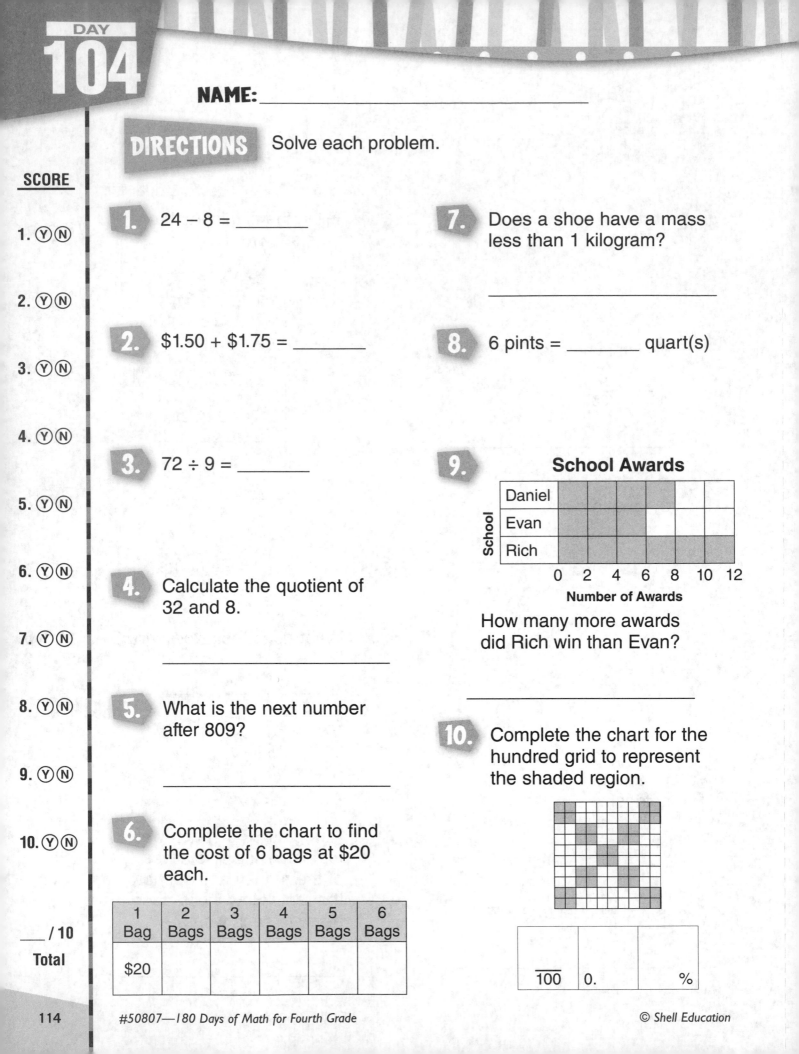

How many more awards did Rich win than Evan?

_____

10. Complete the chart for the hundred grid to represent the shaded region.

$\frac{}{100}$	0.	%

NAME: _____

Solve each problem.

SCORE

1. 19 + 17 = _____

2. Calculate the product of 5 and 10.

_____

3. 56 ÷ 8 = _____

4. 6 ⟌ 54

5. How many digits are in 6,427?

_____

6. 24 − 14 = 10, so

24 − ☐ = 14

7. What is the abbreviation for centimeter squared?

_____

8. 3 feet = _____ yard(s)

9. Circle the solids that have a triangular front view.

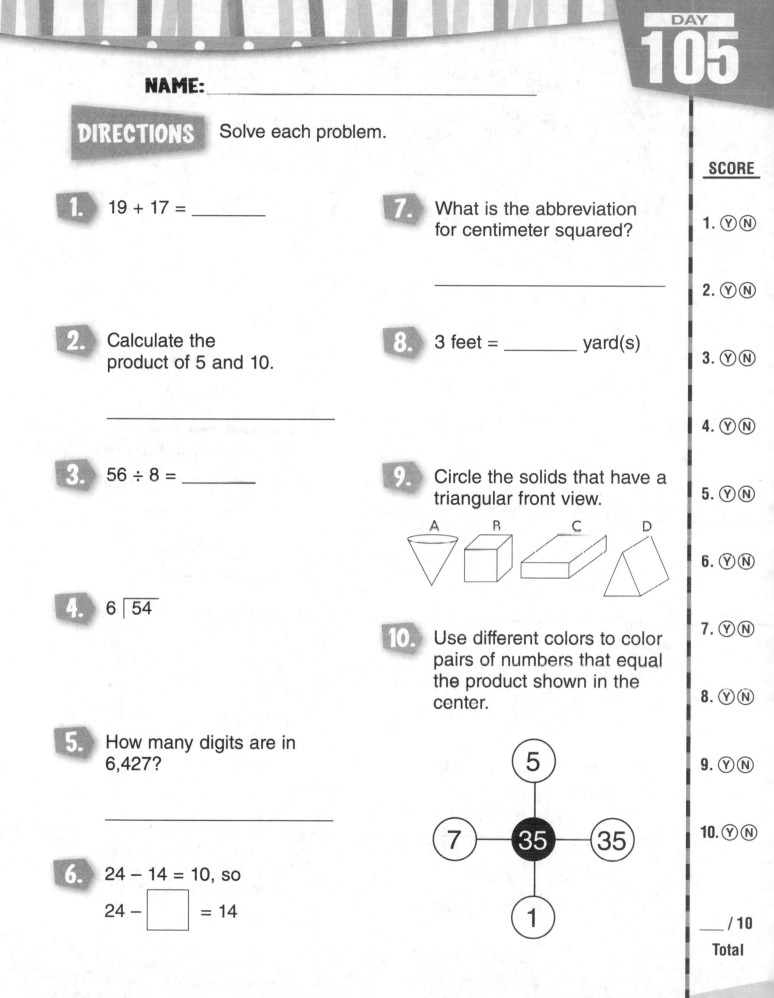

10. Use different colors to color pairs of numbers that equal the product shown in the center.

1. Ⓨ Ⓝ
2. Ⓨ Ⓝ
3. Ⓨ Ⓝ
4. Ⓨ Ⓝ
5. Ⓨ Ⓝ
6. Ⓨ Ⓝ
7. Ⓨ Ⓝ
8. Ⓨ Ⓝ
9. Ⓨ Ⓝ
10. Ⓨ Ⓝ

___ / 10
Total

NAME: _____

SCORE

DIRECTIONS Solve each problem.

1. Ⓨ Ⓝ

1.   16
   − 7

2. Ⓨ Ⓝ

3. Ⓨ Ⓝ

2. Is 0.7 equal to $\frac{7}{10}$?

_____

4. Ⓨ Ⓝ

5. Ⓨ Ⓝ

3. Divide 40 into 5 equal groups.

6. Ⓨ Ⓝ

_____

7. Ⓨ Ⓝ

4. 28 ÷ 7 = _____

8. Ⓨ Ⓝ

9. Ⓨ Ⓝ

5. What is 400 more than 1,609?

10. Ⓨ Ⓝ

_____

6. Fill in the missing number.

___ / 10
Total

_____, 45, 54, 63, 72

7. If 7 ▽ fill a ⬜ and 5 ⬜ fill

a ⬭, then _____ ▽ fill a ⬭.

8. Write the length in inches.

_____ inches

▬▬▬▬▬▬

| | | | | | |
| in. | 1 | 2 | 3 | 4 | 5 |

9. **Sports Played Each Year**

	1st Trimester	2nd Trimester	3rd Trimester
Troy	soccer	basketball	baseball
Jessica	golf	basketball	track
Allison	soccer	diving	swimming

Who does not play basketball?

_____

10. I am a number. If you divide me by 10 and add 4, the answer is 7. What number am I?

_____

NAME: _____

DIRECTIONS Solve each problem.

1. Add 45 and 16. _____

2. Is 0.6 less than 0.58?

_____

3. 9 ⟌ 45

4. Divide 18 into 6 equal groups.

_____

5. What is the next even number after 137?

_____

6. 80 − 37 = ☐ − 22

7. School is scheduled to begin the first weekday in September. What date will school begin?

_____

August						
Sun	Mon	Tues	Wed	Thurs	Fri	Sat
				1	2	3
4	5	6	7	8	9	10
11	12	13	14	15	16	17
18	19	20	21	22	23	24
25	26	27	28	29	30	31

8. Circle the most likely capacity of a large bucket.

15 liters

15 cups

15 inches

9. This prism has:

_____ faces

_____ edges

_____ vertices

10. Double 32, then subtract 12.

_____

1. Ⓨ Ⓝ
2. Ⓨ Ⓝ
3. Ⓨ Ⓝ
4. Ⓨ Ⓝ
5. Ⓨ Ⓝ
6. Ⓨ Ⓝ
7. Ⓨ Ⓝ
8. Ⓨ Ⓝ
9. Ⓨ Ⓝ
10. Ⓨ Ⓝ

___ / 10
Total

NAME: _____

DIRECTIONS Solve each problem.

1. $32 - 9 =$ _____

2. Write $\frac{3}{4}$ as a decimal.

_____

3. List all the factors of 30.

_____

4. $12 \div 6 =$ _____

5. $8000 + 40 + 7 =$ _____

6. $6 + 6 + 6 + \boxed{} = 4 \times 6$

7. Record in milliliters.

_____ mL

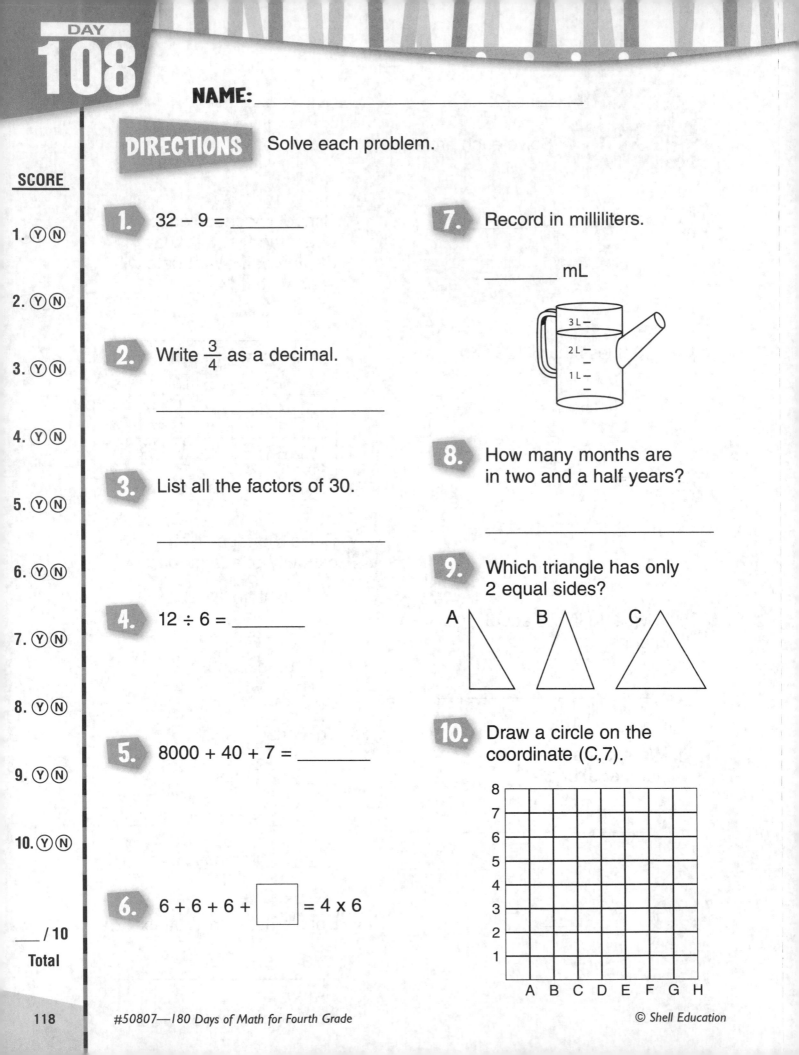

8. How many months are in two and a half years?

_____

9. Which triangle has only 2 equal sides?

A   B   C

10. Draw a circle on the coordinate (C,7).

NAME: _____

DIRECTIONS Solve each problem.

1.
```
   36
+ 15
```

2. $10.00 − $6.50 = _____

3. Share 56 equally among 7.

_____

4. 7 ⟌ 21

5. What is the value of the 9 in 5,439?

_____

6. 4 x 5 = 20 ÷ ☐

7. What is the first month of the year?

_____

What is the last month of the year?

_____

8. Each cube has 1 cm sides. What is the volume of the model?

_____

9. Name this shape.

_____

10. There are 12 squares. Half of them are green and 25% are blue. The rest are orange. How many squares are orange?

_____

1. Ⓨ Ⓝ

2. Ⓨ Ⓝ

3. Ⓨ Ⓝ

4. Ⓨ Ⓝ

5. Ⓨ Ⓝ

6. Ⓨ Ⓝ

7. Ⓨ Ⓝ

8. Ⓨ Ⓝ

9. Ⓨ Ⓝ

10. Ⓨ Ⓝ

___ / 10
Total

NAME: _____

DIRECTIONS Solve each problem.

1.
$$\begin{array}{r} 43 \\ -\ 8 \\ \hline \end{array}$$

2. $7 \times 9 =$ _____

3. How many groups of 8 are in 48?

_____

4. $28 \div 4 =$ _____

5. What ordinal number is after thirtieth?

_____

6. $50 - 32 = 60 - n$

$n =$ _____

7. One side of a square is 9 cm. What is the area?

_____

8. You set your alarm clock to wake up at 6:30 A.M. If you sleep in until 7:28 A.M., how long did you oversleep?

_____

9. Record the data in the bar graph.

Home Runs Hit

Batter						

0 1 2 3 4 5

Harry has hit 4 home runs.

Dean has hit 5 home runs.

Dale has hit 2 home runs.

10. $\frac{1}{8}$ of 48 = 6, so $\frac{5}{8}$ of 48 =

_____

1. Ⓨ Ⓝ

2. Ⓨ Ⓝ

3. Ⓨ Ⓝ

4. Ⓨ Ⓝ

5. Ⓨ Ⓝ

6. Ⓨ Ⓝ

7. Ⓨ Ⓝ

8. Ⓨ Ⓝ

9. Ⓨ Ⓝ

10. Ⓨ Ⓝ

___ / 10
Total

NAME:_____

DIRECTIONS Solve each problem.

1. 27 + 14 = _____

2. $\frac{3}{10}$ of 70 = _____

3. 7 ⟌ 63

4. 35 ÷ 7 = _____

5. Write 7,903 in expanded notation.

_____

_____

6. Fill in the missing number.

30, 36, _____, 48, 54

7. Write the length in centimeters.

_____

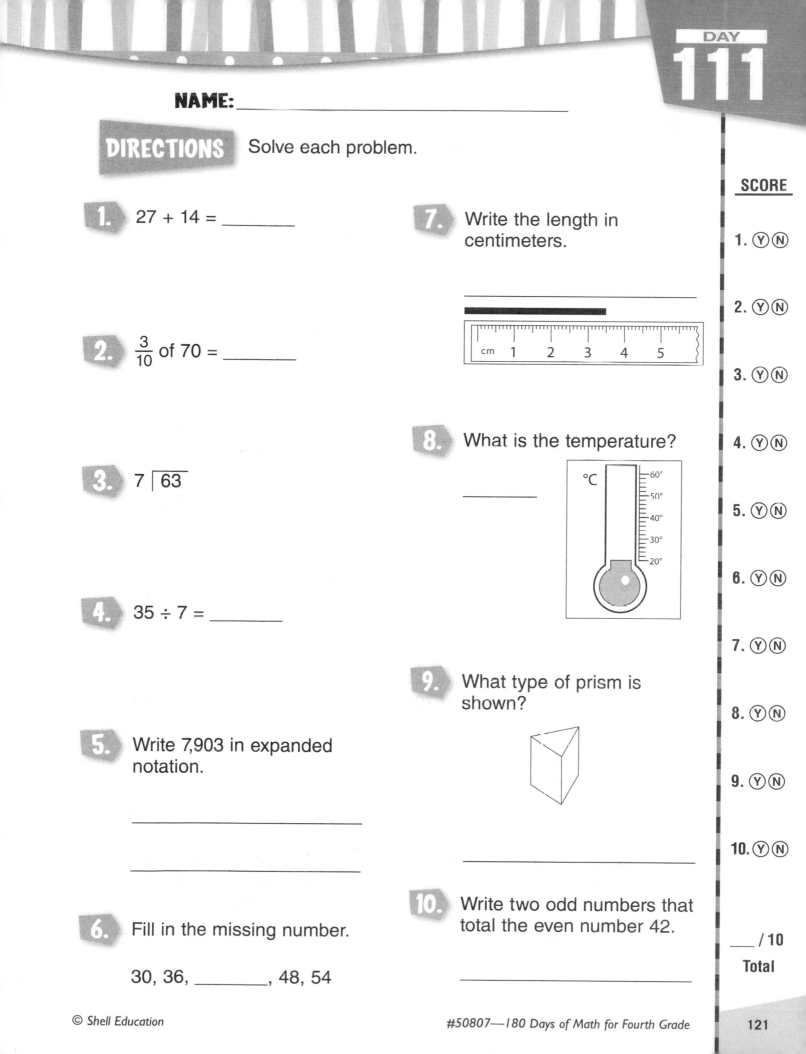

cm 1   2   3   4   5

8. What is the temperature?

_____

°C —60°
    —50°
    —40°
    —30°
    —20°

9. What type of prism is shown?

_____

10. Write two odd numbers that total the even number 42.

_____

1. Ⓨ Ⓝ

2. Ⓨ Ⓝ

3. Ⓨ Ⓝ

4. Ⓨ Ⓝ

5. Ⓨ Ⓝ

6. Ⓨ Ⓝ

7. Ⓨ Ⓝ

8. Ⓨ Ⓝ

9. Ⓨ Ⓝ

10. Ⓨ Ⓝ

___ / 10
Total

NAME: _____

DIRECTIONS Solve each problem.

1. Ⓨ Ⓝ

1. What is the difference between 32 and 19?

_____.

2. Ⓨ Ⓝ

2. Is $\frac{7}{10}$ greater than $\frac{7}{100}$?

3. Ⓨ Ⓝ

_____

4. Ⓨ Ⓝ

5. Ⓨ Ⓝ

3. Divide 54 by 9. _____

6. Ⓨ Ⓝ

7. Ⓨ Ⓝ

8. Ⓨ Ⓝ

4. $63 \div 6 =$ _____

9. Ⓨ Ⓝ

10. Ⓨ Ⓝ

5. Is 4,736 even or odd?

_____

6. $8 + 8 + 8 + 8 =$ ☐ x 8

7. Circle the best estimate for the weight of the object.

100 g   20 kg   5 kg   1 kg

POTATOES

8. 36 inches equals how many yards?

_____

9. Draw the front view.

10. Add 9 tens and 5 ones to the number 43.

_____

___ / 10
Total

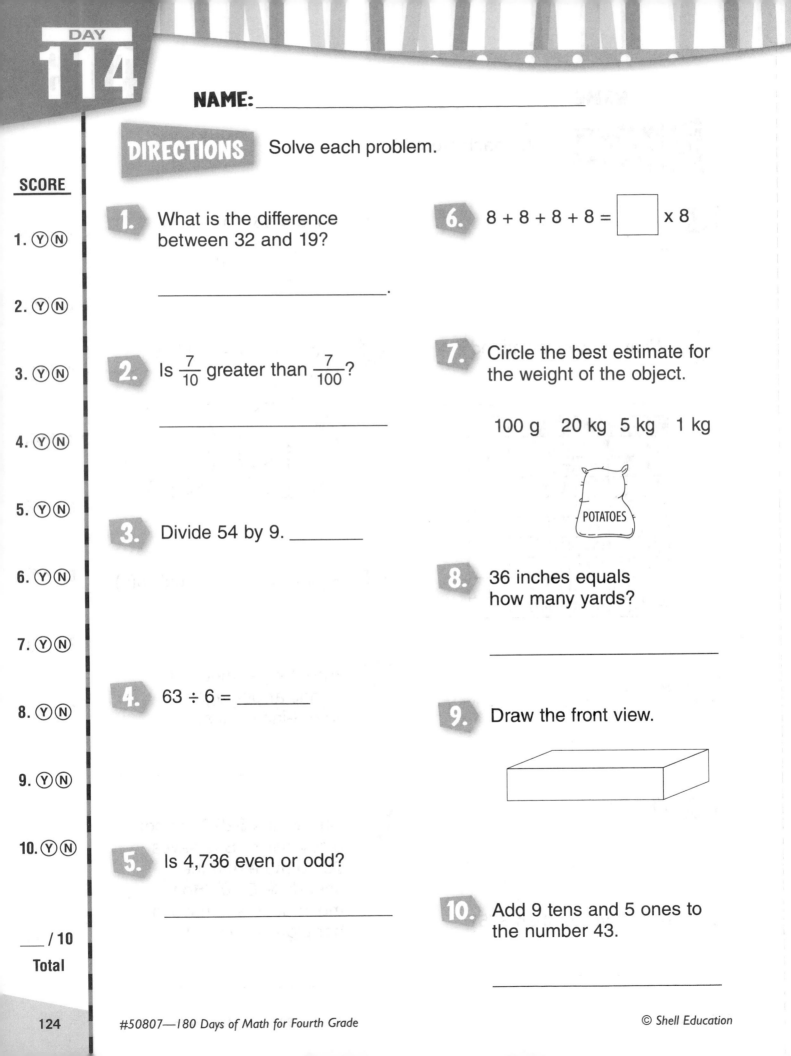

NAME: _____

Solve each problem.

1. 24 + 18 = _____

6. $5 \times 8 = \boxed{} \times 10$

1. Ⓨ Ⓝ

2. Ⓨ Ⓝ

2.
```
    7
  x 8
  ___
```

7. How many cm are in 50 mm?

_____

3. Ⓨ Ⓝ

4. Ⓨ Ⓝ

3. 63 ÷ 9 = _____

8. How many days are in July?

_____

5. Ⓨ Ⓝ

6. Ⓨ Ⓝ

7. Ⓨ Ⓝ

4. 6 ⟌ 48

9. Draw 1 line of symmetry.

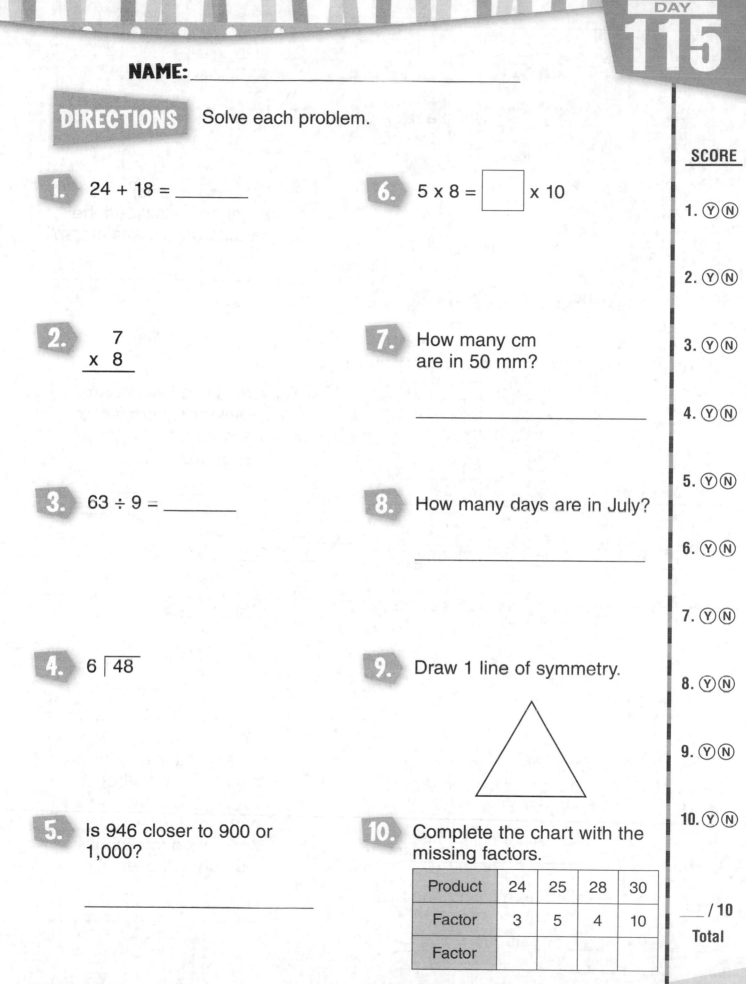

8. Ⓨ Ⓝ

9. Ⓨ Ⓝ

10. Ⓨ Ⓝ

5. Is 946 closer to 900 or 1,000?

_____

10. Complete the chart with the missing factors.

Product	24	25	28	30
Factor	3	5	4	10
Factor				

___ / 10
Total

NAME: _____

DIRECTIONS Solve each problem.

1. Y N

1.   24
       − 9

2. Y N

2. What fraction is shaded?

3. Y N

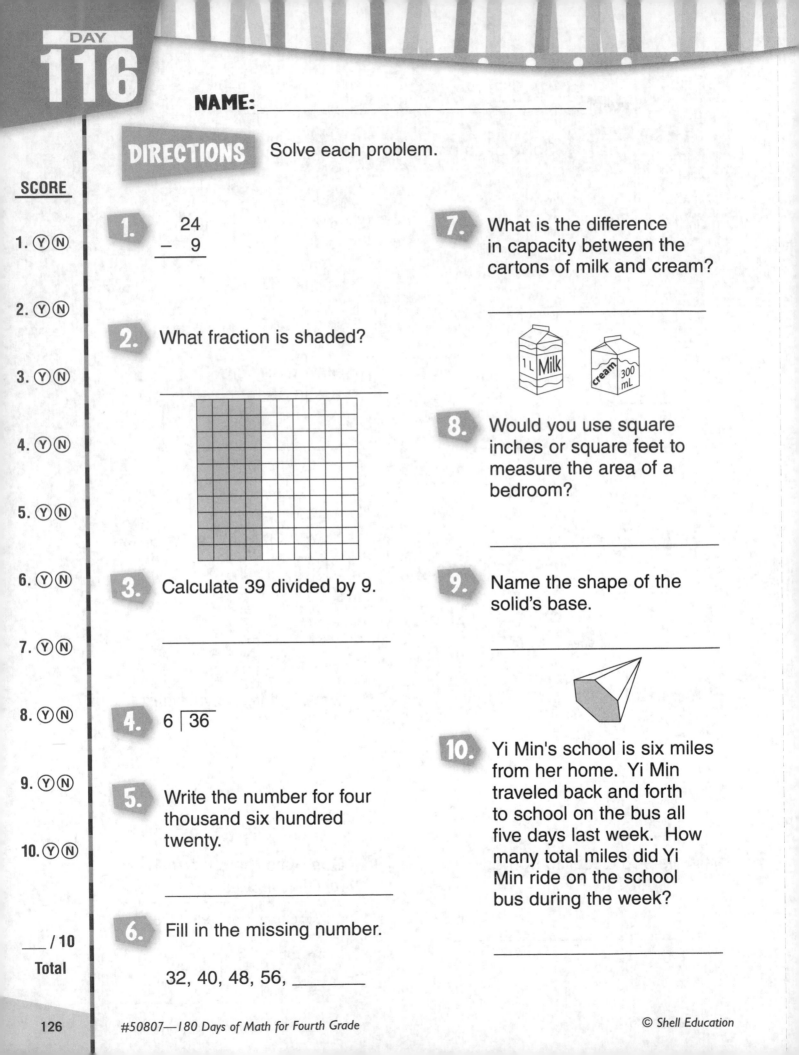

4. Y N

5. Y N

3. Calculate 39 divided by 9.

6. Y N

7. What is the difference in capacity between the cartons of milk and cream?

7. Y N

8. Would you use square inches or square feet to measure the area of a bedroom?

8. Y N

4. 6 ⟌ 36

9. Y N

5. Write the number for four thousand six hundred twenty.

10. Y N

9. Name the shape of the solid's base.

10. Yi Min's school is six miles from her home. Yi Min traveled back and forth to school on the bus all five days last week. How many total miles did Yi Min ride on the school bus during the week?

___ / 10
Total

6. Fill in the missing number.

32, 40, 48, 56, _____

NAME:_____

DIRECTIONS Solve each problem.

1.
$$\begin{array}{r} 15 \\ + 19 \\ \hline \end{array}$$

2. Is $\frac{4}{10}$ equal to $\frac{4}{100}$?

_____

3. $45 \div 9 =$ _____

4. Calculate the quotient of 91 and 10.

_____

5. Round 436 to the nearest ten.

_____

6. 12 seeds are in a packet. Complete the chart to show how many are in 4 packets.

1 Packet	2 Packets	3 Packets	4 Packets
12			

7. Molly's birthday is the 3rd Saturday in August. If today is July 31st, how many days are there until Molly's birthday?

_____

August						
Sun	Mon	Tues	Wed	Thurs	Fri	Sat
				1	2	3
4	5	6	7	8	9	10
11	12	13	14	15	16	17
18	19	20	21	22	23	24
25	26	27	28	29	30	31

8. Which would be the best measure for the lemonade in a full pitcher: a liter, a cup, or a kilogram?

_____

9. What shape is the cross-section?

10. If you multiply me by 8, the product is 96. What number am I?

_____

1. Ⓨ Ⓝ

2. Ⓨ Ⓝ

3. Ⓨ Ⓝ

4. Ⓨ Ⓝ

5. Ⓨ Ⓝ

6. Ⓨ Ⓝ

7. Ⓨ Ⓝ

8. Ⓨ Ⓝ

9. Ⓨ Ⓝ

10. Ⓨ Ⓝ

___/10
Total

NAME: _____

SCORE

DIRECTIONS Solve each problem.

1.
$$\begin{array}{r} 46 \\ -\ 29 \\ \hline \end{array}$$

1. Ⓨ Ⓝ

2. Ⓨ Ⓝ

2. 6 x 40 = _____

3. Ⓨ Ⓝ

4. Ⓨ Ⓝ

5. Ⓨ Ⓝ

3. 72 ÷ 8 = _____

6. Ⓨ Ⓝ

7. Ⓨ Ⓝ

8. Ⓨ Ⓝ

4. 7 ⟌ 63

9. Ⓨ Ⓝ

10. Ⓨ Ⓝ

5. What is the first odd number before 624?

_____

____ / 10
Total

6. 9 x 4 = 36, so

36 ÷ ☐ = 9

7. Is the area of a tennis court measured in cm² or m²?

_____

8. It takes you 12 minutes to get to your friend's house. You leave at 8:10. What time will you arrive at your friend's house?

_____

9. Does this shape tessellate?

_____

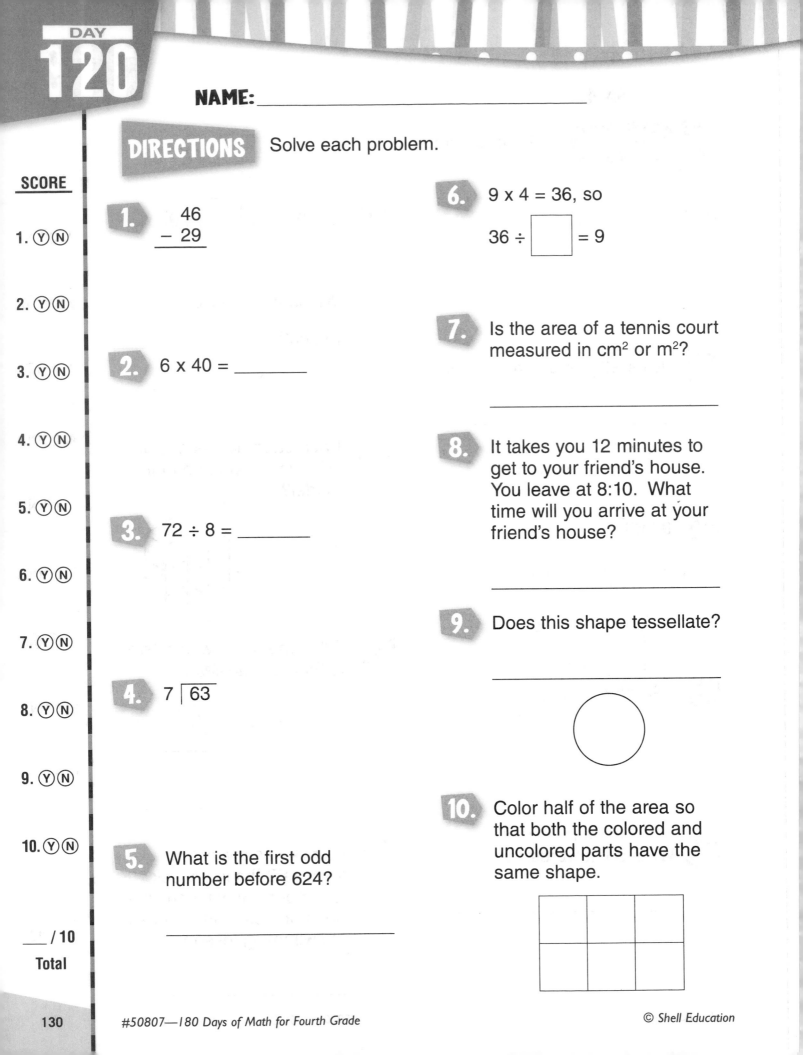

10. Color half of the area so that both the colored and uncolored parts have the same shape.

NAME: _____

DIRECTIONS Solve each problem.

1. What is the sum of 27 and 19?

_____.

2. $\frac{1}{5}$ of 30 = _____

3. 81 ÷ 9 = _____

4. Calculate the quotient of twenty-four and six.

_____

5. 5,000 + 40 + 6 = _____

6. Fill in the missing fraction.

$\frac{1}{8}, \frac{2}{8}, \frac{3}{8},$ _____, $\frac{5}{8}$

7. Write the length in millimeters.

_____

8. Is a 24°F day warm or cold?

_____

9. Draw a line from the real-life object to the solid.

A   B   C   D

10. Follow the pattern in the first circle to complete the second circle.

6
3   9   32

1. Ⓨ Ⓝ

2. Ⓨ Ⓝ

3. Ⓨ Ⓝ

4. Ⓨ Ⓝ

5. Ⓨ Ⓝ

6. Ⓨ Ⓝ

7. Ⓨ Ⓝ

8. Ⓨ Ⓝ

9. Ⓨ Ⓝ

10. Ⓨ Ⓝ

___ / 10
Total

NAME: _____

DIRECTIONS
Solve each problem.

1. 69 – 26 = _____

2. Write 45% as a decimal.

_____

3. 121 ÷ 11 = _____

4. Divide 45 into 9 equal groups.

_____

5. Write 6,802 in expanded notation.

_____

6. 7 + 7 + 7 + 7 = ☐ x 7

7. Calculate the area of a square with 7-cm sides.

_____

7 cm

8. _____ months = 1 year

9. **Books Read in March**

Cathy	📖 📖 📖
Martin	📖 📖 📖 📖 📖
Jose	📖 📖 📖

📖 = 5 books read

Jose's goal was to read 25 books in March. Did he reach his goal?

_____

10. Mick's fishing line was 73 m. He cut off 42 m. How long is it now?

_____

NAME:_____

DIRECTIONS Solve each problem.

1.
$$\begin{array}{r} 25 \\ +\ 8 \\ \hline \end{array}$$

6. $25 + \boxed{} + 12 = 57$

1. Ⓨ Ⓝ

7. Fill in the blanks for the time shown.

2. Ⓨ Ⓝ

2. Is $\dfrac{9}{10}$ equal to $\dfrac{9}{100}$?

_____

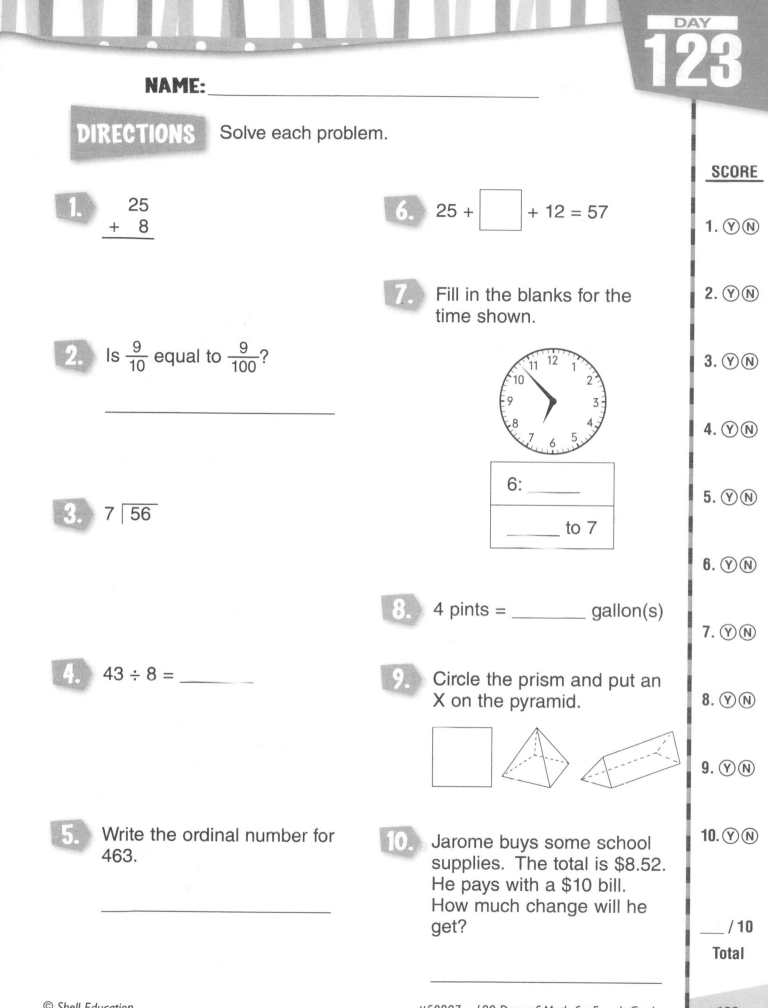

3. Ⓨ Ⓝ

6: _____
_____ to 7

4. Ⓨ Ⓝ

3. $7\overline{)56}$

5. Ⓨ Ⓝ

8. 4 pints = _____ gallon(s)

6. Ⓨ Ⓝ

7. Ⓨ Ⓝ

4. $43 \div 8 =$ _____

9. Circle the prism and put an X on the pyramid.

8. Ⓨ Ⓝ

9. Ⓨ Ⓝ

5. Write the ordinal number for 463.

_____

10. Jarome buys some school supplies. The total is $8.52. He pays with a $10 bill. How much change will he get?

10. Ⓨ Ⓝ

____ / 10

Total

_____

NAME: _____

DIRECTIONS Solve each problem.

1. $27 - 16 =$ _____

2. What percentage is shaded?

_____

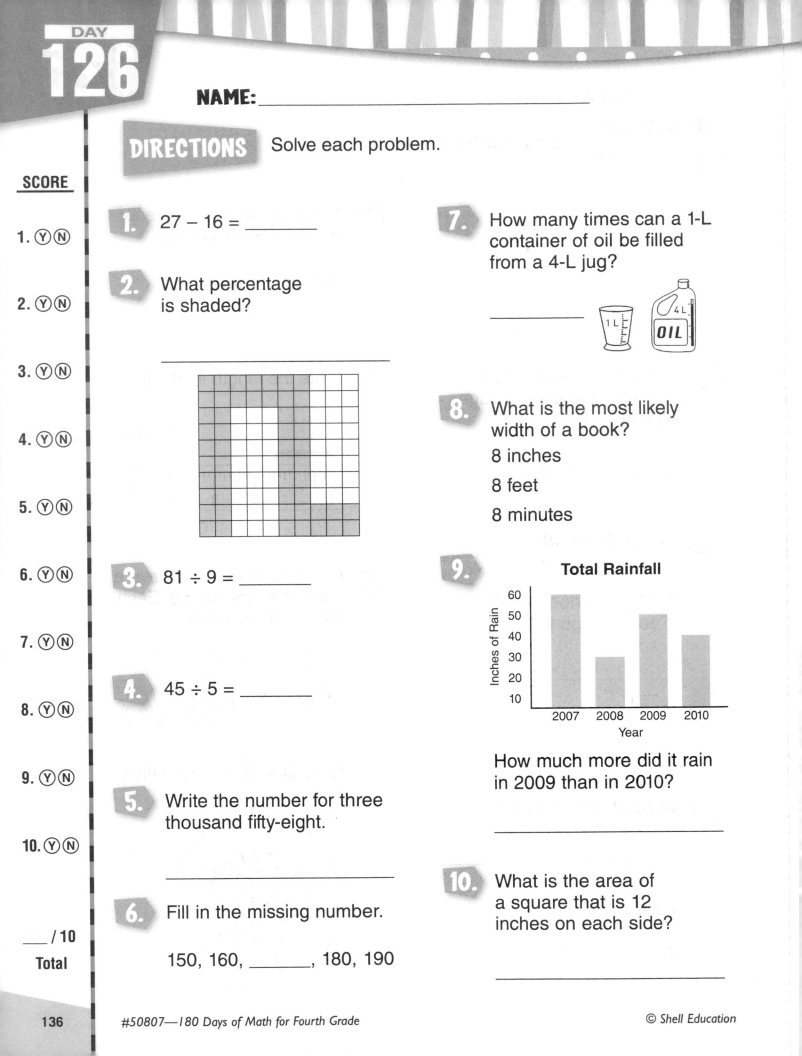

3. $81 \div 9 =$ _____

4. $45 \div 5 =$ _____

5. Write the number for three thousand fifty-eight.

_____

6. Fill in the missing number.

150, 160, _____, 180, 190

7. How many times can a 1-L container of oil be filled from a 4-L jug?

_____

8. What is the most likely width of a book?

8 inches

8 feet

8 minutes

9.
Total Rainfall

How much more did it rain in 2009 than in 2010?

_____

10. What is the area of a square that is 12 inches on each side?

_____

NAME: _____

DIRECTIONS Solve each problem.

1.
24
+ 19

6. Is 6 x 7 equal to 6 x 6 + 6?

_____

1. Ⓨ Ⓝ

2. Ⓨ Ⓝ

7. What day of the week was July 31st?

_____

3. Ⓨ Ⓝ

2. Is $\frac{70}{100}$ equal to $\frac{7}{10}$?

_____

August						
Sun	Mon	Tues	Wed	Thurs	Fri	Sat
				1	2	3
4	5	6	7	8	9	10
11	12	13	14	15	16	17
18	19	20	21	22	23	24
25	26	27	28	29	30	31

4. Ⓨ Ⓝ

5. Ⓨ Ⓝ

3. 72 ÷ 9 = _____

6. Ⓨ Ⓝ

8. How many days are there in 4 years? (Remember leap year!)

_____

7. Ⓨ Ⓝ

4. Calculate the quotient of 35 and 7.

_____

8. Ⓨ Ⓝ

9. What type of prism is shown?

_____

9. Ⓨ Ⓝ

5. What is 10 more than 479?

_____

10. Ⓨ Ⓝ

10. Triple 16, then add 100.

_____

____ / 10
Total

NAME: _____

SCORE

DIRECTIONS Solve each problem.

1. Ⓨ Ⓝ

1. Subtract 21 from 34.

_____

2. Ⓨ Ⓝ

2. Write $\frac{9}{10}$ as a percentage.

3. Ⓨ Ⓝ

_____

4. Ⓨ Ⓝ

3. 24 ÷ 5 = _____

5. Ⓨ Ⓝ

4. 7 ⟌ 28

6. Ⓨ Ⓝ

5. Round 789 to the nearest hundred.

7. Ⓨ Ⓝ

_____

8. Ⓨ Ⓝ

6. 7 x 8 = 56 x ☐

9. Ⓨ Ⓝ

7. I put 700 mL of water in the cup. Next I put a toy in the cup. How much water was displaced by the toy?

10. Ⓨ Ⓝ

_____ mL

_____ / 10
Total

8. Calculate the perimeter.

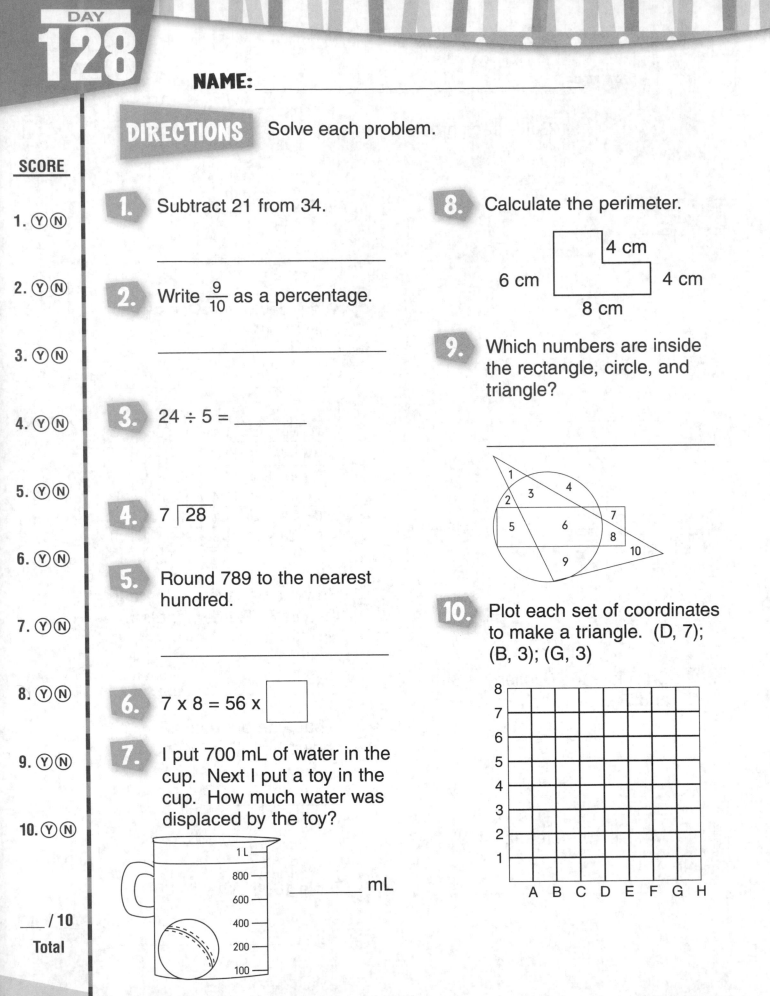

4 cm

6 cm   4 cm

8 cm

9. Which numbers are inside the rectangle, circle, and triangle?

_____

10. Plot each set of coordinates to make a triangle. (D, 7); (B, 3); (G, 3)

NAME: _____

DIRECTIONS Solve each problem.

1. 28 + 29 = _____

7. Which months are in the first quarter of the year?

_____

_____

_____

2. Shade 90%.

8. Calculate the volume of a cube with 2-cm sides.

_____

2 cm

3. 7 | 36

4. 24 ÷ 6 = _____

9. Draw the top view.

5. How many digits are in the number 1,079?

_____

6. Complete the chart. There are 9 nails in a bag. You need 45 nails. How many bags will you buy?

_____

1 Bag	2 Bags	3 Bags	4 Bags	5 Bags	6 Bags
9					

10. Kelly's mom pays her $4.00 an hour to babysit her baby sister. How much money will she make in 4 weeks if she watches her sister 3 hours every week?

_____

1. Ⓨ Ⓝ

2. Ⓨ Ⓝ

3. Ⓨ Ⓝ

4. Ⓨ Ⓝ

5. Ⓨ Ⓝ

6. Ⓨ Ⓝ

7. Ⓨ Ⓝ

8. Ⓨ Ⓝ

9. Ⓨ Ⓝ

10. Ⓨ Ⓝ

____ / 10

Total

NAME: _____

DIRECTIONS Solve each problem.

1. (Y)(N)

1. $46 - 25 =$ _____

2. (Y)(N)

6. $9 + 9 + 9 + \boxed{} = 4 \times 9$

3. (Y)(N)

2. Write 0.5 as a percentage.

7. Calculate the perimeter of a square with 7-cm sides.

4. (Y)(N)

_____

_____

5. (Y)(N)

$\boxed{}$ 7 cm

3. $75 \div 5 =$ _____

6. (Y)(N)

8. _____ hours = 120 minutes

7. (Y)(N)

8. (Y)(N)

4. $8 \overline{)40}$

9. I have one curved surface and no flat surfaces. What solid am I?

9. (Y)(N)

_____

10. (Y)(N)

5. Round 4,506 to the nearest hundred.

10. Sheila bought 3 dozen eggs. How many eggs did she buy?

___/ 10
Total

_____

_____

NAME:_____

DIRECTIONS Solve each problem.

1.
```
   18
+   6
```

1. Ⓨ Ⓝ

2. $\frac{1}{10}$ of 20 = _____

2. Ⓨ Ⓝ

7. Draw the time that is 16 minutes later.

3. Ⓨ Ⓝ

4. Ⓨ Ⓝ

3. Divide 15 into 3 equal groups.

_____

8. _____ gallon(s) = 2 quarts

5. Ⓨ Ⓝ

6. Ⓨ Ⓝ

9. **Sports Played Each Year**

	1st Trimester	2nd Trimester	3rd Trimester
Troy	soccer	basketball	baseball
Jessica	golf	basketball	track
Allison	soccer	diving	swimming

4. 82 ÷ 6 = _____

7. Ⓨ Ⓝ

How many children play soccer?

8. Ⓨ Ⓝ

5. Write 4,825 in words.

_____

_____

9. Ⓨ Ⓝ

_____

10. Haru gets $2.50 each week for allowance. How much does he get in 4 weeks?

10. Ⓨ Ⓝ

6. 23 − 15 = ▢ + 8

___/10

Total

NAME: _____

DIRECTIONS Solve each problem.

SCORE

1. Ⓨ Ⓝ

2. Ⓨ Ⓝ

3. Ⓨ Ⓝ

4. Ⓨ Ⓝ

5. Ⓨ Ⓝ

6. Ⓨ Ⓝ

7. Ⓨ Ⓝ

8. Ⓨ Ⓝ

9. Ⓨ Ⓝ

10. Ⓨ Ⓝ

___ / 10
Total

1.
$$\begin{array}{r} 53 \\ -\ 22 \\ \hline \end{array}$$

2. $\frac{3}{4}$ of 16 = _____

3. $25 \div 5 =$ _____

4. $2\overline{\smash{)}17}$

5. Write 624 in expanded notation.

_____

_____

6. $218 + 12 = 240 -$ ☐

7. Joe's mass is half the mass of Sam, whose mass is 46 kg. What is Joe's mass?

_____

8. 6 inches = _____ foot

9. A rectangle has:

_____ angles

_____ sides

_____ axes of symmetry

10. Subtract 7 tens and 0 ones from the number 83.

_____

NAME:_____

DIRECTIONS Solve each problem.

1. 37 + 24 = _____

6. Is 4 x 3 equal to 6 x 2?

_____

2. 8 x 6 = _____

7. How many meters are in 600 centimeters?

_____

3. 40 ÷ 4 = _____

8. What month comes before August?

_____

4. 19 ÷ 3 = _____

9. Is a square a rectangle?

_____

5. 600 + 70 = _____

10. Complete the chart with the missing factors.

Product	32	36	40	42
Factor	4	6	5	6
Factor				

1. Ⓨ Ⓝ

2. Ⓨ Ⓝ

3. Ⓨ Ⓝ

4. Ⓨ Ⓝ

5. Ⓨ Ⓝ

6. Ⓨ Ⓝ

7. Ⓨ Ⓝ

8. Ⓨ Ⓝ

9. Ⓨ Ⓝ

10. Ⓨ Ⓝ

___ / 10
Total

NAME: _____

1. Ⓨ Ⓝ

2. Ⓨ Ⓝ

3. Ⓨ Ⓝ

4. Ⓨ Ⓝ

5. Ⓨ Ⓝ

6. Ⓨ Ⓝ

7. Ⓨ Ⓝ

8. Ⓨ Ⓝ

9. Ⓨ Ⓝ

10. Ⓨ Ⓝ

___ / 10
Total

DIRECTIONS Solve each problem.

1. $68 - 34 =$ _____

2. 10% of 30 = _____

3. $9\overline{)45}$

4. Divide 37 by 3. _____

5. What is the value of the hundreds place in 1,743?

_____

6. Fill in the missing number.

0.85, 0.80, _____, 0.70

7. I drink 250 mL of milk each day. How much milk do I drink in 5 days?

_____

8. How many minutes are there between 5:38 A.M. and 9:42 P.M.?

_____

9. This prism has:

_____ faces

_____ edges

A _____ for a base

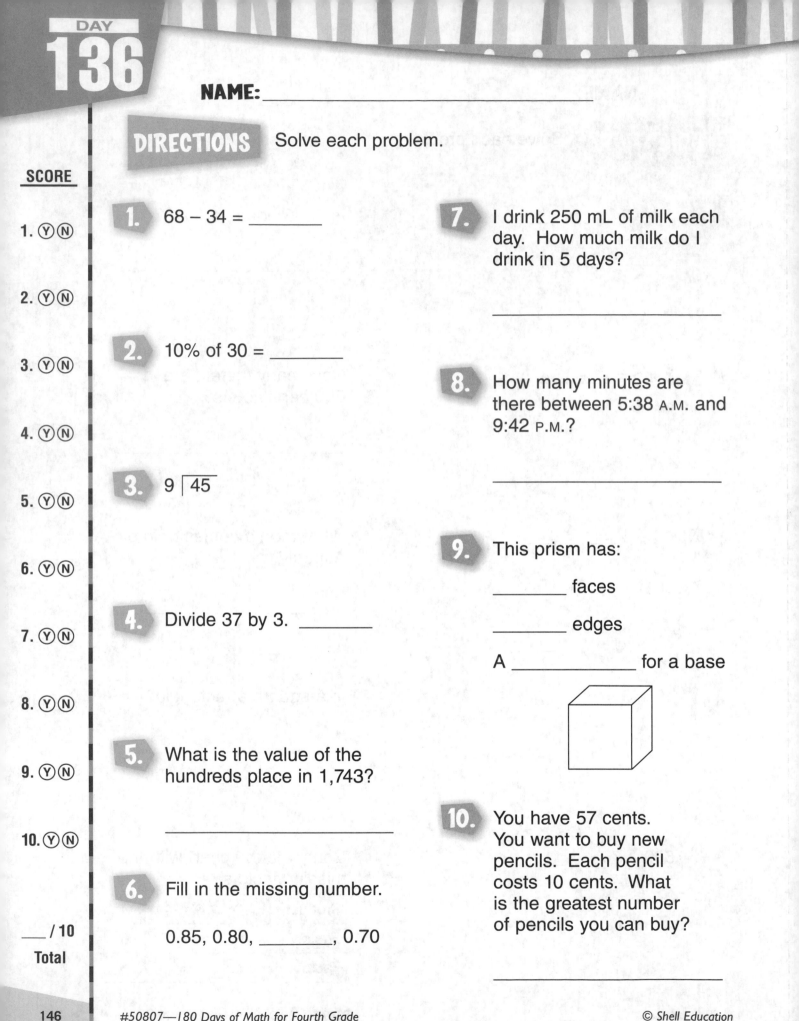

10. You have 57 cents. You want to buy new pencils. Each pencil costs 10 cents. What is the greatest number of pencils you can buy?

_____

NAME: _____

DIRECTIONS Solve each problem.

1.
$$\begin{array}{r} 24 \\ + 14 \\ \hline \end{array}$$

2. Is $\frac{1}{8}$ less than $\frac{1}{4}$?

_____

3. Calculate the quotient of 26 and 13.

_____

4. $65 \div 10 =$ _____

5. What is the place value of 6 in 216?

_____

6. $27 \div n = 9$

$n =$ _____

7. What day of the week is the first day in December?

_____

December						
Sun	Mon	Tues	Wed	Thurs	Fri	Sat
	1	2	3	4	5	6
7	8	9	10	11	12	13
14	15	16	17	18	19	20
21	22	23	24	25	26	27
28	29	30	31			

8. Would you use a thermometer or a ruler to measure distance?

_____

9. Name a two-dimensional shape that has two equal acute angles and two equal obtuse angles.

_____

10. If you divide me by 8, you get 6. What number am I?

_____

SCORE

1. Ⓨ Ⓝ
2. Ⓨ Ⓝ
3. Ⓨ Ⓝ
4. Ⓨ Ⓝ
5. Ⓨ Ⓝ
6. Ⓨ Ⓝ
7. Ⓨ Ⓝ
8. Ⓨ Ⓝ
9. Ⓨ Ⓝ
10. Ⓨ Ⓝ

___ / 10
Total

NAME: _____

DIRECTIONS Solve each problem.

SCORE

1. Ⓨ Ⓝ

2. Ⓨ Ⓝ

3. Ⓨ Ⓝ

4. Ⓨ Ⓝ

5. Ⓨ Ⓝ

6. Ⓨ Ⓝ

7. Ⓨ Ⓝ

8. Ⓨ Ⓝ

9. Ⓨ Ⓝ

10. Ⓨ Ⓝ

___ / 10
Total

1.
$$\begin{array}{r} 28 \\ -\ 13 \\ \hline \end{array}$$

2. Calculate 50 percent of 40.

_____

3. $76 \div 8 =$ _____

4. $6\overline{)89}$

5. How many digits are in 9,092?

_____

6. $100 \div 2 = \boxed{} \times 5$

7. How many 250-milliliter scoops of ice cream are in a 6-liter carton?

_____

8. 48 hours = _____ days

9. Is this a right angle?

_____

10. Write the directions for the path the counter moved.

_____

_____

_____

_____

start

NAME: _____

DIRECTIONS Solve each problem.

1. 27 + 15 = _____

6. 7 + 7 + 7 + 7 + ☐ =
5 x 7

1. Ⓨ Ⓝ

2. Ⓨ Ⓝ

7. How many days are in

January? _____

May? _____

August? _____

2. $\frac{1}{8}$ of 40 is _____.

3. Ⓨ Ⓝ

4. Ⓨ Ⓝ

3. 50 ÷ 10 = _____

8. 10 mm = _____ cm

5. Ⓨ Ⓝ

6. Ⓨ Ⓝ

9. Label with *reflection*,
rotation, or *translation*.

7. Ⓨ Ⓝ

4. 9 ⟌ 38

_____

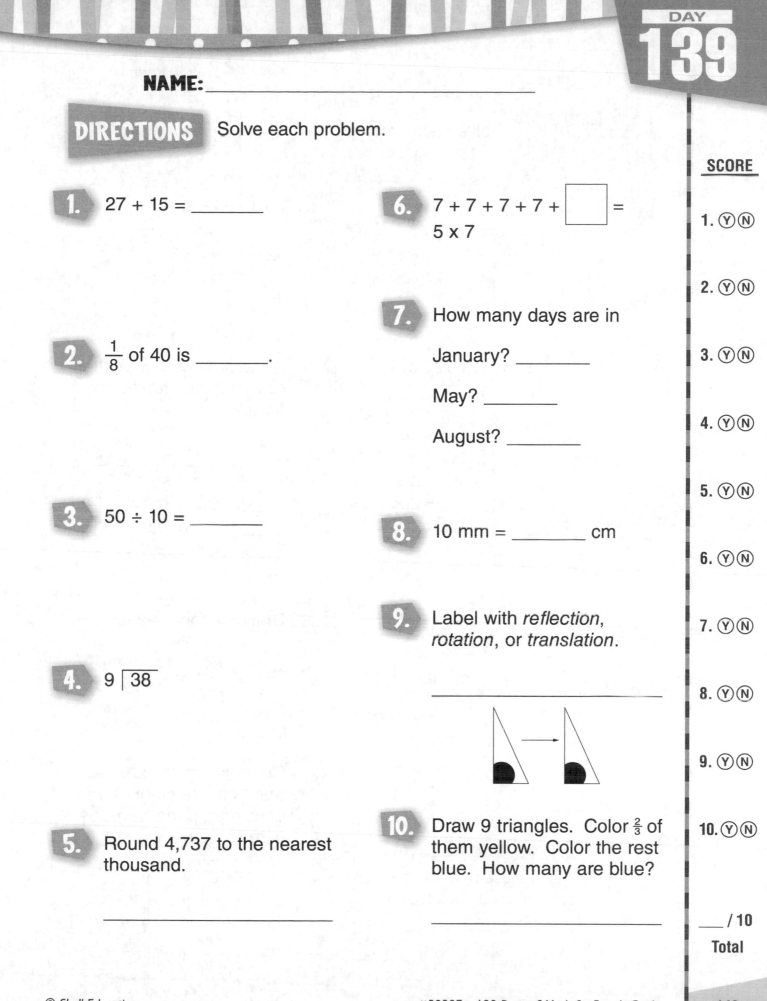

8. Ⓨ Ⓝ

9. Ⓨ Ⓝ

10. Draw 9 triangles. Color $\frac{2}{3}$ of
them yellow. Color the rest
blue. How many are blue?

5. Round 4,737 to the nearest
thousand.

10. Ⓨ Ⓝ

_____

_____

___ / 10

Total

NAME: _____

SCORE

1. Ⓨ Ⓝ

2. Ⓨ Ⓝ

3. Ⓨ Ⓝ

4. Ⓨ Ⓝ

5. Ⓨ Ⓝ

6. Ⓨ Ⓝ

7. Ⓨ Ⓝ

8. Ⓨ Ⓝ

9. Ⓨ Ⓝ

10. Ⓨ Ⓝ

___ / 10
Total

1. $28 - 16 =$ _____

2. List the first 3 multiples of 7.

_____ _____ _____

3. $43 \div 7 =$ _____

4. $6 \overline{)27}$

5. Is 421 even or odd?

_____

6. $7 \times 6 = 42$, so

$42 \div \boxed{} = 6$

7. Is the area of a computer screen measured in cm^2 or m^2?

_____

8. _____ seconds = 14 minutes

9. Draw the top view.

10. Color half of the area so that both the colored and uncolored parts have the same shape.

NAME: _____

DIRECTIONS Solve each problem.

1.
33
+ 25

6. Fill in the missing fraction.

$$\frac{6}{10}, \frac{7}{10}, \underline{\hspace{1.5cm}}, \frac{9}{10}$$

2. 10% of 20 is _____.

7. Write the length in millimeters. _____

3. 77 ÷ 11 = _____

8. _____ yards = 12 feet

4. Divide 4 into 90. _____

9. Name the polygon that has five vertices.

_____

5. Write 8,931 in words.

_____

_____

_____

10. Use each of the five numbers once and any operations to solve the problem below.

| 10 | 13 | 1 | 4 | 12 |

☐ ☐ ☐ ☐ ☐ = 20

1. Ⓨ Ⓝ
2. Ⓨ Ⓝ
3. Ⓨ Ⓝ
4. Ⓨ Ⓝ
5. Ⓨ Ⓝ
6. Ⓨ Ⓝ
7. Ⓨ Ⓝ
8. Ⓨ Ⓝ
9. Ⓨ Ⓝ
10. Ⓨ Ⓝ

___/ 10
Total

NAME: _____

SCORE

DIRECTIONS Solve each problem.

1. Ⓨ Ⓝ

1.   36
        − 24

2. Ⓨ Ⓝ

3. Ⓨ Ⓝ

2. $10 − $4.50 = _____

4. Ⓨ Ⓝ

5. Ⓨ Ⓝ

3. 55 ÷ 11 = _____

6. Ⓨ Ⓝ

7. Ⓨ Ⓝ

8. Ⓨ Ⓝ

4. 7⟌66

9. Ⓨ Ⓝ

10. Ⓨ Ⓝ

5. What is the next odd number after 893?

_____

___ / 10
Total

6. Complete the chart. There are six sides on a cube. How many sides are on 6 cubes?

_____

1 Cube	2 Cubes	3 Cubes
6		

4 Cubes	5 Cubes	6 Cubes

7. Calculate the perimeter of the rectangle.

4 cm

2 cm

_____

8. 104 weeks = _____ years

9. How many lines of symmetry does a pentagon have?

_____

10. Beth can jump rope twice as many times as Veronica. Veronica can jump 132 times. How many times can Beth jump?

_____

NAME: _____

DIRECTIONS Solve each problem.

1. 34 + 28 =

_____

6. 36 + ☐ = 72 − 14

1. Ⓨ Ⓝ

2. Ⓨ Ⓝ

2. Is 50% equal to $\frac{1}{2}$?

_____

7. Show 5 past 6 on both clocks.

3. Ⓨ Ⓝ

4. Ⓨ Ⓝ

5. Ⓨ Ⓝ

3. 12 ÷ 3 = _____

8. What month comes after June?

_____

6. Ⓨ Ⓝ

7. Ⓨ Ⓝ

4. 44 ÷ 5 = _____

9. True or false? All plane shapes are polygons.

_____

8. Ⓨ Ⓝ

9. Ⓨ Ⓝ

5. Is 928 greater than 982?

_____

10. Tickets for a movie are $\frac{1}{2}$ off if you buy the tickets early. If the full-price ticket costs $12.00, how much will you save by buying a ticket early?

_____

10. Ⓨ Ⓝ

_____ / 10
Total

NAME: _____

SCORE

DIRECTIONS   Solve each problem.

1. Ⓨ Ⓝ

2. Ⓨ Ⓝ

3. Ⓨ Ⓝ

4. Ⓨ Ⓝ

5. Ⓨ Ⓝ

6. Ⓨ Ⓝ

7. Ⓨ Ⓝ

8. Ⓨ Ⓝ

9. Ⓨ Ⓝ

10. Ⓨ Ⓝ

___ / 10
Total

1. 54 − 23 = _____

2. 50% of 20 is _____.

3. 78 ÷ 12 = _____

4. 8 ⟌ 53

5. Write the number for seven thousand, five hundred one.

_____

6. 6 x [   ] = 8 x 3

7. One pack of nails has a mass of 250 grams. What is the mass of 3 packs?

_____

8. Write the length in inches.

_____ inches

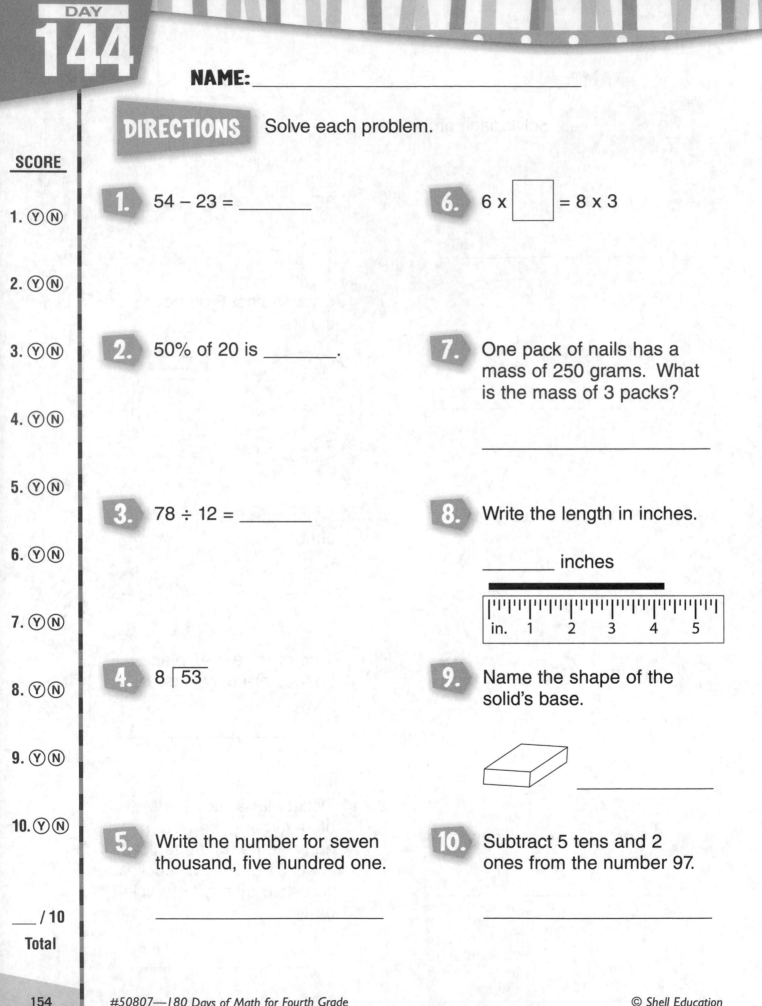

in.   1   2   3   4   5

9. Name the shape of the solid's base.

_____

10. Subtract 5 tens and 2 ones from the number 97.

_____

NAME: _____

DIRECTIONS Solve each problem.

1.
37
+ 26

2. 5 x 60 = _____

3. Divide 5 into 52. _____

4. 67 ÷ 10 = _____

5. Write 1,857 in expanded notation.

_____

_____

6. 7 x 6 = 42 ÷ ☐

7. What is the abbreviation for cubic meter?

_____

8. Which would be the best tool for measuring the width of a book: a ruler, a clock, or a meter stick?

_____

9.

Dollars Earned in May

Audrey	$15
Dameon	$23
Jason	$12
Lauren	$18

Audrey wants to buy a new CD that costs $13.99. Did she earn enough money in May to buy the CD?

_____

10. Use different colors to color pairs of numbers that equal the product shown in the center.

40 1 2
20 40 4
10 8 5

SCORE

1. Ⓨ Ⓝ

2. Ⓨ Ⓝ

3. Ⓨ Ⓝ

4. Ⓨ Ⓝ

5. Ⓨ Ⓝ

6. Ⓨ Ⓝ

7. Ⓨ Ⓝ

8. Ⓨ Ⓝ

9. Ⓨ Ⓝ

10. Ⓨ Ⓝ

___ / 10
Total

NAME: _____

Solve each problem.

SCORE

1. Ⓨ Ⓝ

2. Ⓨ Ⓝ

3. Ⓨ Ⓝ

4. Ⓨ Ⓝ

5. Ⓨ Ⓝ

6. Ⓨ Ⓝ

7. Ⓨ Ⓝ

8. Ⓨ Ⓝ

9. Ⓨ Ⓝ

10. Ⓨ Ⓝ

___ / 10
Total

1.
$$\begin{array}{r} 68 \\ -\ 27 \\ \hline \end{array}$$

2. Is $\frac{1}{2}$ more than $\frac{1}{8}$?

_____

3. $9\overline{)39}$

4. $91 \div 7 =$ _____

5. What is the value in the tens place in 3,827?

_____

6. Fill in the missing number.

749, 742, _____, 728, 721

7. How many liters are in 6,000 milliliters?

_____

8. ___ minutes = 360 seconds

9. Draw a line that is parallel to the line below.

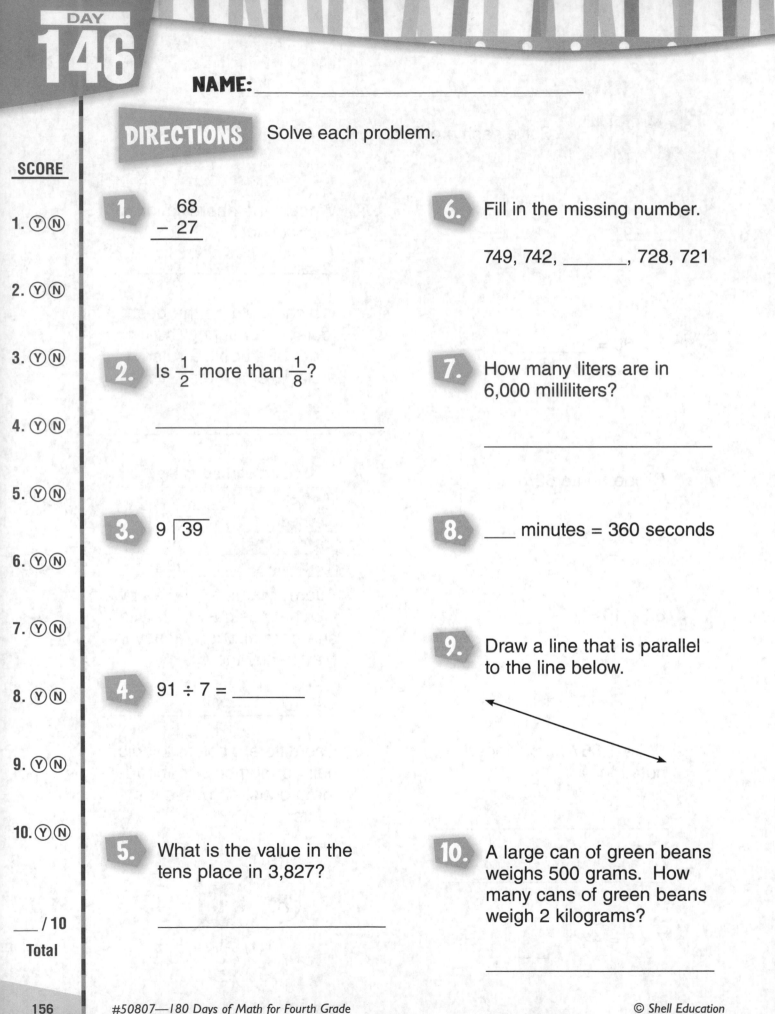

10. A large can of green beans weighs 500 grams. How many cans of green beans weigh 2 kilograms?

_____

NAME: _____

DIRECTIONS Solve each problem.

1. 43 + 28 = _____

6. 245 = 200 + _____ + 5

1. Ⓨ Ⓝ

2. Ⓨ Ⓝ

2. 50% of 10 is _____.

7. What is the date of the 3rd Sunday in December?

_____

3. Ⓨ Ⓝ

December						
Sun	Mon	Tues	Wed	Thurs	Fri	Sat
	1	2	3	4	5	6
7	8	9	10	11	12	13
14	15	16	17	18	19	20
21	22	23	24	25	26	27
28	29	30	31			

4. Ⓨ Ⓝ

3. 60 ÷ 6 = _____

5. Ⓨ Ⓝ

8. How many days are in August?

_____

6. Ⓨ Ⓝ

7. Ⓨ Ⓝ

4. Divide 40 into 10 equal groups.

_____

8. Ⓨ Ⓝ

9. Does this shape tessellate?

_____

9. Ⓨ Ⓝ

10. Ⓨ Ⓝ

5. Is 432 closer to 400 or 500?

_____

10. Halve 64, then add 12.

_____

___ / 10
Total

NAME:_____

DIRECTIONS Solve each problem.

SCORE

1. (Y)(N)

2. (Y)(N)

3. (Y)(N)

4. (Y)(N)

5. (Y)(N)

6. (Y)(N)

7. (Y)(N)

8. (Y)(N)

9. (Y)(N)

10. (Y)(N)

___ / 10
Total

1. 25 − 14 = _____

2. $\frac{1}{2}$ of 20 = _____

3. 6 ⟌ 54

4. How many 5s are in 15?

_____

5. 1,000 + 600 + 30 + 2 =

_____

6. 10 x 6 = 6 x ☐

7. Record in liters: _____ L

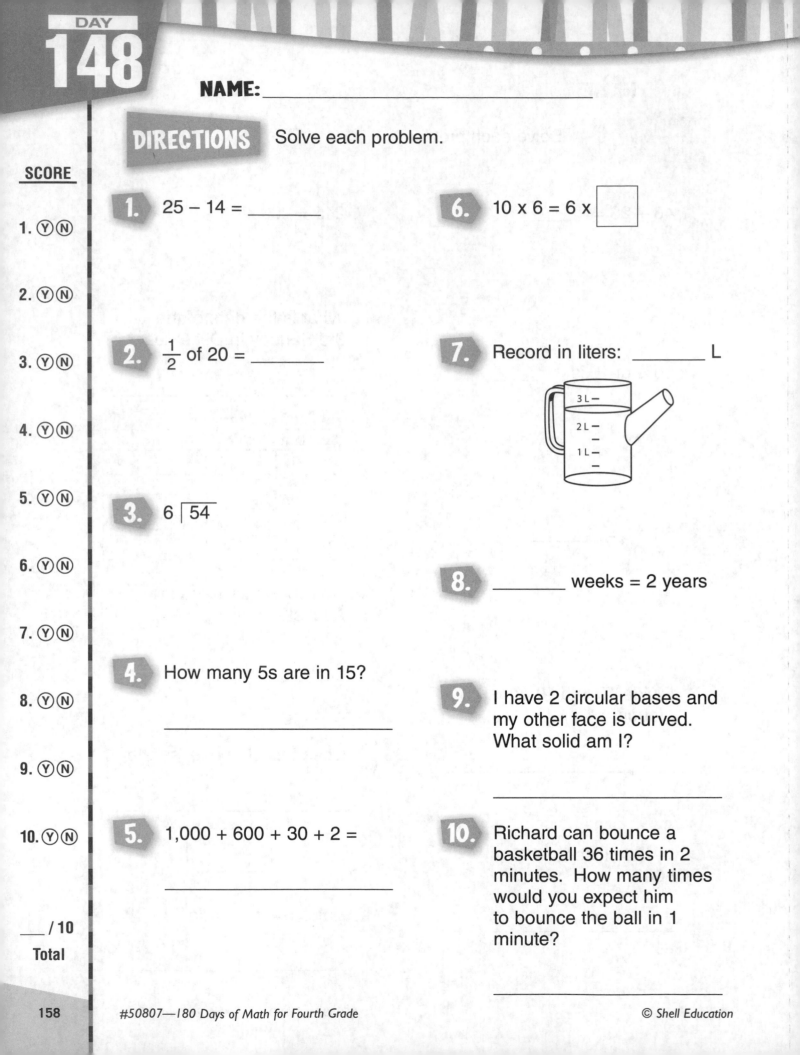

8. _____ weeks = 2 years

9. I have 2 circular bases and my other face is curved. What solid am I?

_____

10. Richard can bounce a basketball 36 times in 2 minutes. How many times would you expect him to bounce the ball in 1 minute?

_____

NAME:_____

DIRECTIONS Solve each problem.

1.
   18
+   9

2. Is 0.6 greater than 0.59?

_____

3. 8 ⟌ 16

4. 68 ÷ 9 = _____

5. Write 7,490 in expanded notation.

_____

6. Is 5 x 9 equal to 9 + 9 + 9 + 9 + 9 + 9?

_____

7. Which months are in the last quarter of the year?

_____

_____

8. Record the volume if the side of each cube is 5 cm.

_____

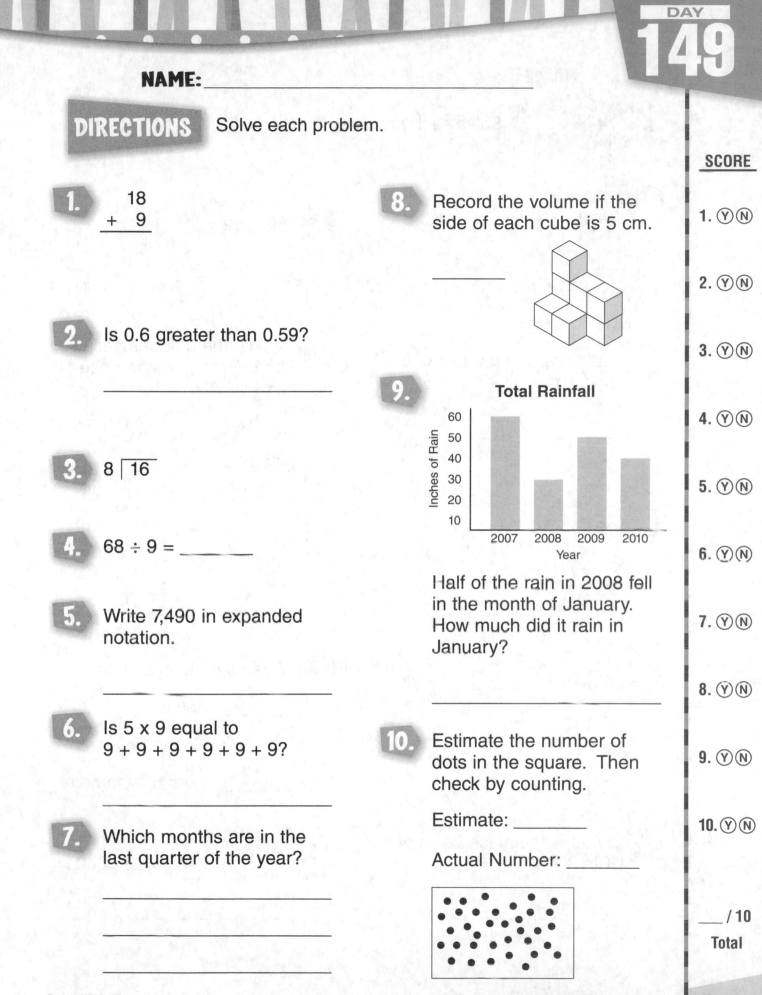

9. **Total Rainfall**

Half of the rain in 2008 fell in the month of January. How much did it rain in January?

_____

10. Estimate the number of dots in the square. Then check by counting.

Estimate: _____

Actual Number: _____

1. Ⓨ Ⓝ

2. Ⓨ Ⓝ

3. Ⓨ Ⓝ

4. Ⓨ Ⓝ

5. Ⓨ Ⓝ

6. Ⓨ Ⓝ

7. Ⓨ Ⓝ

8. Ⓨ Ⓝ

9. Ⓨ Ⓝ

10. Ⓨ Ⓝ

___ / 10
Total

NAME: _____

SCORE

1. Ⓨ Ⓝ

2. Ⓨ Ⓝ

3. Ⓨ Ⓝ

4. Ⓨ Ⓝ

5. Ⓨ Ⓝ

6. Ⓨ Ⓝ

7. Ⓨ Ⓝ

8. Ⓨ Ⓝ

9. Ⓨ Ⓝ

10. Ⓨ Ⓝ

___ / 10
Total

1.
$$\begin{array}{r} 28 \\ -\ 15 \\ \hline \end{array}$$

2. Calculate the product of 5 and 70.

_____

3. $12 \div 4 =$ _____

4. $55 \div 5 =$ _____

5. What is the place value of 1 in 8,126?

_____

6. $45 + 45 = 90 \times \boxed{}$

7. Would the unit of measure for the area of a hand be cm² or m²?

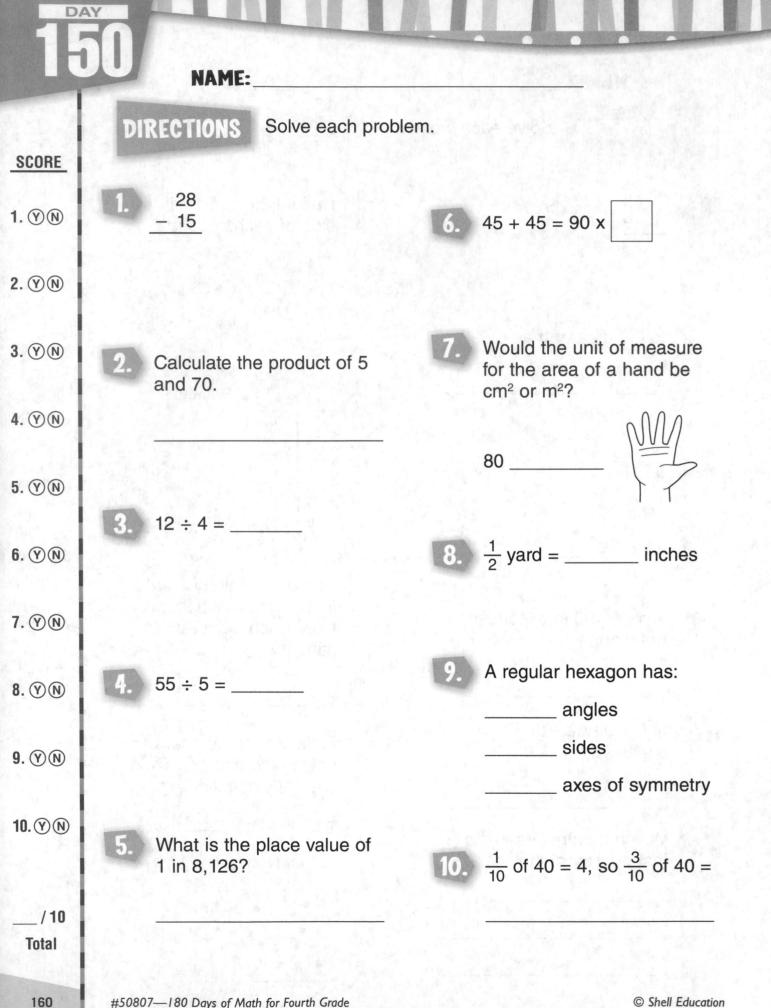

80 _____

8. $\frac{1}{2}$ yard = _____ inches

9. A regular hexagon has:

_____ angles

_____ sides

_____ axes of symmetry

10. $\frac{1}{10}$ of 40 = 4, so $\frac{3}{10}$ of 40 =

_____

NAME: _____

DIRECTIONS Solve each problem.

1. 25 + 13 = _____

6. Fill in the missing number.

318, 321, _____, 327, 330

1. Ⓨ Ⓝ

2. Ⓨ Ⓝ

2. $1.50
  + $2.25

7. Write the length in centimeters.

_____

3. Ⓨ Ⓝ

4. Ⓨ Ⓝ

3. 5 ⟌ 20

8. Would you be more likely to use a ruler or a yardstick to measure the length of a room?

_____

5. Ⓨ Ⓝ

6. Ⓨ Ⓝ

7. Ⓨ Ⓝ

4. 41 ÷ 9 = _____

9. A square has:

_____ axes of symmetry

and _____ right angles.

8. Ⓨ Ⓝ

9. Ⓨ Ⓝ

5. Round 2,747 to the nearest hundred.

_____

10. Follow the pattern in the first circle to complete the second circle.

10. Ⓨ Ⓝ

___ / 10

Total

NAME:_____

1. Ⓨ Ⓝ

2. Ⓨ Ⓝ

3. Ⓨ Ⓝ

4. Ⓨ Ⓝ

5. Ⓨ Ⓝ

6. Ⓨ Ⓝ

7. Ⓨ Ⓝ

8. Ⓨ Ⓝ

9. Ⓨ Ⓝ

10. Ⓨ Ⓝ

___ / 10
Total

DIRECTIONS Solve each problem.

1. Subtract 29 from 68.

_____

2. Write 81% as a fraction.

_____

3. $80 \div 8 =$ _____

4. Divide 6 into 92. _____

5. How many digits are in the number 237?

_____

6. $20 \div 1 = \boxed{} \times 5$

7. Calculate the perimeter of a square with 4-cm sides.

_____

4 cm

8. 4 days = _____ hours

9. Circle the solids that have a triangular top view.

A   B   C   D

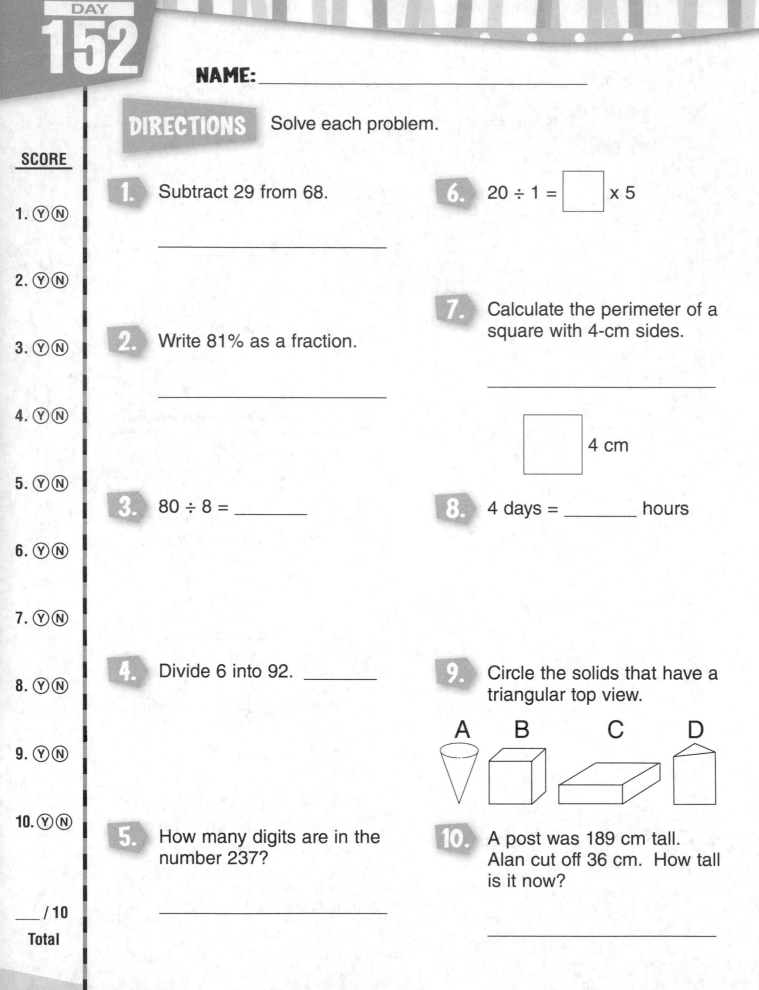

10. A post was 189 cm tall. Alan cut off 36 cm. How tall is it now?

_____

NAME: _____

DIRECTIONS Solve each problem.

1.
$$\begin{array}{r} 26 \\ + 18 \\ \hline \end{array}$$

1. Ⓨ Ⓝ

2. 50% of 30 is _____

2. Ⓨ Ⓝ

3. 16 ÷ 8 = _____

3. Ⓨ Ⓝ

4. 7 ⟌ 69

5. Write 9,058 in words.

_____

_____

6. 29 − 17 = ☐ x 4

7. Complete the clocks for the time 15 past 9.

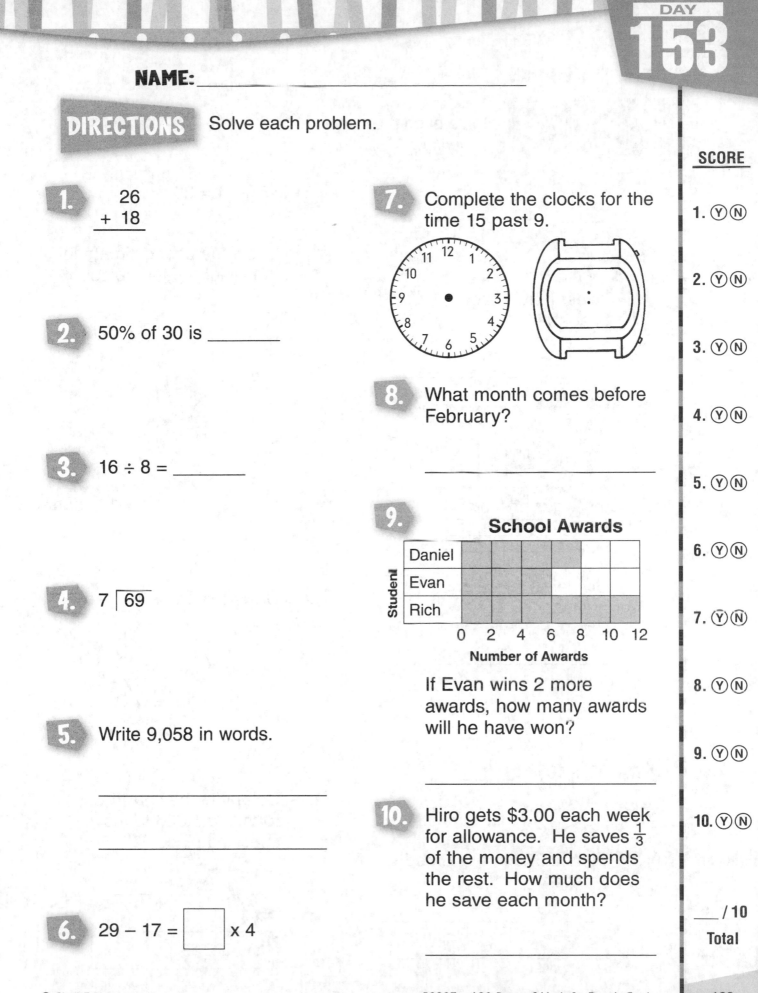

8. What month comes before February?

_____

9.

School Awards

Student						
Daniel						
Evan						
Rich						

0   2   4   6   8   10   12
Number of Awards

If Evan wins 2 more awards, how many awards will he have won?

_____

10. Hiro gets $3.00 each week for allowance. He saves $\frac{1}{3}$ of the money and spends the rest. How much does he save each month?

_____

4. Ⓨ Ⓝ

5. Ⓨ Ⓝ

6. Ⓨ Ⓝ

7. Ⓨ Ⓝ

8. Ⓨ Ⓝ

9. Ⓨ Ⓝ

10. Ⓨ Ⓝ

___ / 10
Total

NAME: _____

DIRECTIONS Solve each problem.

SCORE

1. Y N

2. Y N

3. Y N

4. Y N

5. Y N

6. Y N

7. Y N

8. Y N

9. Y N

10. Y N

___ / 10
Total

1.
$$\begin{array}{r} 17 \\ -\ 15 \\ \hline \end{array}$$

2. What percentage is shaded?

_____

3. Divide 18 into 2 equal groups.

_____

4. $93 \div 10 =$ _____

5. Write 2,573 in expanded notation.

_____

_____

6. $46 + 14 = 20 \times$ ☐

7. Circle the best estimate for the weight of the object.

100 g   2 kg   5 kg   10 kg

Sudso

8. _____ months = 10 years

9. Draw 1 line of symmetry.

10. Complete the chart by rounding 1,326 to the specified place.

Ten	
Hundred	
Thousand	

NAME:_____

DIRECTIONS Solve each problem.

1. Add 34 and 37.

_____

1. Ⓨ Ⓝ

2. 6 x 7 = _____

2. Ⓨ Ⓝ

6. $\frac{1}{4}$ of 36 = 4 + ☐

7. Is 10 mm equal to 1 cm?

_____

3. Ⓨ Ⓝ

3. 81 ÷ 9 = _____

8. 4 pints = _____ quart(s)

4. Ⓨ Ⓝ

5. Ⓨ Ⓝ

6. Ⓨ Ⓝ

4. 7$\overline{)56}$

9. How many angles are in this shape?

_____

7. Ⓨ Ⓝ

8. Ⓨ Ⓝ

9. Ⓨ Ⓝ

10. Ⓨ Ⓝ

5. 4,000 + 50 + 3 = _____

10. Complete the chart with the missing factors.

Product	48	56	60	81
Factor	8	7	6	9
Factor				

___ / 10
Total

NAME: _____

DIRECTIONS   Solve each problem.

SCORE

1. Ⓨ Ⓝ

2. Ⓨ Ⓝ

3. Ⓨ Ⓝ

4. Ⓨ Ⓝ

5. Ⓨ Ⓝ

6. Ⓨ Ⓝ

7. Ⓨ Ⓝ

8. Ⓨ Ⓝ

9. Ⓨ Ⓝ

10. Ⓨ Ⓝ

___ / 10
Total

1. 28 − 17 = _____

2. Is 0.7 less than 0.59?

_____

3. 42 ÷ 2 = _____

4. 21 ÷ 4 = _____

5. What is the even number before 1,802?

_____

6. Write the next two numbers in the pattern.

0.6, 0.7, 0.8, _____, _____

7. How many buckets will it take to empty the tank?

_____

60 L   10 L

8. How many days are in November?

_____

9. This pyramid has:

_____ faces

_____ vertices

A _____ for a base

10. Joel's pencil was 13.2 cm long. Ming's pencil was 15.45 cm long. How much longer was Ming's pencil?

_____

DIRECTIONS Solve each problem.

1.
    46
  + 25

2. Write $\frac{1}{4}$ as a decimal.

_____

3. 70 ÷ 7 = _____

4. 46 ÷ 6 = _____

5. What is the value of the tens place in 2,504?

_____

6. When Amy walks, she covers 58 cm with each step. Complete the chart to find the distance she covers in 5 steps.

_____

Step 1	Step 2	Step 3	Step 4	Step 5
58				

7. Which day of the week is New Year's Eve?

_____

December						
Sun	Mon	Tues	Wed	Thurs	Fri	Sat
	1	2	3	4	5	6
7	8	9	10	11	12	13
14	15	16	17	18	19	20
21	22	23	24	25	26	27
28	29	30	31			

8. 24 months = _____ years

9. What is another name for a right angle?

_____

10. If you multiply me by 13, you get 52. What number am I?

_____

1. Ⓨ Ⓝ
2. Ⓨ Ⓝ
3. Ⓨ Ⓝ
4. Ⓨ Ⓝ
5. Ⓨ Ⓝ
6. Ⓨ Ⓝ
7. Ⓨ Ⓝ
8. Ⓨ Ⓝ
9. Ⓨ Ⓝ
10. Ⓨ Ⓝ

___ / 10
Total

NAME: _____

DIRECTIONS   Solve each problem.

1. Ⓨ Ⓝ

1.
$$\begin{array}{r} 36 \\ -\ 25 \\ \hline \end{array}$$

2. Ⓨ Ⓝ

3. Ⓨ Ⓝ

2. Write 0.71 as a fraction.

_____

4. Ⓨ Ⓝ

5. Ⓨ Ⓝ

3. 24 ÷ 8 = _____

6. Ⓨ Ⓝ

4. 8)‾8‾2‾

7. Ⓨ Ⓝ

8. Ⓨ Ⓝ

5. Is 2,567 greater than or less than 2,675?

9. Ⓨ Ⓝ

_____

10. Ⓨ Ⓝ

6. 1,467 =
1,000 + _____ + 60 + 7

7. How many 4 liter bottles can be filled with 36 liters of juice?

_____

8. Circle the most likely length of a vacation.

7 days

7 months

7 meters

9. Draw in the diagonals for the shape.

10. Draw a square on the coordinates (G,5).

___ / 10
Total

NAME: _____

DIRECTIONS Solve each problem.

1. 38 + 23 = _____

6. 10 − 2 = ☐ x 4

1. Ⓨ Ⓝ

2. Ⓨ Ⓝ

2. Shade 85%.

7. How many days are in a year?

_____

3. Ⓨ Ⓝ

4. Ⓨ Ⓝ

8. _ _____ m = 1 km

5. Ⓨ Ⓝ

6. Ⓨ Ⓝ

3. 6 ‾9‾4‾

9. Fill in the blank with *rotation*, *reflection*, or *translation*.

7. Ⓨ Ⓝ

8. Ⓨ Ⓝ

4. 43 ÷ 7 = _____

_____

☐ → ◇

9. Ⓨ Ⓝ

10. There are 8 circles. 25% are blue. 50% are red. The rest are orange. What fraction of the circles are orange?

10. Ⓨ Ⓝ

___/10

Total

5. 1,000 + 50 + 6 = _____

_____

NAME:_____

DIRECTIONS Solve each problem.

1. $47 - 8 =$ _____

1. Ⓨ Ⓝ

2. Ⓨ Ⓝ

2. 50% of $60 =$ _____

3. Ⓨ Ⓝ

4. Ⓨ Ⓝ

3. Calculate the quotient of 525 and 7.

5. Ⓨ Ⓝ

_____

6. Ⓨ Ⓝ

4. $57 \div 5 =$ _____

7. Ⓨ Ⓝ

8. Ⓨ Ⓝ

5. What is the number after 4,989?

9. Ⓨ Ⓝ

10. Ⓨ Ⓝ

_____

6. $81 \div 9 = 9 \times \boxed{}$

7. The floor has an area of 16 m². It is covered with a mat of 9 m². What area is uncovered?

_____

8. 1 _____ = 60 minutes

9. What type of prism is shown?

_____

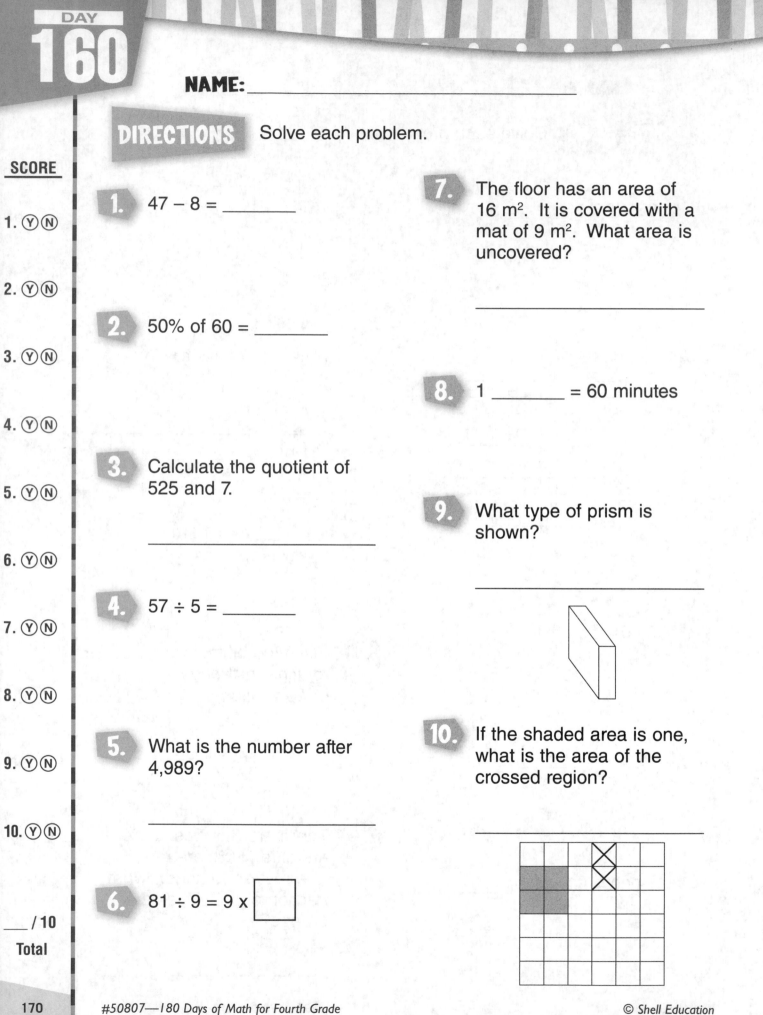

10. If the shaded area is one, what is the area of the crossed region?

_____

NAME: _____

DIRECTIONS Solve each problem.

1.
```
   29
+  14
```

2. Write 25% as a fraction.

_____

3. Calculate 71 divided by 10.

_____

4. 24 ÷ 6 = _____

5. Write 1,414 in expanded notation.

_____

6. Fill in the missing fraction.

$$\frac{1}{100}, \frac{2}{100}, \frac{3}{100}, \underline{\hspace{1cm}}, \frac{5}{100}$$

7. Write the length in millimeters.

_____

_____

| cm | 1 | 2 | 3 | 4 | 5 |

8. 16 pints = _____ gallons

9. How many faces does a square pyramid have?

_____

10. Use each of the five numbers once and any operations to solve the problem below.

_____

| 10 | 13 | 1 | 4 | 12 |

☐ ☐ ☐ ☐ ☐ = 10

1. (Y)(N)

2. (Y)(N)

3. (Y)(N)

4. (Y)(N)

5. (Y)(N)

6. (Y)(N)

7. (Y)(N)

8. (Y)(N)

9. (Y)(N)

10. (Y)(N)

___/10
Total

NAME: _____

DIRECTIONS Solve each problem.

1. Ⓨ Ⓝ

2. Ⓨ Ⓝ

3. Ⓨ Ⓝ

4. Ⓨ Ⓝ

5. Ⓨ Ⓝ

6. Ⓨ Ⓝ

7. Ⓨ Ⓝ

8. Ⓨ Ⓝ

9. Ⓨ Ⓝ

10. Ⓨ Ⓝ

___ / 10
Total

1.
$$\begin{array}{r} 26 \\ -\ 13 \\ \hline \end{array}$$

2. Write $\frac{73}{100}$ as a percentage.

_____

3. $95 \div 5 =$ _____

4. Divide 8 into 44.

5. What is the place value of 2 in 2,647?

_____

6. $3 \times 3 = \frac{1}{3}$ of ☐

7. Calculate the perimeter of a square with 6-cm sides.

_____

☐ 6 cm

8. 2 yards = _____ inches

9. Is a hexagon a plane shape or a solid?

_____

10. Mom bakes 24 cookies for the soccer team. One-half of the cookies are eaten. How many are not eaten?

_____

NAME:_____

DIRECTIONS Solve each problem.

1. Calculate the sum of 25 and 17.

_____

2. Is $\frac{4}{5}$ greater than, less than, or equal to $\frac{4}{50}$?

_____

3. $83 \div 6 =$ _____

4. Calculate the quotient of 56 and 7.

_____

5. Write four thousand seven hundred with numerals.

_____

6. $100 \times 1 = 10 \times$ ☐

7. Show 7:50 on both clocks.

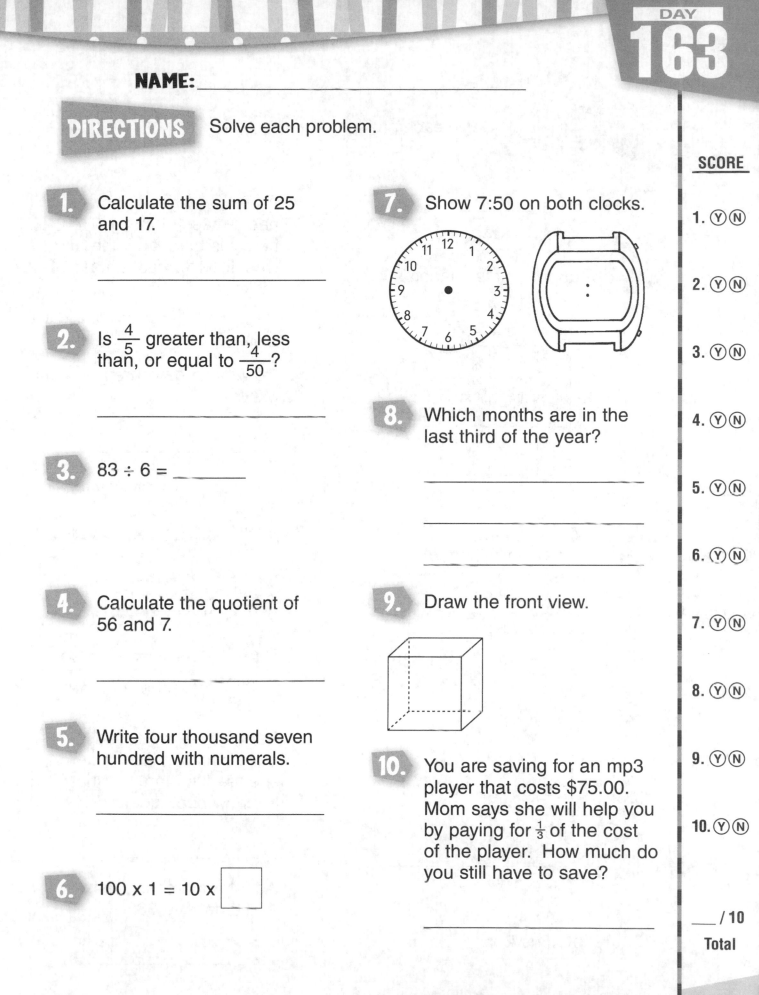

8. Which months are in the last third of the year?

_____

_____

9. Draw the front view.

10. You are saving for an mp3 player that costs $75.00. Mom says she will help you by paying for $\frac{1}{3}$ of the cost of the player. How much do you still have to save?

_____

1. Ⓨ Ⓝ

2. Ⓨ Ⓝ

3. Ⓨ Ⓝ

4. Ⓨ Ⓝ

5. Ⓨ Ⓝ

6. Ⓨ Ⓝ

7. Ⓨ Ⓝ

8. Ⓨ Ⓝ

9. Ⓨ Ⓝ

10. Ⓨ Ⓝ

___ / 10
Total

NAME: _____

SCORE

DIRECTIONS Solve each problem.

1. (Y) (N)

2. (Y) (N)

3. (Y) (N)

4. (Y) (N)

5. (Y) (N)

6. (Y) (N)

7. (Y) (N)

8. (Y) (N)

9. (Y) (N)

10. (Y) (N)

___ / 10
Total

1. $42 - 8 =$ _____

2. What percent is shaded?

_____

3. Divide 63 into 7 equal groups.

_____

4. $5 \overline{)25}$

5. What is the number after 4,799?

_____

6. $\frac{1}{8}$ of 48 is 2 x ☐

7. An empty wheelbarrow has a mass of 12 kg. How heavy is the load if the full wheelbarrow has a mass of 22 kg?

_____

8. How many days are in May?

_____

9.

Books Read in March

Cathy	📖 📖 📖
Martin	📖 📖 📖 📖
Jose	📖 📖 📖

📖 = 5 books read

Cathy's goal is to read 10 more books in April than she read in March. What is her new book goal?

_____

10. Add 4 hundreds, 3 tens, and 0 ones to 362.

_____

NAME: _____

DIRECTIONS Solve each problem.

1. 38
    + 34

2. Is 49 a square number?

_____

3. 2 | 14

4. 45 ÷ 9 = ___ ___

5. What is the value of the hundreds place in 2,604?

_____

6. Complete the chart to find the cost of 5 pens at 25¢ each.

_____

1 Pen	2 Pens	3 Pens	4 Pens	5 Pens
25¢				

7. How many millimeters are there in 8 centimeters?

_____

8. How many times in a year is the date the 31st?

_____

9. Draw 1 line of symmetry.

10. A pound of ground beef costs $2.00. You have a coupon for 25% off. How much will you save?

_____

1. Ⓨ Ⓝ

2. Ⓨ Ⓝ

3. Ⓨ Ⓝ

4. Ⓨ Ⓝ

5. Ⓨ Ⓝ

6. Ⓨ Ⓝ

7. Ⓨ Ⓝ

8. Ⓨ Ⓝ

9. Ⓨ Ⓝ

10. Ⓨ Ⓝ

___ / 10
Total

NAME: _____

DIRECTIONS Solve each problem.

SCORE

1. Ⓨ Ⓝ

2. Ⓨ Ⓝ

3. Ⓨ Ⓝ

4. Ⓨ Ⓝ

5. Ⓨ Ⓝ

6. Ⓨ Ⓝ

7. Ⓨ Ⓝ

8. Ⓨ Ⓝ

9. Ⓨ Ⓝ

10. Ⓨ Ⓝ

___ / 10
Total

1.
$$\begin{array}{r} 23 \\ -5 \\ \hline \end{array}$$

2. Write 37% as a decimal.

_____

3. Divide 20 into 4 equal groups.

_____

4. 59 ÷ 7 = _____

5. Write 3,014 in expanded notation.

_____

_____

6. Fill in the missing number.

642, 648, 654, _____, 666

7. If 8 [glass] fill a [pitcher] and

5 [pitcher] fill a [bucket], then

_____ [glass] fill a [bucket].

8. Which would be the best measure for the length of a commercial on TV: an hour, a minute, or a kilogram?

_____

9. What shape is the cross-section?

_____

10. What is the next number in the pattern?

1, 5, 9, 13, _____

#50807—180 Days of Math for Fourth Grade

NAME:_____

DIRECTIONS Solve each problem.

1. 44 + 27 = _____

6. 27 ÷ 9 = 3 x ☐

1. Ⓨ Ⓝ

7. What date is it one day after December 31st?

2. Ⓨ Ⓝ

2. 50% of 50 is _____.

3. Ⓨ Ⓝ

December						
Sun	Mon	Tues	Wed	Thurs	Fri	Sat
	1	2	3	4	5	6
7	8	9	10	11	12	13
14	15	16	17	18	19	20
21	22	23	24	25	26	27
28	29	30	31			

4. Ⓨ Ⓝ

3. Calculate the quotient of 72 and 7.

_____

8. Which would be the best measure for the capacity of a bucket: cup, kilogram, or liter?

5. Ⓨ Ⓝ

6. Ⓨ Ⓝ

7. Ⓨ Ⓝ

_____

4. 96 ÷ 9 = _____

9. What is the name for lines that intersect to form right angles?

8. Ⓨ Ⓝ

9. Ⓨ Ⓝ

_____

5. Is 1,427 closer to 1,400 or 1,500?

10. Ⓨ Ⓝ

10. If you divide me by 12, you get 5. What number am I?

_____

_____ / 10

_____

Total

NAME: _____

DIRECTIONS Solve each problem.

SCORE

1. Ⓨ Ⓝ

2. Ⓨ Ⓝ

3. Ⓨ Ⓝ

4. Ⓨ Ⓝ

5. Ⓨ Ⓝ

6. Ⓨ Ⓝ

7. Ⓨ Ⓝ

8. Ⓨ Ⓝ

9. Ⓨ Ⓝ

10. Ⓨ Ⓝ

___ / 10
Total

1. Calculate the difference between 27 and 16.

_____

2. Shade 62%.

3. 8 ⟌ 84

4. 28 ÷ 7 = _____

5. What is 400 more than 3,570?

_____

6. 2,473 = 2,000 + _____ + 70 + 3

7. How many milliliters are in a quarter of a liter?

_____

8. _____ seconds = 4 minutes

9. True or false? Parallel lines never meet.

_____

10. Commercials are half a minute long, with 5 commercials every commercial break. How long is each commercial break?

_____

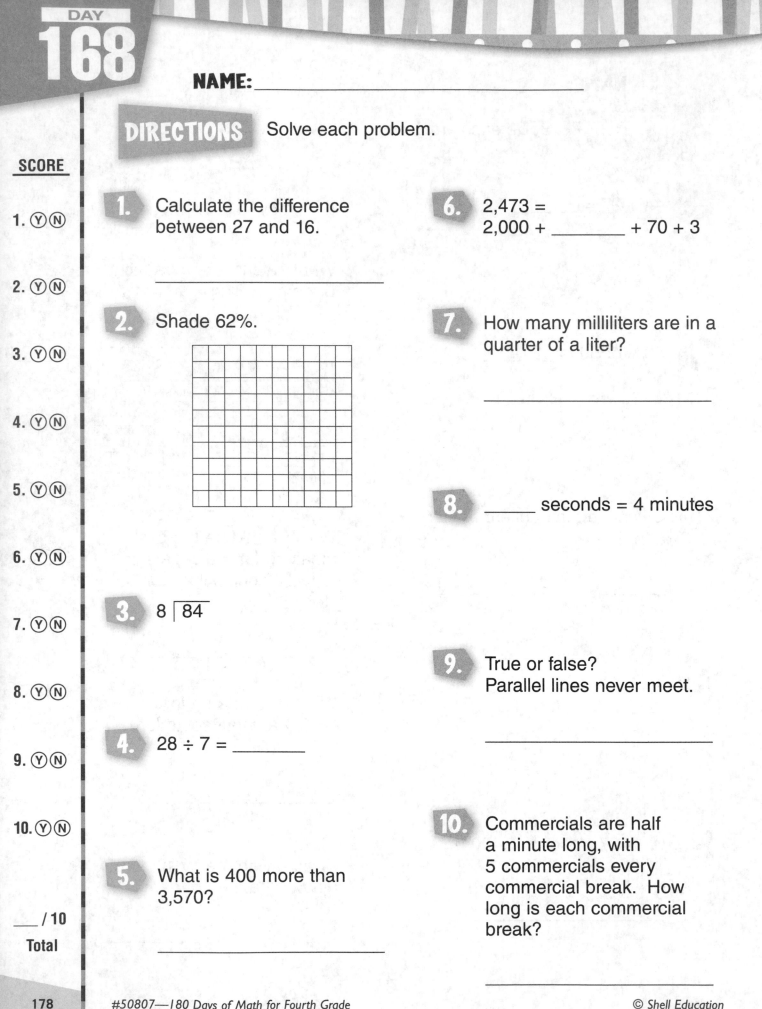

NAME: _____

DIRECTIONS Solve each problem.

SCORE

1.
```
   31
    3
+  19
```

7. What is the day before January 1?

_____

2. Write $\frac{3}{10}$ as a percentage.

_____

8. Calculate the perimeter of a hexagon with 5-cm sides.

_____

3. $8\,\overline{)\,24}$

9. Draw a line from the real-life object to the matching solid.

4. $60 \div 10 =$ _____

5. Is 5,243 less than 5,234?

_____

6. Marcia saves $2.50 every week. In what week will she have $8.00?

_____

10. Kaylee pays $4.00 for 8 daisies. What is the price of each daisy?

_____

Week 1	Week 2	Week 3	Week 4	Week 5
$2.50				

1. Ⓨ Ⓝ
2. Ⓨ Ⓝ
3. Ⓨ Ⓝ
4. Ⓨ Ⓝ
5. Ⓨ Ⓝ
6. Ⓨ Ⓝ
7. Ⓨ Ⓝ
8. Ⓨ Ⓝ
9. Ⓨ Ⓝ
10. Ⓨ Ⓝ

___ / 10
Total

NAME: _____

DIRECTIONS Solve each problem.

1. $\begin{array}{r} 32 \\ -\ 9 \\ \hline \end{array}$

2. Write 0.35 as a percentage.

_____

3. $4\overline{)23}$

4. $46 \div 12 =$ _____

5. Round 1,276 to the nearest ten.

_____

6. $42 \div 6 = 14 \div \boxed{}$

7. _____ is the amount of surface covered or enclosed by any two-dimensional shape.

8. Matthew wakes up at 7:00 A.M. He got 10 hours sleep. What time did he go to bed?

_____

9. Label with *reflection*, *rotation*, or *translation*.

_____

10. $\frac{1}{5}$ of 35 = 7, so $\frac{3}{5}$ of 35 =

_____

 #50807—180 Days of Math for Fourth Grade

NAME:_____

DIRECTIONS Solve each problem.

1. 35 + 45 = _____

2. Is $\frac{3}{10}$ greater than $\frac{3}{100}$?

_____

3. 27 ÷ 12 = _____

4. 5 ⟌ 85

5. Is 9,018 greater than 9,081?

_____

6. Fill in the missing number.

854, _____, 840, 833, 826

7. Write the length in centimeters.

_____

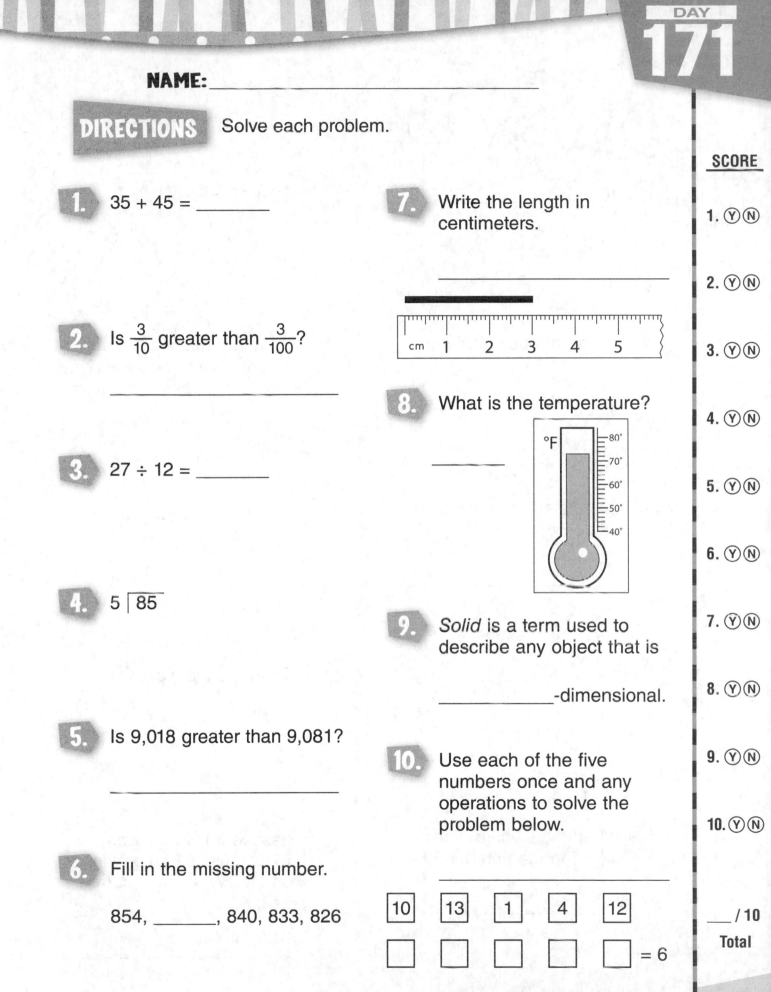

8. What is the temperature?

_____

°F

9. *Solid* is a term used to describe any object that is

_____-dimensional.

10. Use each of the five numbers once and any operations to solve the problem below.

_____

10	13	1	4	12
☐	☐	☐	☐	☐ = 6

1. Ⓨ Ⓝ

2. Ⓨ Ⓝ

3. Ⓨ Ⓝ

4. Ⓨ Ⓝ

5. Ⓨ Ⓝ

6. Ⓨ Ⓝ

7. Ⓨ Ⓝ

8. Ⓨ Ⓝ

9. Ⓨ Ⓝ

10. Ⓨ Ⓝ

___ / 10
Total

NAME:_____

DIRECTIONS Solve each problem.

1. $46 - 34 =$ _____

6. $60 \div 10 = \frac{1}{2}$ of ☐

2. Write 30% as a fraction.

_____

7. A square has a perimeter of 12 cm. What is its area?

_____

3. Calculate the quotient of 97 and 6.

_____

8. $100 \text{ cm} = 1$ _____

4. $73 \div 5 =$ _____

9. Draw the top view.

5. What is the value of the digit 4 in the number 2,643?

_____

10. Last year my tree was 67 cm tall. It has grown 34 cm. What is its current height?

_____

NAME: _____

DIRECTIONS Solve each problem.

1.
$$\begin{array}{r} 47 \\ + 23 \\ \hline \end{array}$$

6. $7 \times \boxed{}$ is $\frac{1}{4}$ of 56

1. Ⓨ Ⓝ

2. Write 0.84 as a percentage.

_____

7. Complete the clocks for the time 25 to 2.

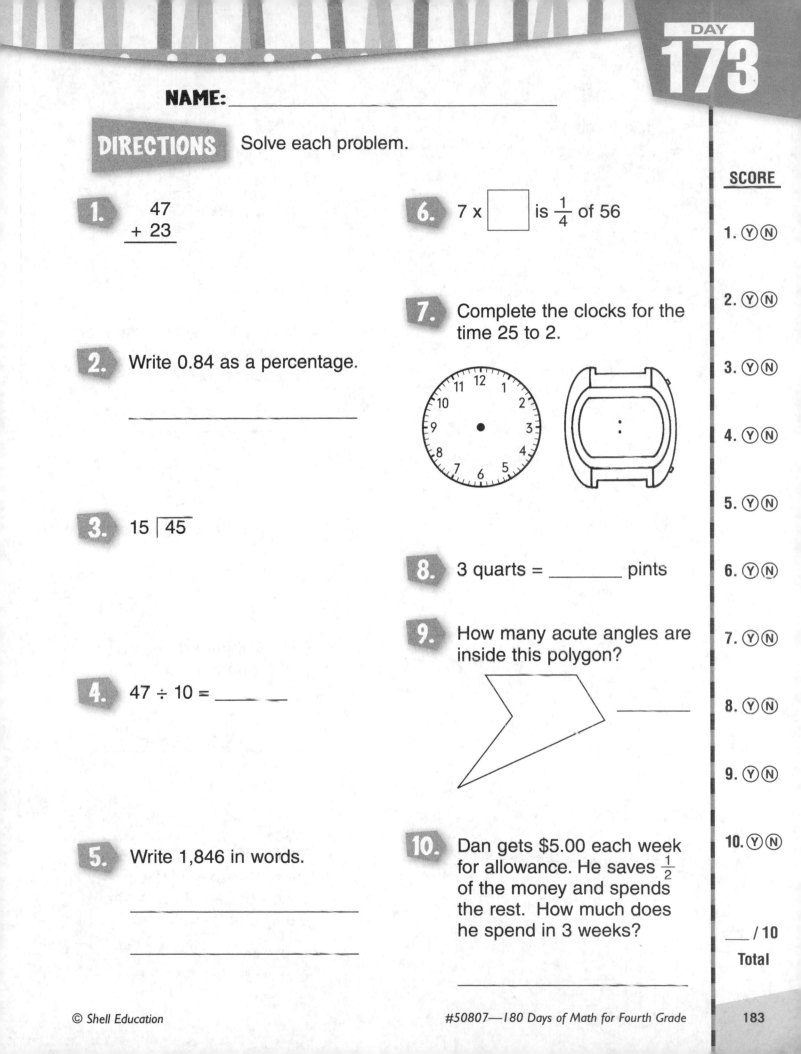

2. Ⓨ Ⓝ

3. Ⓨ Ⓝ

3. 15 $\overline{)45}$

8. 3 quarts = _____ pints

4. Ⓨ Ⓝ

5. Ⓨ Ⓝ

6. Ⓨ Ⓝ

9. How many acute angles are inside this polygon?

_____

4. 47 ÷ 10 = _____ _____

7. Ⓨ Ⓝ

8. Ⓨ Ⓝ

9. Ⓨ Ⓝ

5. Write 1,846 in words.

_____

_____

10. Dan gets $5.00 each week for allowance. He saves $\frac{1}{2}$ of the money and spends the rest. How much does he spend in 3 weeks?

_____

10. Ⓨ Ⓝ

____ / 10

Total

NAME: _____

SCORE

1. Ⓨ Ⓝ

2. Ⓨ Ⓝ

3. Ⓨ Ⓝ

4. Ⓨ Ⓝ

5. Ⓨ Ⓝ

6. Ⓨ Ⓝ

7. Ⓨ Ⓝ

8. Ⓨ Ⓝ

9. Ⓨ Ⓝ

10. Ⓨ Ⓝ

___ / 10
Total

1.
$$\begin{array}{r} 42 \\ -\ 23 \\ \hline \end{array}$$

2. $9 \times 8 =$ _____

3. $30 \div 5 =$ _____

4. $6\overline{)61}$

5. $3{,}000 + 40 + 7 =$ _____

6. $\frac{1}{5}$ of $45 = 3 \times$ ☐

7. Would you use kilograms or grams to measure the mass of a soccer ball?

_____

8. _____ hours = 180 minutes

9. Draw a line perpendicular to the one below.

⟷

10. Trish eats one box of cereal every 2 weeks. How many boxes of cereal does she eat in 8 weeks?

_____

NAME: _____

Solve each problem.

1. 32 + 7 + 28 = _____

6. 23 − 15 = _____ − 48

1. Ⓨ Ⓝ

2. Ⓨ Ⓝ

2. Write 25% as a decimal.

_____

7. Write the abbreviation for square meter.

_____

3. Ⓨ Ⓝ

4. Ⓨ Ⓝ

3. Calculate the quotient of 32 and 8.

_____

8. _____ yards = 9 feet

5. Ⓨ Ⓝ

6. Ⓨ Ⓝ

4. 98 ÷ 7 = _____

9. Draw the front view.

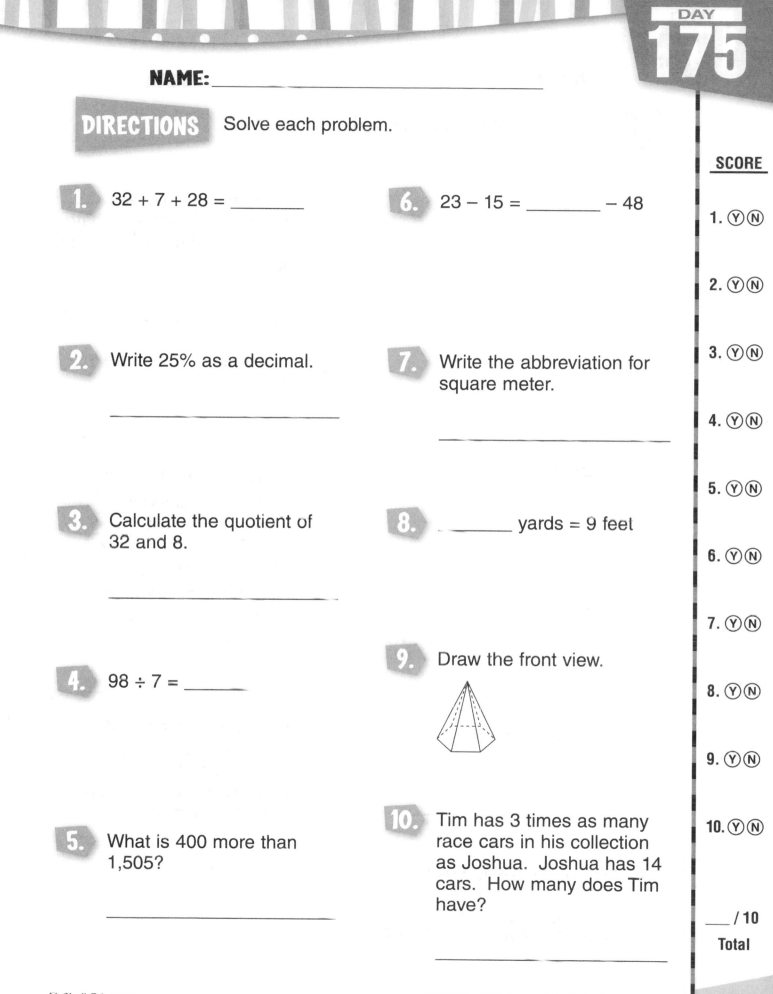

7. Ⓨ Ⓝ

8. Ⓨ Ⓝ

9. Ⓨ Ⓝ

5. What is 400 more than 1,505?

_____

10. Tim has 3 times as many race cars in his collection as Joshua. Joshua has 14 cars. How many does Tim have?

_____

10. Ⓨ Ⓝ

_____ / 10
Total

NAME: _____

NAME

DIRECTIONS Solve each problem.

SCORE

1. Ⓨ Ⓝ

2. Ⓨ Ⓝ

3. Ⓨ Ⓝ

4. Ⓨ Ⓝ

5. Ⓨ Ⓝ

6. Ⓨ Ⓝ

7. Ⓨ Ⓝ

8. Ⓨ Ⓝ

9. Ⓨ Ⓝ

10. Ⓨ Ⓝ

___ / 10
Total

1.
$$\begin{array}{r} 47 \\ -\ 28 \\ \hline \end{array}$$

2. Write 47% as a fraction.

_____

3. $35 \div 5 =$ _____

4. $8\overline{)48}$

5. $2{,}000 + 500 + 30 + 6 =$

_____

6. $7 + 8 = 18 -$ _____

7. How many 250-mL mugs are in 5 L of water?

_____

8. Write the length in inches.

_____ inches

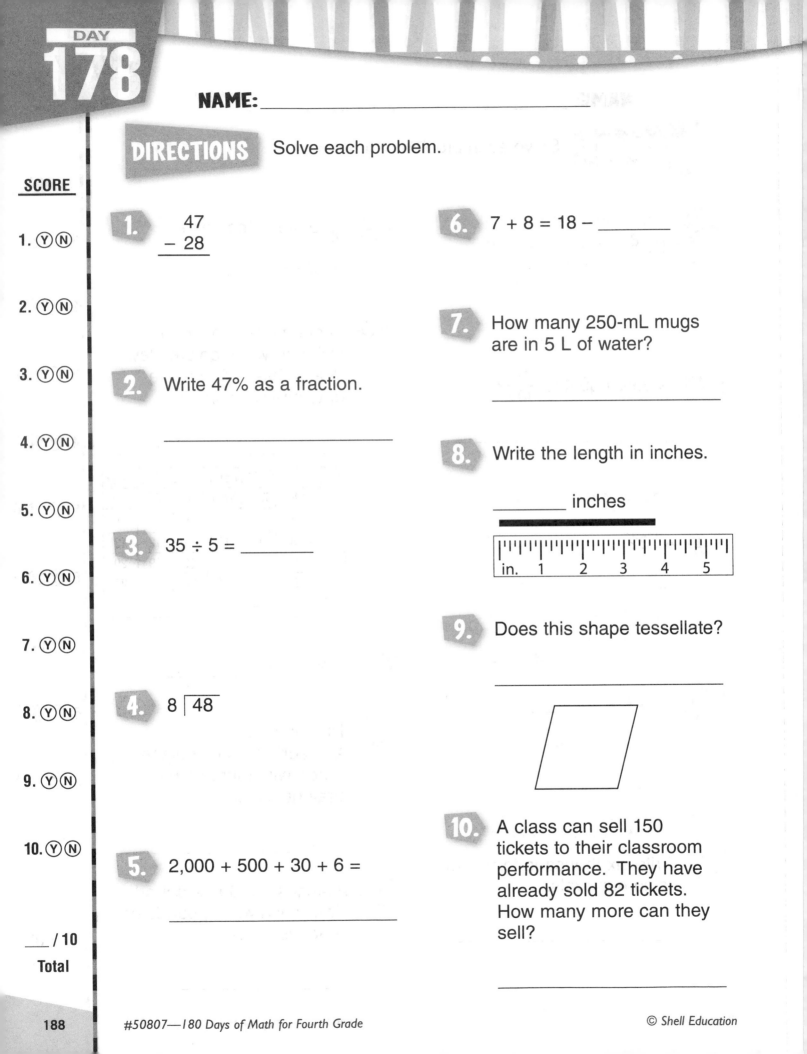

9. Does this shape tessellate?

_____

10. A class can sell 150 tickets to their classroom performance. They have already sold 82 tickets. How many more can they sell?

_____

NAME: _____

DIRECTIONS Solve each problem.

1. 26 + 16 = _____

6. 3,039 = 3,000 + _____

1. Ⓨ Ⓝ

7. Would you use square inches or square feet to measure the area of an area rug?

2. Ⓨ Ⓝ

2. Is 3% equal to $\frac{3}{10}$?

_____

3. Ⓨ Ⓝ

_____

8. What is the volume of a cube with 1-cm sides?

4. Ⓨ Ⓝ

3. 10 ⟌ 74

_____.

5. Ⓨ Ⓝ

9. How many obtuse angles are inside this polygon?

6. Ⓨ Ⓝ

_____

4. 99 ÷ 11 = _____

7. Ⓨ Ⓝ

8. Ⓨ Ⓝ

9. Ⓨ Ⓝ

10. Tina practices the piano twice as long as her sister Jenny. Jenny practices the piano 25 minutes every day. How long does Tina practice each day?

10. Ⓨ Ⓝ

5. Is 2,386 closer to 2,300 or 2,400?

_____

____ / 10

_____

Total

NAME: _____

SCORE

DIRECTIONS Solve each problem.

1. Ⓨ Ⓝ

1. 36 – 19 = _____

2. Ⓨ Ⓝ

7. Are 2,000 milliliters and 2 liters equivalent?

_____

3. Ⓨ Ⓝ

2. Write 81% as a decimal.

_____

8. What is the most likely temperature inside of a house?

4. Ⓨ Ⓝ

7°F   70°F   –70°F

3. How many 5s are in 90?

5. Ⓨ Ⓝ

_____

9. I have a square base and all my other faces are triangular. What solid am I?

6. Ⓨ Ⓝ

4. 87 ÷ 12 = _____

_____

7. Ⓨ Ⓝ

10. Draw the mirror image of this shape so it is symmetrical.

8. Ⓨ Ⓝ

5. What is the place value of 7 in 3,972?

9. Ⓨ Ⓝ

_____

6. How much do 6 pens cost if 1 pen costs 30¢?

10. Ⓨ Ⓝ

_____

___/ 10
Total

1 Pen	2 Pens	3 Pens	4 Pens	5 Pens	6 Pens
30¢					

ANSWER KEY

Day 1
1. 23
2. 4 out of 5 boxes should be shaded.
3. 4
4. 2
5. yes
6. 60
7. 4.5 centimeters
8. A.M.
9. 5 sides
10.

+	8	14	17	19	22	36
19	27	33	36	38	41	55
29	37	43	46	48	51	65
39	47	53	56	58	61	75

Day 2
1. 11
2. 24
3. 2
4. 4
5. 4 tens or 40
6. 9
7. 12 cm
8. 92°F
9. face or square
10. 29 kg

Day 3
1. 900
2. 8
3. 2
4. 8
5. 417 should be circled.
6. 2
7. six minutes past seven o'clock
8. 60
9. no
10. $6.00

Day 4
1. 17
2. $3.25
3. 5
4. 8
5. 64
6. 4
7. volume
8. 4
9. pentagon
10. 6

Day 5
1. 100
2. 40
3. 1 R4
4. 4
5. three hundred six
6. 1
7. 2 m²
8. Monday
9. 3, 6, 0, 2, 3
10. Clockwise, from the top: 8, 24, 40, 12, 28, 36, 16, 4, 20, 32

Day 6
1. 11
2. 9
3. 7
4. 7 R7
5. 3 hundreds or 300
6.
7. 5 buckets
8. 12
9. circle
10. 95 stacks

Day 7
1. 15
2. 3 pentagons should be colored
3. 9
4. 2
5. 200 + 40 + 7
6. 4
7. February 7
8. September
9. yes
10. 34

Day 8
1. 35
2. yes
3. 4
4. 7
5. yes
6. 8
7. 1.1 Liters
8. 4.5 inches
9. rotation
10. Estimate: Answers will vary; Actual Number: 17 dots

Day 9
1. 24
2. 8 eighths
3. 4
4. 9
5. 963 should be circled.
6. 6
7. 10
8. yardstick
9. the square and triangle should be colored.
10. 71 cm

Day 10
1. 19
2. 54
3. 8
4. 3
5. 6 or 6 ones
6. 2
7. perimeter
8. 2
9. a line should be drawn to the sphere.
10. D

ANSWER KEY *(cont.)*

Day 11
1. 25
2. Yes
3. 8
4. 2
5. 47
6. 12
7. 30 mm
8. 25 minutes
9.
10. Answers may vary: 1 and 11; 3 and 9; 5 and 7

Day 12
1. 29
2. 7
3. 6
4. 7
5. 1 ten or 10
6. 20
7. 16 cm^2
8. scale
9. 48 cm^2
10. 4 boys

Day 13
1. 27
2. no
3. There should be 2 pens in each row.
4. 2
5. tens
6. 4
7. 8 to 10
8. 24
9. parallelogram or quadrilateral
10. $4

Day 14
1. 35
2. no
3. 8
4. 5 fours
5. 33, 43, 73
6. 6
7. grams
8. 2
9. B, C, and D should be circled.
10. Tens: 420; Hundreds: 400

Day 15
1. 31
2. 54
3. 4
4. 9
5. 9 ten thousands or 90,000
6. 6
7. yes
8. 3
9. Triangle A
10. The following pairs should be colored: 1 and 15; 3 and 5

Day 16
1. 25
2. 4
3. 2 sevens
4. 4
5. 500 + 60 + 3
6. 39
7. The brick should be circled.
8. 31 days
9. $18
10. 3 hr. 48 minutes

Day 17
1. 52
2. 4 fourths
3. 2
4. 6
5. 6 tens or 60
6. 2
7. the 21st
8. yardstick
9. yes
10. 46

Day 18
1. 15
2. 0.25
3. 4
4. 10
5. 70
6. 4
7. yes
8. 5 kilograms should be circled.
9. pentagon
10.

Day 19
1. 35
2. 6
3. 4
4. 12
5. 6
6. 22
7. 9 cm^3
8. A.M.
9. 15 books
10. 40 minutes

Day 20
1. 15
2. 64
3. 10
4. 2
5. 66
6. 2
7. cm^2
8. 1
9. 2 and 4
10. The 3 left or the 3 right squares should be shaded.

Day 21
1. 39
2. 3
3. 4
4. 7
5. hundreds
6. 20
7. 3 cm
8. Cup
9.
10. Answers will vary: 1 and 7; 3 and 5

ANSWER KEY (cont.)

Day 22
1. 6
2. 0.3
3. 7
4. 6
5. no
6. 2
7. 18 cm
8. 32°C
9. a sphere
10. 700 g

Day 23
1. 49
2. 0.35
3. 4
4. 4
5. 34
6. 6
7. 4:01; 1 past 4
8. 1
9. 2007
10. $6.25

Day 24
1. 3
2. $\frac{27}{100}$
3. 9
4. 2
5. 386
6. 16
7. 10 kg
8. 8
9. triangle
10. $\frac{19}{100}$, 0.19, 19%

Day 25
1. 58
2. 12
3. 10 threes
4. 10
5. 1,000 + 60 + 1
6. 10
7. 50 mm
8. 36
9. 4; 0
10. 4, 8, 12, 16, 20, 24, 28, 32, 36, and 40 should be colored.

Day 26
1. 5
2. 0.16
3. 7
4. 5
5. no
6. 92
7. 6
8. February
9. Rich
10. 3,863 ants

Day 27
1. 61
2. 9
3. 3
4. 3
5. 1,568
6. 2
7. Thursday
8. 2
9. A should be circled
10. 5 and 6

Day 28
1. 17
2. 12 fourths
3. 4
4. 2
5. hundreds
6. 5
7. 200 mL
8. ruler
9. yes
10. A triangle should be drawn on the coordinate (G,3).

Day 29
1. 52
2. 0.5
3. 8 twos
4. 4
5. 147
6. 2
7. cubic units or units^3
8. 35 minutes
9.

10. no

Day 30
1. 21
2. 35
3. 4
4. 4
5. 60
6. 6
7. 36 m^2
8. no
9. baseball
10. 42

Day 31
1. 26
2. 9
3. 4
4. 5
5. 2,078
6. 80
7. 25 mm
8. bathing suit
9. triangular prism
10.

−	44	48	53	61	72	75
19	25	29	34	42	53	56
29	15	19	24	32	43	46
39	5	9	14	22	33	36

Day 32
1. 26
2. $\frac{3}{10}$
3. 3
4. 6
5. 3,000 + 400 + 20 + 6
6. 11
7. 9 cm^2
8. 52
9. B
10. 50¢

ANSWER KEY *(cont.)*

Day 33
1. 30
2. 6 triangles should be colored.
3. 4
4. 8
5. two thousand, four hundred sixty-seven
6. 27
7. 2:40, analog and digital time
8. 4
9.

	Pizza	Tacos
Sharon		X
Sue	X	X

10. 75¢

Day 34
1. 11
2. 0.60
3. 6
4. 14
5. no
6. 15
7. 78 kg
8. 48
9. reflection
10. 81

Day 35
1. 61
2. 45
3. 3 nines
4. 2
5. 400
6. 4
7. yes
8. June
9. A, B and D should be circled.
10. The following pairs should be colored: 21 and 1, 3 and 7.

Day 36
1. 12
2. 7
3. 10
4. 1, 2, 3, 6
5. 894
6. 750
7. 7 liters
8. ruler
9. A circle should be drawn.
10. 11 inches

Day 37
1. 72
2. 0.75
3. 2
4. 9 nines
5. 800
6. 3
7. Monday
8. 6 feet should be circled.
9. An angle greater than 90° should be drawn.
10. 227

Day 38
1. 12
2. $\frac{1}{10}$
3. 4
4. 6 groups
5. 1,374
6. 20
7. 7,000 millimeters
8. P.M.
9. trapezoid
10.

Day 39
1. 41
2. 5
3. 6
4. 1, 2, 4
5. no
6. 6
7. cm
8. warm
9. 4
10. 2 squares should be red.

Day 40
1. 17
2. 42
3. 5
4. 2
5. 1,320
6. 8
7. length
8. 1
9. 3; 2
10. 1

Day 41
1. 53
2. 0.6
3. 1, 3, 9
4. 10
5. 3 digits
6. 56
7. 2 cm
8. 8
9. Dameon
10. Answers will vary: 1 and 19; 3 and 17; 5 and 15; 7 and 13; or 9 and 11.

Day 42
1. 21
2. 30 boxes should be shaded.
3. 2
4. 1, 2, 3, 4, 6, 12
5. 17th
6. 3
7. 20 cm
8. 6
9. false
10. 100 cm or 1 m

Day 43
1. 39
2. 6
3. 1, 2, 4, 8, 16
4. 8
5. 0.3
6. 4
7. 12:09; 9 past 12
8. 30 days
9.
10. $10.00

ANSWER KEY *(cont.)*

Day 44
1. 14
2. 53 boxes should be shaded.
3. 4 sevens
4. 8
5. 6 tens or 60
6. 3
7. no
8. 5
9. rectangle
10. 4

Day 45
1. 38
2. 30
3. 9
4. 1, 2, 3, 6, 9, 18
5. 2,975
6. 9
7. cm³
8. thermometer
9. Cathy and Jose
10. Clockwise, from the top:
    40 56 16 64 80
    24 48 72 32 0

Day 46
1. 7
2. 9
3. 6 sixes
4. 8
5. 34
6. 159
7. 2
8. 24
9. 8; 8; 8
10. 1/4 pizza

Day 47
1. 17
2. 0.32
3. 7 threes
4. 10
5. No
6. 9
7. March 6
8. 2 hours 15 minutes
9. 2 pairs
10. 8 and 9

Day 48
1. 26
2. 3
3. 7 rows
4. 7
5. no
6. 42
7. 5 liters
8. 34°F
9. 2008
10. Answers will vary.

Day 49
1. 24
2. 9
3. 1, 2, 4, 8
4. 5
5. 4 hundreds or 400
6. 4
7. 8 cm³
8. 120
9. cube
10. 72 in. or 6 ft. tall

Day 50
1. 19
2. 54
3. 9 twos
4. 1, 2, 3, 4, 6, 8, 12, 24
5. 3,900
6. 6
7. 20 mm
8. 2
9. A and C should be circled.
10. 36

Day 51
1. 38
2. yes
3. 9
4. 6
5. 423
6. 1
7. 55 mm
8. $\frac{1}{2}$ or 0.5
9.
10. Answers will vary: 1 and 15; 3 and 13; 5 and 11; or 7 and 9.

Day 52
1. 33
2. $2.75
3. 5 sixes
4. 8
5. 2,634
6. 6
7. 81 cm²
8. 12 months
9. 8 awards
10. 2 possible patterns: Add 4 to get 20, 24; Multiply by 2, then by 3 to get 32, 48.

Day 53
1. 33
2. 24
3. 9
4. 4
5. 0
6. 30
7. 11:00, analog and digital time
8. square inches
9. edge
10. $15.00

Day 54
1. 38
2. $\frac{67}{100}$
3. 8
4. 7
5. 36th
6. 6
7. kilograms
8. 1 kilometer should be circled.
9. reflection
10. 870; 900

Day 55
1. 1,280
2. 24
3. 2
4. 9
5. yes
6. 3
7. 1,000 steps
8. 2
9. Soccer, Diving, Swimming
10. 1, 30; 2, 15; and 5, 6 should be colored.

ANSWER KEY (cont.)

Day 56
1. 54
2. 3 boxes should be shaded.
3. 7 sixes
4. 10
5. thousands
6. 30
7. B
8. Wednesday
9.

10. 7 with 9 feet remaining

Day 57
1. 68
2. $2.75
3. 9
4. 7
5. 130
6. 7
7. Wednesday
8. P.M.
9. A line should be drawn from the cube to the die.
10. 728

Day 58
1. 46
2. $\frac{99}{100}$
3. 3
4. 10 sevens
5. 128
6. 8
7. 1,100 mL
8. 24°C
9. Jahir: 23
   Olivia: 15
   Gerald: 35
   Mimi: 3
10.

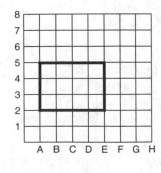

Day 59
1. 43
2. 72
3. 7
4. 6
5. 1,900
6. 39
7. 9 cm³
8. 2
9. no
10. $1.14

Day 60
1. 9
2. 21
3. 4
4. 9
5. 7 tens or 70
6. 60
7. cm²
8. 4
9. 1 and 10
10. A

Day 61
1. 64
2. 30 boxes should be shaded.
3. 10
4. 7
5. 79
6. 600
7. 3.5 cm
8. 2
9. circle
10.

+	7	15	18	23	25	28
19	26	34	37	42	44	47
29	36	44	47	52	54	57
39	46	54	57	62	64	67

Day 62
1. 8
2. 0.2
3. 7
4. 6
5. 2,000 + 300 + 60 + 5
6. 27
7. 8 cm
8. 6 faces
9. Answers will vary
10. 4 liters

Day 63
1. 34
2. 56
3. 10
4. 9
5. 5 hundreds or 500
6. 2
7. 7:26; 26 past 7
8. 1.5 or $1\frac{1}{2}$ inches
9. no
10. $4.75

Day 64
1. 17
2. no
3. 9
4. 9
5. 1,264; 1,426; 1,624
6. 8
7. 100 g
8. centimeter
9. no
10. $\frac{46}{100}$; 0.46; 46%

Day 65
1. 31
2. 60
3. 9
4. 8
5. yes
6. 3
7. 75 cm²
8. 3
9. cube or rectangular
10. Clockwise, from top:
    3 15 27 9 24 18
    12 30 21 6

Day 66
1. 14
2. 21
3. 5
4. 8
5. 2,003
6. 12
7. 20 bottles
8. 120
9. $3
10. 19 cm

ANSWER KEY *(cont.)*

Day 67
1. 40
2. 7
3. 7
4. 5
5. 4 digits
6. 5
7. 4 Mondays
8. 40 minutes
9. trapezoid
10. 7 and 6

Day 68
1. 9
2. .42
3. 16
4. 5
5. 4 hundreds or 400
6. 7
7. 16 cups of 250 mL each
8. July, August, September
9.
10. D

Day 69
1. 61
2. 7
3. 4 threes
4. 9 R4
5. 7,532
6. 15
7. yes
8. build a snowman
9. A and C should be colored.
10. 3 times

Day 70
1. 26
2. 81
3. 8
4. 8
5. 1,400
6. 20¢; 30¢; 40¢; 50¢; 60¢; 70¢
7. 60 m²
8. 60
9. B should be colored.
10. Three cubes on either the right or left should be shaded.

Day 71
1. 55
2. 8
3. 4 sixes
4. 9
5. two thousand, forty-seven
6. 24
7. 5.5 cm
8. 16
9. 5 books
10. Answers will vary: 1 and 23; 3 and 21; or 5 and 19; 7 and 17; 9 and 15; 11 and 13.

Day 72
1. 15
2. $\frac{3}{10}$
3. 8
4. 8
5. 2,907; 2,097; 2,079
6. 7
7. 36 cm²
8. 9
9. right angle
10. 2 possible answers: Add 4 to get 25, 29; Multiply by 2, then by 3 to get 42, 63

Day 73
1. 40
2. 65 boxes should be shaded.
3. 3 R 5
4. 5
5. 2 hundreds or 200
6. 7
7. The clock should read 1:10.
8. 24 months
9. hexagon
10. $4.50

Day 74
1. 17
2. no
3. 4 sixes
4. 5 R 1
5. 4 digits
6. 6
7. 43 kg
8. 243 cm³
9. 2007
10. 35

Day 75
1. 50
2. 72
3. 7
4. 9 groups
5. three thousand, fifty-eight
6. 9
7. yes
8. yardstick
9. yes
10. The following pairs should be colored: 8, 4; 16, 2; 32, 1

Day 76
1. 24
2. 6
3. 9
4. 8
5. tens
6. 240
7. 200 mL
8. meter stick
9. 5; 5; 5
10. 2 hr. 50 minutes

Day 77
1. 30
2. $\frac{53}{100}$
3. 7 R3
4. 6
5. 500
6. 45
7. the 19th
8. 4 inches
9. Answers may vary. Possible answers include sphere and egg.
10. 559

Day 78
1. 2
2. yes
3. 6 R4 or 6.8
4. 7
5. yes
6. 9
7. yes
8. 108
9. Evan
10. Answers will vary.

ANSWER KEY *(cont.)*

Day 79
1. 60
2. 0.6
3. 7 R5 or 7.5
4. 8
5. 7 tens or 70
6. 3
7. 72 cm³
8. 15 hours and 2 minutes
9. rotating
10. 375 beads

Day 80
1. 18
2. 63
3. 5
4. 8 R7 or 8.7
5. 9,710
6. 4
7. cm²
8. thermometer
9.

10. 2

Day 81
1. 60
2. No
3. 5
4. 10
5. 289
6. 48
7. 45 mm
8. 120
9. 3, 0, 2
10. Answers will vary. Examples: 1, 49; 25, 25.

Day 82
1. 33
2. 20
3. 6 R2
4. 7
5. 4 digits
6. 3
7. 8 cm
8. 3
9. Troy and Allison
10. 3,000 mL or 3 L

Day 83
1. 70
2. $\frac{1}{4}$ is greater than $\frac{1}{8}$
3. 8 R1
4. 4 R2
5. 2,500
6. 7
7. 4:07; 7 past 4
8. 12
9. yes
10. 3 for $6.00

Day 84
1. 17
2. $\frac{3}{10}$
3. 3 R3
4. 5 R7 or 5.7
5. 1,806
6. 5
7. grams
8. 31 days
9. 3 angles
10. 2,180; 2,200; 2,000

Day 85
1. 70
2. 56
3. 2 R1
4. 5 R2
5. hundreds
6. 6
7. m²
8. 4.5 or $4\frac{1}{2}$ inches
9. a square
10. 3, 6, 9, 12, 15,18, 21, 24, 27, 30, 33, 36, and 39 should be colored.

Day 86
1. 16
2. 5
3. 9 R2
4. 9 R7
5. 7 hundreds or 700
6. 48
7. 4.5 containers
8. 45 kilograms
9. Cheryl: 2 smiley faces; Brooke: 4 smiley faces
10. 53,210

Day 87
1. 33
2. 60¢
3. 5 R4
4. 2 R6
5. yes
6. 4
7. Sunday
8. 14 days
9. yes
10. 11 and 12

Day 88
1. 37
2. 10
3. 3 R3
4. 7 R5
5. two thousand, sixty-four
6. 10
7. 100 mL
8. Friday
9. B and C
10. a square should be added

Day 89
1. 31
2. no
3. 7
4. 8 R4
5. 4 digits
6. 24
7. 4 seasons
8. 1
9. A straight line should be drawn.
10. $1.50

Day 90
1. 16
2. 28
3. 6 R6
4. 4 R4
5. 400
6. 7
7. m
8. P.M.
9. yes
10. 18

ANSWER KEY *(cont.)*

Day 91
1. 57
2. $1.25
3. 3 R6
4. 9
5. 746
6. 42
7. 2.5 cm
8. 58°F
9. rectangular prism
10.

–	45	47	56	63	77	82
19	26	28	37	44	58	63
29	16	18	27	34	48	53
39	6	8	17	24	38	43

Day 92
1. 19
2. 0.05
3. 5 R2
4. 4 R3
5. 5 hundreds or 500
6. $1.00, $1.50, $2.00, $2.50
7. Area measures surface.
8. 12 cm3
9.

10. 2 possible answers: Add 3 to get 33, 36; Multiply by 2, then by 3 to get 60, 90

Day 93
1. 37
2. $\frac{4}{10}$
3. 4 R4 or 4.5
4. 4
5. 124
6. 2
7. Clock should show 3:35.
8. minute
9. $68
10. 6 tickets

Day 94
1. 54
2. 3
3. 8 R1
4. 8 R3
5. 400
6. 8
7. 42 kg
8. 1
9. octagon
10. 4,830; 4,800; 5,000

Day 95
1. 33
2. 36
3. 6
4. 9 R5
5. 2,776
6. 0
7. 600 cm
8. January
9. A square should be drawn.
10. The following pairs should be colored: 45, 1; 3, 15; 5, 9

Day 96
1. 19
2. $2.35
3. 7 R4 or 7.5
4. 14
5. 3,000 + 600 + 40 + 2
6. 49
7. 8 liters
8. 4
9. rotation or reflection
10. $35.38

Day 97
1. 26
2. 0.7
3. 4 fours
4. 6 R4 or 6.5
5. 447
6. yes
7. Saturday
8. ruler
9. Martin
10. 1,015

Day 98
1. 18
2. no
3. 2 R4 or 2.5
4. 10 R2 or 10.5
5. 5,253
6. 6
7. 500 milliliters
8. 12 minutes should be circled.
9.

10. Estimate: Answers may vary. Actual Number: 24 dots

Day 99
1. 61
2. $\frac{62}{100}$ or $\frac{31}{50}$
3. 1, 2, 4, 5, 10, 20
4. 3
5. forty-second
6. 9
7. April, May, June
8. 8 cm³
9. 2 surfaces; 1 edge
10. 10 toys

Day 100
1. 8
2. 42
3. 7
4. 1, 2, 3, 4, 6, 9, 12, 18, 36
5. 7 tens or 70
6. 18
7. 8 m²
8. 5 weekdays
9. 180 inches
10. C

Day 101
1. 52
2. 6
3. 8
4. 8
5. 800
6. 35
7. 30 mm
8. 40 minutes
9. A and C
10. Answers may vary. Possibilities include (13 + 12 + 4 + 1) ÷ 10 = 3 or 13 – 12 + 10 ÷ (4 + 1) = 3

ANSWER KEY *(cont.)*

Day 102
1. 54
2. yes
3. 5 R3
4. 2 eights
5. eight thousand, ninety-one
6. 48
7. 25 cm^2
8. jacket
9.

10. 6 pencils

Day 103
1. 61
2. $\frac{9}{100}$
3. 6
4. 9
5. 300 + 80 + 6
6. yes
7. 5:16; 16 past 5
8. day
9. vertex
10. $1.00

Day 104
1. 16
2. $3.25
3. 8
4. 4
5. 810
6. $40; $60; $80; $100; $120
7. yes
8. 3
9. 6 more awards
10. $\frac{36}{100}$; 0.36; 36%

Day 105
1. 36
2. 50
3. 7
4. 9
5. 4 digits
6. 10
7. cm^2
8. 1
9. A and D should be circled.
10. The following pairs should

be colored: 35, 1; 7, 5

Day 106
1. 9
2. yes
3. 8
4. 4
5. 2,009
6. 36
7. 35
8. 2.5 or $2\frac{1}{2}$ inches
9. Allison
10. 30

Day 107
1. 61
2. No
3. 5
4. 3
5. 138
6. 65
7. September 2
8. 15 liters should be circled.
9. 8; 18; 12
10. 52

Day 108
1. 23
2. 0.75
3. 1, 2, 3, 5, 6, 10, 15, 30
4. 2
5. 8,047
6. 6
7. 2,500
8. 30 months
9. B
10. A circle should be drawn at coordinate (C,7).

Day 109
1. 51
2. $3.50
3. 8
4. 3
5. 9
6. 1
7. January; December
8. 8 cm^3
9. hexagon
10. 3

Day 110
1. 35
2. 63
3. 6 eights
4. 7
5. thirty-first
6. 42
7. 81 cm^2
8. 58 minutes
9.

Batter						
Harry						
Dean						
Dale						
	0	1	2	3	4	5

10. 30

Day 111
1. 41
2. 21
3. 9
4. 5
5. 7,000 + 900 + 3
6. 42
7. 3.5 cm
8. 20°C
9. triangular prism
10. Answers will vary. Possibilities include: 1, 41; 3, 39; 5, 37, etc.

Day 112
1. 46
2. $\frac{25}{100}$ or $\frac{1}{4}$
3. 2
4. 8
5. thousands
6. yes
7. 22 cm
8. days
9. 3; 3; 3
10. 700 grams

Day 113
1. 31
2. 70%
3. 2 R7
4. 2
5. no
6. 7
7. The clock should read 6:29.
8. 1
9. 15 inches
10. $16.00

ANSWER KEY *(cont.)*

Day 114
1. 13
2. yes
3. 6
4. 10 R3 or 10.5
5. even
6. 4
7. 5 kg
8. 1
9. A rectangle should be drawn.
10. 138

Day 115
1. 42
2. 56
3. 7
4. 8
5. 900
6. 4
7. 5 cm
8. 31 days
9. A line of symmetry should be drawn from any vertex.
10. 8; 5; 7; 3

Day 116
1. 15
2. $\frac{2}{5}$ or $\frac{4}{10}$ or $\frac{40}{100}$
3. 4 R3
4. 6
5. 4,620
6. 64
7. 700 mL
8. square feet
9. hexagon
10. 60

Day 117
1. 34
2. no
3. 5
4. 9 R1
5. 440
6. 24, 36, 48; 48
7. 17 days
8. liter
9. circle
10. 12

Day 118
1. 16
2. 7 rows or 70 squares should be shaded.
3. 2
4. 12
5. 5,734
6. 4
7. 4 250 mL cups
8. Thursday
9. $17
10. rotating

Day 119
1. 53
2. 50%
3. 7
4. 4
5. fifty-six
6. 3
7. April; June
8. 9 cm³
9. translate
10. 6 hours

Day 120
1. 17
2. 240
3. 9
4. 9
5. 623
6. 4
7. m²
8. 8:22
9. no
10. There are 8 possible correct designs involving either a line, a V, or an L shape.

Day 121
1. 46
2. 6
3. 9
4. 4
5. 5,046
6. $\frac{4}{8}$
7. 20 mm
8. cold
9. There should be a line drawn between the ice cream cone and the cone.
10. 2 possible answers: Add 3 to get 35, 38; Multiply by 2, then by 3 to get 64, 96

Day 122
1. 43
2. 0.45
3. 11
4. 5
5. 6,000 + 800 + 2
6. 4
7. 49 cm²
8. 12
9. no
10. 31 m

Day 123
1. 33
2. no
3. 8
4. 5 R3
5. 463rd
6. 20
7. 6:53; 7 minutes to 7
8. $\frac{1}{2}$
9. The prism (far right) should be circled and pyramid (center) should be crossed out.
10. $1.48

Day 124
1. 4
2. $2.75
3. 5
4. 9
5. hundreds
6. 30
7. grams
8. 4
9. yes
10. $\frac{48}{100}$; 0.48; 48%

Day 125
1. 64
2. 32 apples
3. 6
4. 9
5. odd
6. 4
7. 150 cm²
8. 1.5 or $1\frac{1}{2}$ inches
9. A and C should be circled.
10. Clockwise, from top:

18	48	54	24	60
30	6	36	12	42

ANSWER KEY *(cont.)*

Day 126
1. 11
2. 52%
3. 9
4. 9
5. 3,058
6. 170
7. 4 times
8. 8 inches should be circled.
9. 10"
10. 144 in²

Day 127
1. 43
2. yes
3. 8
4. 5
5. 489
6. yes
7. Wednesday
8. 1.461 days
9. pentagonal prism
10. 148

Day 128
1. 13
2. 90%
3. 4 R4
4. 4
5. 800
6. 1
7. 200 mL
8. 28 cm
9. 6
10.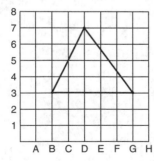

Day 129
1. 57
2. 9 rows or 90 squares should be shaded.
3. 5 R1
4. 4
5. 4 digits
6. 18, 27, 36, 45, 54, 5 bags
7. January, February, March
8. 8 cm³
9. A circle should be drawn.
10. $48

Day 130
1. 11
2. 24
3. 10 R1
4. 10
5. no
6. 2
7. 36 m²
8. 2:50
9. 4 awards
10. 27

Day 131
1. 62
2. yes
3. 8
4. 16
5. odd
6. 900
7. centimeters
8. 73°F
9. One of the following lines should be drawn:

10. Answers will vary. Possibilities include: 1, 57; 3, 55, etc.

Day 132
1. 21
2. 50%
3. 15
4. 5
5. 4,500
6. 9
7. 28 cm
8. 2
9. Answers may vary. Possible answers include sphere and egg.
10. 36 eggs

Day 133
1. 24
2. 2
3. 5
4. 13 R4
5. four thousand, eight hundred twenty-five
6. 0
7. The clock should read 6:37.
8. $\frac{1}{2}$
9. 2 children
10. $10

Day 134
1. 31
2. 12
3. 5
4. 8 R1
5. 600 + 20 + 4
6. 10
7. 23 kg
8. $\frac{1}{2}$
9. 4; 4; 2
10. 13

Day 135
1. 61
2. 48
3. 10
4. 6 R1
5. 670
6. yes
7. 6 meters
8. July
9. yes
10. 8; 6; 8; 7

ANSWER KEY *(cont.)*

Day 136
1. 34
2. 3
3. 5
4. 12 R1
5. 7 hundreds or 700
6. 0.75
7. 1,250 mL
8. 964 minutes
9. 6 faces; 12 edges; a square base
10. 5 pencils

Day 137
1. 38
2. yes
3. 2
4. 6 R5
5. ones
6. 3
7. Monday
8. ruler
9. parallelogram or rhombus
10. 48

Day 138
1. 15
2. 20
3. 9 R4
4. 14 R5
5. 4 digits
6. 10
7. 24
8. 2
9. yes
10. left 4, down 5, right 2, down 2, right 6, up 3, left 2, up 4.

Day 139
1. 42
2. 5
3. 5
4. 4 R2
5. 5,000
6. 7
7. 31; 31; 31
8. 1
9. translation
10. 6 triangles should be colored yellow; 3 triangles should be colored blue.

Day 140
1. 12
2. 7, 14, 21
3. 6 R1
4. 4 R3
5. odd
6. 7
7. cm^2
8. 840
9. A square should be drawn.
10. or

Day 141
1. 58
2. 2
3. 7
4. 22 R2
5. Eight thousand, nine hundred thirty-one
6. $\frac{8}{10}$
7. 50 mm
8. 4
9. pentagon
10. Answers will vary. Possibilities include: 13 −10 + 12 +4 + 1

Day 142
1. 12
2. $5.50
3. 5
4. 9 R3
5. 895
6. 12, 18, 24, 30, 36, 36 sides
7. 12 cm
8. 2
9. 5
10. 264 times

Day 143
1. 62
2. yes
3. 4
4. 8 R4
5. no
6. 22
7. The clocks should read 6:05.
8. July
9. false
10. $6.00

Day 144
1. 31
2. 10
3. 6 R6
4. 6 R5
5. 7,501
6. 4
7. 750 g
8. $4\frac{1}{4}$ inches or 4.25
9. rectangle
10. 45

Day 145
1. 63
2. 300
3. 10 R2
4. 6 R7
5. 1,000 + 800 + 50 + 7
6. 1
7. m^3
8. ruler
9. yes
10. 40,1; 20,2; 8,5; 10,4

Day 146
1. 41
2. yes
3. 4 R3
4. 13
5. 2 tens or 20
6. 735
7. 6 liters
8. 6
9. A parallel line should be drawn.
10. 4

Day 147
1. 71
2. 5
3. 10
4. 4
5. 400
6. 40
7. December 21
8. 31 days
9. yes
10. 44

ANSWER KEY (cont.)

Day 148
1. 11
2. 10
3. 9
4. 3 fives
5. 1,632
6. 10
7. 2.5 or $2\frac{1}{2}$ liters
8. 104
9. cylinder
10. 18 times

Day 149
1. 27
2. yes
3. 2
4. 7 R5
5. 7,000 + 400 + 90
6. no
7. October, November, December
8. 1,125 cm^3
9. 15 inches
10. Estimate: Answers will vary. Actual Number: 35 dots

Day 150
1. 13
2. 350
3. 3
4. 11
5. hundreds
6. 1
7. cm^2
8. 18
9. 6; 6; 6
10. 12

Day 151
1. 38
2. $3.75
3. 4
4. 4 R5
5. 2,700
6. 324
7. 5.5 or $5\frac{1}{2}$ cm
8. yardstick
9. 4; 4
10. 2 possible answers: Add 10 to get 50, 60; Multiply by 3, then 5 to get 120, 200

Day 152
1. 39
2. $\frac{81}{100}$
3. 10
4. 15 R2
5. 3 digits
6. 4
7. 16 cm
8. 96
9. D should be circled.
10. 153 cm

Day 153
1. 44
2. 15
3. 2
4. 9 R6
5. nine thousand, fifty-eight
6. 3
7. The clocks should read 9:15.
8. January
9. 8 awards
10. $4.00

Day 154
1. 2
2. 68%
3. 9
4. 9 R3
5. 2000 + 500 + 70 + 3
6. 3
7. 2 kg
8. 120
9. A line of symmetry should be drawn from vertex to vertex or side to side.
10. 1,330; 1,300; 1,000

Day 155
1. 71
2. 42
3. 9
4. 8
5. 4,053
6. 5
7. yes
8. 2
9. 5 angles
10. 6; 8; 10; 9

Day 156
1. 11
2. no
3. 21
4. 5 R1
5. 1,800
6. 0.9, 1.0
7. 6 buckets
8. 30 days
9. 5 faces; 5 vertices; a square base
10. 2.25 cm

Day 157
1. 71
2. 0.25
3. 10
4. 7 R4
5. 0
6. 116, 174, 232, 290; 290 cm
7. Wednesday
8. 2
9. 90° angle
10. 4

Day 158
1. 11
2. $\frac{71}{100}$
3. 3
4. 10 R2
5. 2,567 is less than 2, 675
6. 400
7. 9 bottles
8. 7 days
9. 2 diagonals should be drawn from vertex to vertex.
10. A square should be drawn in (G,5).

Day 159
1. 61
2. 85 squares should be shaded.
3. 15 R4
4. 6 R1
5. 1,056
6. 2
7. 365 days
8. 1,000
9. rotation
10. $\frac{1}{4}$

ANSWER KEY *(cont.)*

Day 160
1. 39
2. 30
3. 75
4. 11 R2
5. 4,990
6. 1
7. 7 m²
8. hour
9. rectangular prism
10. $\frac{1}{2}$

Day 161
1. 43
2. $\frac{25}{100}$ or $\frac{1}{4}$
3. 7 R1
4. 4
5. 1,000 + 400 + 10 + 4
6. $\frac{4}{100}$
7. 20 mm
8. 2
9. 5
10. Answers will vary. Possibilities include: 12 + 13 − 10 − 4 − 1

Day 162
1. 13
2. 73%
3. 19
4. 5 R4
5. thousands
6. 27
7. 24 cm
8. 72
9. yes
10. 12 cookies

Day 163
1. 42
2. greater than
3. 13 R5
4. 8
5. 4,700
6. 10
7. The clock should read 7:50; 10 to 8
8. September, October, November, December
9. A square should be drawn.
10. $50

Day 164
1. 34
2. 45%
3. 9
4. 5
5. 4,800
6. 3
7. 10 kg
8. 31 days
9. 25 books
10. 792

Day 165
1. 72
2. yes
3. 7
4. 5
5. 6 hundreds or 600
6. 50¢, 75¢, $1.00, $1.25
7. 80 mm
8. 7
9. A line of symmetry should be drawn from vertex to vertex or side to side.
10. 50¢

Day 166
1. 18
2. 0.37
3. 5
4. 8 R3
5. 3,000 + 10 + 4
6. 660
7. 40
8. a minute
9. a circle
10. 17

Day 167
1. 71
2. 25
3. 10 R2
4. 10 R6
5. 1,400
6. 1
7. January 1
8. liter
9. perpendicular lines
10. 60

Day 168
1. 11
2. 62 squares should be shaded.
3. 10 R4
4. 4
5. 3,970
6. 400
7. 250 milliliters
8. 240
9. true
10. $2\frac{1}{2}$ minutes

Day 169
1. 53
2. 30%
3. 3
4. 6
5. no
6. $5.00; $7.50; $10.00; Week 4
7. December 31
8. 30 cm
9. A line should be drawn from the can to the cylinder.
10. 50¢

Day 170
1. 23
2. 35%
3. 5 R3
4. 3 R10
5. 1,280
6. 2
7. area
8. 9:00 P.M.
9. rotation
10. 21

ANSWER KEY *(cont.)*

Day 171
1. 80
2. yes
3. 2 R3
4. 17
5. no
6. 847
7. 3 cm
8. 73°F
9. 3
10. Answers will vary. Possibilities include: 13 − 4 + 10 − 12 − 1

Day 172
1. 12
2. $\frac{30}{100}$ or $\frac{3}{10}$
3. 16 R1
4. 14 R3
5. 4 tens or 40
6. 12
7. 9 cm²
8. meter
9.
10. 101 cm

Day 173
1. 70
2. 84%
3. 3
4. 4 R7
5. one thousand, eight hundred forty-six
6. 2
7. The clocks should read 1:35.
8. 6
9. 3 acute angles
10. $7.50

Day 174
1. 19
2. 72
3. 6
4. 10 R1
5. 3,047
6. 3
7. grams
8. 3
9. A perpendicular line should be drawn.
10. 4 boxes

Day 175
1. 67
2. 0.25
3. 4
4. 14
5. 1,905
6. 56
7. m²
8. 3
9. A triangular front view should be drawn.
10. 42 race cars

Day 176
1. 15
2. 10¢
3. 8
4. 9 R5
5. no
6. 20/100
7. 5 liters
8. 6 months
9. 7 different sports are played
10. 12

Day 177
1. 32
2. yes
3. 8
4. 6 R8
5. 6,042
6. 10
7. December 24
8. km
9. false
10. $2.67

Day 178
1. 19
2. $\frac{47}{100}$
3. 7
4. 6
5. 2,536
6. 3
7. 20
8. $3\frac{3}{4}$ or 3.75 inches
9. yes
10. 68 tickets

Day 179
1. 42
2. no
3. 7 R4
4. 9
5. 2,400
6. 39
7. square feet
8. 1 cm³
9. 1 obtuse angle
10. 50 minutes

Day 180
1. 17
2. 0.81
3. 18 fives
4. 7 R3
5. tens
6. $0.60, $0.90, $1.20, $1.50, $1.80; 6 pens cost $1.80
7. yes
8. 70°F
9. square pyramid
10.

REFERENCES CITED

Kilpatrick, J., J. Swafford, and B. Findell, eds. 2001. *Adding it up: Helping children learn mathematics.* Washington, DC: National Academies Press.

Marzano, R. 2010. When practice makes perfect...sense. *Educational Leadership* 68 (3): 81–83.

McIntosh, M. E. 1997. Formative assessment in mathematics. *Clearing House* 71 (2): 92–96.

DIGITAL RESOURCES

Accessing the Digital Resources

The digital resources can be downloaded by following these steps:

1. Go to **www.tcmpub.com/digital**

2. Sign in or create an account.

3. Click **Redeem Content** and enter the ISBN number, located on page 2 and the back cover, into the appropriate field on the website.

4. Respond to the prompts using the book to view your account and available digital content.

5. Choose the digital resources you would like to download. You can download all the files at once, or you can download a specific group of files.

Please note: Some files provided for download have large file sizes. Download times for these larger files will vary based on your download speed.

ISBN:
9781425808075

CONTENTS OF THE DIGITAL RESOURCES

Teacher Resources

- Practice Page Item Analysis Chart
- Student Item Analysis Chart

Student Resources

- Practice Pages
